ST. DAVID'S AND DEWISLAND

A SOCIAL HISTORY

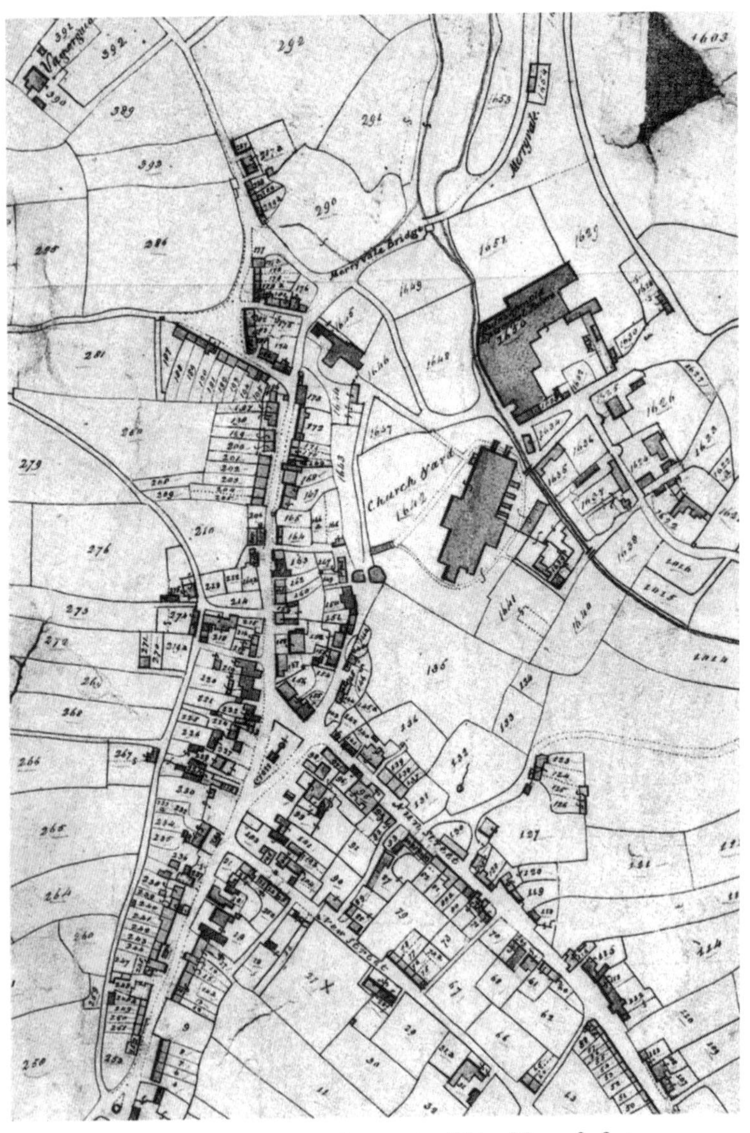

City of St. David's according to the Tithe Map of 1840

National Library of Wales

St. David's and Dewisland

A Social History

DAVID W. JAMES

CARDIFF
UNIVERSITY OF WALES PRESS

Reprinted, 2013

www.uwp.co.uk

British Library Cataloguing-in-Publication Data
A catalogue record for this book is available from the British Library.

ISBN 978-1-7831-6001-3

Printed by CPI Antony Rowe, Chippenham

To Dorothy,
and to our children,
Mary, Ann and Richard

Contents

Place-names of the Parish

In 1967 the University of Wales Press published a third edition of *A Gazetteer of Welsh Place-names*, the result of work done by the Board of Celtic Studies over a long period on the orthography of these names. A list of some of these that belong to the parish of St. David's is given below as a guide to their correct spelling. This list includes instances of places that have inherited both a Welsh and an English name, and of attempts to transcribe into English the sounds of a Welsh original.

O. S. Sheet 157 (1974)	*Gazetteer (1967)*	*Local Forms*
Abercastle	Abercastell	
Abereiddy	Abereiddi	
Brawdy	Breudeth	
Carnllidi	Carn Llidi	
Castle Morris	Casmorys	
Clegyr-Boia	Clegyrfwya	Clegyrfwya
Llandruidion	Llandridian	
Llanvirn	Llanfyrn	
Llanrian	Llanrhian	
Maesymynydd		Maesymwni
Mathry	Mathri	
Penberry	Penbiri	
Pointz Castle	Cas-bwnsh	
Porth-clais	Porth Glais	
Porthllisky (bay)	Porth Lisgi	
Porthlysgi (farm)		
Porthstinian (St. Justinian)	Porth Stinan	
Priskilly	Prysgili	
Pwllcaerog		Pwllcawrog
Ramsey Island	Ynys Dewi	
St. Brides	Sain Ffraid	
St. David's Head	Penmaendewi	
Skyfog		Ysgeifiog
Solva	Solfach	
Trellwyd		Treliwyd
Tremynydd		Tremwni
Treginnis	Treginis	
Tretio	Treteio	Treteio
Trevine	Tre-fin	
Vachelych	Fachelych	
Whitchurch	Tregroes	Tregrwes

Foreword

Professor Emeritus E. G. Bowen, M.S., D.Litt., Ll.D., Hon.D.Univ. (Open) F.S.A. (Formerly Professor of Geography and Anthropology in the University College of Wales, Aberystwyth.)

The Parish of St. David's (including that of the Cathedral Close) is one of the largest parishes in the whole of Dyfed. The parish occupies the land that was once the Cantref of Pebidiog, later to be known as Dewisland – The Land of David. The essential features of the territory are its extreme westerly location and its pronounced peninsular character. This is true not only of the region as a whole but also of its several parts. The major peninsula forming Dewisland is clearly broken up into three smaller peninsulas – St. David's Head, Point St. John and Porthtaflod, while right around the coast of the entire parish from Abereiddy Bay in the north-east to Penrhyn St. Elvis in the south-west, the repeated occurrence of place names including the terms *Trwyn*, or *Pen* alternating with *Aber*, *Porth* or *Traeth* tell the same story of the power of the Atlantic breakers working upon the relative hardness and resistance of the rocks. As is to be expected, the extreme western face of the peninsula receives the full force of the Atlantic gales and has long been even more shattered by the waves. Large blocks, like Ramsey Island, have become detached; the sea rushes through the Sound which separates it from the mainland. Here the tidal race is both strong and dangerous. Further out to sea are smaller rocky islets, themselves but shattered remnants of the peninsula, known characteristically as the Bishops and Clerks.

In sharp contrast to the natural beauty of the coastal scenery the bare, open wind-swept surface of the interior seems, at first sight, to be rather unattractive. Basically, this country represents the extreme south-westward continuation of the uplands of Central Wales, orientated on an E.N.E.–W.S.W. axis parallel to the Welsh coast, and falling south-westward with steadily decreasing elevation. It has been eroded into a series of plateau surfaces much broken by the present drainage pattern. Within the Parish itself the plateau is made up of the 200 ft surface relieved by the massive upstanding igneous masses of Penbiri, Carn Llidi and others. To add to the uniformity of the scene the strong sea winds, laden with salt, have kept down any thick forest cover so that moorland and scrubland abound.

It is not the purpose of the author to attempt to tie up in any detail the physical and human scene, or, indeed, to set out a strictly chronological description of the major episodes in the long and fascinating history of the Parish, but, on the contrary, to try and isolate the several facets of social life that have characterised the Parish over the centuries. It is these, in turn, which are closely interwoven with the distinctive natural endowments of the region. The historical geographer can in this case do no better than to quote Wordsworth,

'Two Voices are there; one is of the Sea,
One of the Mountains; each a mighty Voice.'

Archaeologists and prehistorians agree that movement by sea in early times was much easier than movement by land in Atlantic Europe. It is clear that the many peninsulas and tidal inlets around the Dewisland peninsula made movement by sea easy, and after entry, the open country offered further access. There is evidence that coastal landings were used throughout Prehistoric times and well beyond the Roman period into the Dark Ages. It was in this later period that the missionaries of the Celtic Church (usually known as the Celtic Saints) passed through the countryside on their journeys partly by land and partly by sea to Ireland, Cornwall and Brittany. Their names have survived associated with many churches and villages in the Celtic lands. Linked with this movement was the establishment of a monastic cell in Glyn Rhosyn – a small but well sheltered valley sunk into the southernmost tip of the Dewisland peninsula. This was to become the site of the later Cathedral of St. David's in the little village-city that gathered around it. According to the story, as we have it, St. David was the son of a King of Ceredigion and of the family of Cunedda, thereby linking him with the founder of a Welsh tribal group hostile to the Irish branch of the Celtic Stock. David was said to have studied at Henfynyw (Old Mynyw) in his native land of Ceredigion and seems to have made his first contact with the future Dewisland while on a missionary crusade with a party from Henfynyw which moved south-westwards on a route roughly parallel to the coast, establishing churches on the way. When David arrived in Glyn Rhosyn he found that an Irish tribe from across the sea had settled in the neighbourhood and he himself had to face a confrontation with the local Irish Chieftain who resisted his coming. Nevertheless, the saint's will prevailed and he called his newly established monastery Mynyw (Menevia) after the Old Mynyw in Ceredigion. Menevia thus became the Medieval Latin name for St. David's.

The Saint's name spread far and wide in Wales and also in South-eastern Ireland, and further afield in Cornwall and Brittany. Pilgrims from these areas gathered in large numbers in medieval times. Many obviously came by sea and we find the main peninsula dotted on all sides with little medieval chapels, ten in all, arranged in a circular manner around the Cathedral with its shrine. Most of these chapels are either on the water's edge or on a cliff top above a landing place. Here pilgrims would offer a short prayer for a safe passage or offer thanks for a safe landing before proceeding to the Saint's shrine. So it would seem that the traffic along the western seaways would naturally focus on the little Cathedral City which thus became in its day and age a veritable Piccadilly Circus. St. David's is no longer a Piccadilly Circus but we must remember that the great tradition of the sea lived on beyond medieval times until the coming of the steamship in modern times. So the coastlands of Dewisland are laden with tales of trade and plunder and of shipwrecks and gallant seamen who faced the terrors of the Deep near at home or in far-off lands. The chapters in this book tell their story.

We can now look away from the sea and at the ancient Cantref of Pebidiog and we are reminded straightaway that we are in a thoroughly Welsh area, very much in the tradition of Dewi Sant, who like most of his contemporaries lived very close to the soil. When Norman Bishops reigned at St. David's Pebidiog became an episcopal lordship, and it figures as such prominently in the survey of Bishop Martyn's lands drawn up in 1326 and commonly known as the Black Book of St. David's. The social and economic picture at this time was more complex. We can distinguish the semi-urban settlement of St. David's with its township and open fields; then there were the demesne lands of the Bishop himself. Here the serf-tenants lived in tiny nucleated villages with their large open fields around, tilled in common by the peasants as was customary in an Anglo-Norman village at this time. The peasants did reaping and cartage duties for the Bishop as in Norman Law. Then there were Knights' fees as at Pointz Castle and Castle Morris. Mingled with all this were the lands of the free tenants who rendered no agricultural services and worked under Welsh Law. They lived in small hamlets and isolated farms. These isolated farmsteads were the fountain-heads of the real Welsh life and culture. The really important feature revealed by the Black Book of St. David's, therefore, is that most of the hamlets, villages and large farms of modern Dewisland were in existence in the early fourteenth century and have survived in modified form down to our own times. As the early population increased in numbers by the late sixteenth century much fractionation of holdings took place especially among the *tyddynod*, closely related to the native pattern of land inheritance in Wales. In this way every portion of land was being settled and squatting on the waste land was rife. This explains why portions of the rain-swept, wind-swept, storm-battered island of Ramsey were farmed and as we read in Mr James's narrative the farmer had to be boatman first of all to negotiate the tide race and great swells of Ramsey Sound. It is obvious and, indeed, important that this book should elaborate on the agricultural side. The author has selected a number of long established farmsteads such as Pwllcaerog and Treginnis Isha with Hendre and Treleddyn and examined in the closest detail the everyday life and husbandry of the farmer and his family. He has shown that in the darkness of a winter's night around the fire there was much serious thought about religious, agricultural and economic matters and it is with this background in the end that Pebidiog farmers and their families and servants responded in large numbers to the call of, firstly, the older Dissenters, and later the fervour of Hywel Harris and his followers and, in time, chapels large and small dotted the Parish and became the centres of the social and religious life of the community. In this way the author shows how the spirit of nonconformist Wales grew in this area from its grass roots. It was the ministers of these little chapels and the farmers in their congregations that became so keen on educational matters as the school records of the nineteenth century indicate. Mr James, as a long serving Head Teacher in the area, writes of these and allied matters with direct firsthand knowledge. It was these Welsh nonconformists who became Liberal and Progressive in politics and who realized the need not only for knowledge but for economic progress and strove so hard with the Town Traders to work for the coming of the railway to the Parish – which never came. Here, therefore, in this Parish are the two mighty voices – the ever present voice of the Sea and the voice of the mountain land of Wales, for as is well known, the heart of Welsh Nonconformity and Liberalism in the nineteenth century was not in the new industrial areas but in *Cymru Fynyddig*.

The story of Dewisland, however, is not complete unless we take into full account the presence of the separate parish of the Cathedral Close set in the midst of this rural-maritime scene. The primitive huts of the Celtic Christian period were replaced with the coming of the Normans and even a wooden structure might have existed before

Bernard, the first Norman Bishop, built the first stone cathedral early in the twelfth century. Later in that century the earliest Norman work was replaced when Bishop Peter de Leia began the building of the present Cathedral on a scale and magnificence that places it in a national rather than in a local class – it is beyond all question the finest church in all Wales. Around the Cathedral are the remains of the Chapel, Cloister and College of St. Mary, and to the south-westward the ruins of Bishop Gower's magnificent Palace. The Cathedral together with the Bishop's Palace and the Houses of the Canons and Dignitaries and officers of the Diocese thus all lay together in an enclosed area called the Close or Citadel, and are surrounded by a stone wall well over a thousand yards in circumference. Here, therefore, is a magnificent, self-contained ecclesiastical complex set as an enclave in this remote and sometimes barren land.

One of the fascinating social problems of Dewisland, which has been fully examined in this book is the interaction and final balance achieved between these three elements: the coastal zone with its present rapidly developing tourist industry and its long tradition of the sea; the dominantly Welsh Nonconformist community of the interior; and the literally walled off ecclesiastical enclave. The balance and interplay of these communities is not easy to assess at different periods of time, but in this book this has been attempted for the first time. The author comes to the conclusion that in the end the Welsh rural community is dominant. Its influence reaches right up to the coastal margins of the Peninsula itself, more strongly of course, before an exotic tourist industry took possession. Likewise, it reached up to the very walls of the Cathedral Close in the mid-nineteenth century, when a very intelligent Master of the Cathedral Grammar School within could write to his Dean, 'I am no favourer of Dissent, yet I keep coming to the conclusion that we are under infinite obligations to Dissenters for keeping alive a sense of religion in the minds of men, especially in places like St. David's where from the extent of the Parish it is physically impossible for the inhabitants to attend their Parish Church. Had two or three Chapels of Ease been erected fifty years ago and pious men appointed with sufficient incomes to minister to their pulpits and go about among the people during the week as diligent pastors of their flock, Dissent would be almost unknown at the present day in the Parish of St. David's.'

Acknowledgements

I am deeply grateful to the following: the Librarian and staff of our own County (now Regional) Library in Haverfordwest, and in particular to H. J. Dickman, now retired Librarian of many years, who helped me at the beginning, and to those of the staff who have the good fortune to belong to St. David's; the Dean and Archdeacon and staff of the Cathedral Library; the Archivist and staff of the Records Office in Haverfordwest; the Librarian and staff of the National Library of Wales, Aberystwyth, and in particular the Keepers of Manuscripts and Maps and Prints; the Curator of the County Museum in Haverfordwest; the Chairman, Clerk and members of the Community Council of St. David's, who gave me the freedom of the Parish Chest and Vestry and Council Minutes; and the Headmaster of Ysgol Dewi Sant, who allowed me to use the School Library and the Davies Williams Memorial Library.

I am also deeply indebted to many of the people of City and Parish (who told me of old family traditions and showed me precious documents and family histories) and to many outside the Parish: J. H. M. Bateman; Sidney Beer; Wilkin and Rahel Beynon; George Bird; Peter Boorman; Byron Davies; Elwyn Davies; Evan Davies; Jenkin Davies; Lettice Davies; M. E. and Janet Davies; Nurse Davies; Davieses of Hendre; Peter Davies; Wynford Davies; R. and P. Driver; John Edwards; Bryn Evans; D. Watts Evans; Joan Evans; Mali Evans; Richard Evans; Wyn Evans; Henry Evans of New Ffynnon; Grays of Glasfryn; Ivor Griffiths; Sidney Gronow; Canon and Kay Halliwell; Captain George Harries; George Harries; W. E. Harries; Mervyn Harries; Hemingways of Middle Mill; E. Hurley; Mary Medlicott; Talfryn James; Thomas James of Skyfog; Johns of Tretio; Tommy John; Mair Jones; Perkin Jones; Winston Jones; Frank Lamb; Dai Lewis; Eiluned Lewis; Stanley Lewis; W. Llewellyn; H. V. Lloyd; I. O. Martin; Dr Middleton; Edna Morgan; Gwilym Morgan; Verdun Morgan; Lena Morris; William Morris; Coxwain Morris; D. A. and Gerald Nash; M. Ogdon; Gilbert Owen; Ann Pelham; E. Preece; Tommy Phillips;

Morris Price; Bowen Rees; Bryn Rees; C. M. Rees; Ogwen Rees; M. J. Richards; Maurice Riley; Herbert Roach; Mabel Roberts; Percy and Phillip Roberts; Marion Roderick; Dewi Rowlands; David Salmon; Mattie and J. O. Stephens; Ivor Thomas; Nurse Thomas; Mabel Thomas; M. Nicholas Thomas; G. M., Dorothy and Mervyn Walters; Ralph Warren; Billy Williams; Mattie Williams; Owen Williams; and ex-Chief Coastguard Williams.

There were many others, unnamed, but who, perhaps completely unaware of their contribution, said something or other in daily conversation that kindled a thought here or confirmed something there on the thousand and one things that make, and have made, the life history of a community within a parish. They too have had their part in this book, whose existence is the best of all acknowledgements. I am grateful to them, and to those who showed me their collections of old photographs – Gerald Nash, Mair Jones, and Desmond Hampson (whose very rich collection includes that of W. Morris Mendus). The sketch album of Geoffrey Platt showed land and buildings in quite a different and revealing light.

I gratefully acknowledge permission to quote from the poetry of Waldo Williams; the poetry of James Nicholas, the St. David's-born National Eisteddfod Chaired Bard of 1969; *The Captain's Wife*, the late Eiluned Lewis's novel of nineteenth-century St. David's; and the graphic manuscript diary of Ivor Arnold.

I am grateful to Mr J. Iorwerth Davies, the Regional Librarian of Dyfed County Council Regional Library, Haverfordwest, and Mr R. H. Williams, photographer, also of Haverfordwest, for their assistance in securing photographic prints of material in the Regional Library for reproduction in the volume.

I thank T. E. Jenkins, one-time Dean of St. David's, who read my first feeble efforts; and my wife, who read the proof sheets with patience and with care; and Emeritus Professor E. G. Bowen, who supplied the maps, wrote the Foreword, and encouraged and corrected throughout, and read the typescript. Lastly, I thank the University of Wales Press Board for accepting the work, and the Director, Mr John Rhys, M.A., and his Assistant Editor, Mr Alun Treharne, who with patient care and courtesy brought it safely to print.

David W. James

Preface

This is the story of a village which is also a city. It is a story that makes no claim to be a detailed, annotated, academic history, least of all of the cathedral church which is its centrepiece. Notwithstanding, it does attempt to depict the motley history of a community, or stories of many groups of common and sometimes uncommon people within the community, against the backcloth of the broader history of Wales and England and Western Europe.

It is the story of a parish which is commensurate with an ancient division of a Celtic kingdom, part of the cantref (land of a hundred homes) of Pebidiog, itself part of the ancient Celtic kingdom of Dyfed. Who Pebid was we do not know, except that he was probably a chieftain ruling under a king of Dyfed.

Through this parish runs the river Alun, six miles long, now itself little more than a streamlet, but of greater significance than its size. As it flows down to the sea through a valley which suggests a river of greater size than now, it bisects a walled city of immense historical importance, a religious *civitas*, the origin of most of the later history of the place. Christianity had come here before the time of David, but it was his character and missionary work that made his monastery one of the great centres of Celtic times, a cradle of Celtic Christianity in Wales. David is Dewi in Welsh, and this is why the place is called Tyddewi – the monastery or house of David. Centuries later the names Dewisland and Dewsland appeared and continued to appear side by side with Pebidiog until a general anglicisation made Dewisland more popular than Pebidiog.

In the Lives of the Celtic Saints, the House of David, Tyddewi, was called Cell Muni (deriving from an Irish word meaning 'wood') or in Latin Civitas Kellmunnensis, the monastery of the grove. From this came the Welsh name Mynyw, the name given to the Cathedral and to the land around. When Latin became the language of the church, Mynyw became Menevia, the name sometimes given to the parish, and to the See.

Around the monastic settlement of the Grove on which the

Cathedral now stands, and on which in pre-Christian times may well have been a pagan circle of stones or trees, was later built the wall of the Close, with four gates in its roundness, facing the four points of the compass. And it was around this wall, and mostly on the high ground above it, that there grew the cluster of houses which now make up the City of St. David's.

Around all this are villages and the remains of villages, and the cottage homes or ruins of homes of rustic craftsmen and mariners and farm labourers who at one time made up most of the population. Sloping down from the granite wall on the north towards the sea and the splendid-curving Bay of St. Brides are the farmlands, and farmhouses whose names belong to pre-Norman times. This is the ancient farmland, and on St. David's Head is the earliest farm of all, an Iron Age settlement still traceable in rock and stony soil. Around all this, and beyond the granite wall, is the coastline, magnificent in texture and colour and shape, cliffs guarded by a crowd of ancient field forts whose names are full of the sound of danger. The sea surrounds this westward looking land on three sides, leaving little more than five miles of landward boundary, and that too was once fortified by bank and ditch.

All this is ancient history. The cruel contortion of cliff, the outline of the *carn*, the emanation of the land, even the burdensome bending of every bush away from the west – all these suggest age, and endurance, and a primeval strength. But the significance of St. David's belongs to that past, and neither this story nor any other can ignore it.

The story is primarily of two communities. One is the story of the Celtic farmer who came and settled on higher ground, following his Neolithic predecessor, and slowly and laboriously gained cultivable land for himself and his kinship from high stony slope and marsh. The other is the story of a Celtic missionary monk who saw something good in a hump of a mound in a well-wooded bowl of a valley bisected by the running living water of a little stream which took him safe and sheltered to a creek in a bay. One, the community of the farmer. The other, the community of the priest. They have co-existed and interacted for fourteen hundred years; have known poverty and prosperity; and both have had a very close interest in the land which was the sustenance of them all.

They and their successors were in their time and season the only employers of labour, of craftsmen, of servants male and female, of farm labourers living in tied cottages. It will be part of this story to tell how these supporting communities lived and got on with one another and with their masters; how they housed themselves and ate, how after centuries of being tied to the soil they lifted up their eyes and looked for better things.

Even more significant have been the separate histories of church and farm. Four revolutions in a century and a half transformed the life of the farmer, his farm, and his workers. It took eight hundred years to strip the feudal church, which took over from the Celtic Saints, of its autocratic power, its control over land and administration. The tribal bishop of the Celtic Church was usurped by a Norman feudal bishop who was lord and master of everything in St. David's, lord even of life and death: here in particular, because the See of St. David's was the largest and richest, and its capital was this City. Here was a cathedral church which was also a parish church for a very large parish and for a very small and isolated rural community, dominated by the church and ruled by the bishop. How that changed must also be significant. The autocracy of bishop and chapter meant an extreme conservatism. It meant peace for the parish, for the Norman bishops protected it over the centuries from any involvement with war, and the immunity of the church protected it from any civil disturbance. And that meant continuity. Old customs, old offices of administration, old systems of holding land, stayed on. Dewsland, said Francis Jones, represents the oldest lordship in Wales, one which has remained to our times in the unbroken possession of the heirs and successors of those in whom it was originally vested. That continuity must also be part of our story.

The geography of the Dewisland Peninsula, its extreme western location, has influenced its history immensely, not only in the early days of Celtic civilisation and Christianity but throughout and up to recent times. Norman and English kings came to St. David's as pilgrims, and for other reasons. They looked towards Ireland, forty miles away, a land best conquered, and always a base from which others could endanger their safety. The physical and psychological awareness of Ireland, old linkages of the Celtic Church, long genealogical links of princely families across the water, Irishmen on the soil of Dyfed, questions of naval defence, smuggling – all form part of the Irish element which cannot be forgotten in the story of St. David's.

Here, therefore, is the history of a parish grounded in a rich antiquity; intensely conservative and at the same time subjected by history to enormous change; central, and isolated; Celtic, and Norman; austere; once rich, then poor. And throughout, in some form or other, a place of pilgrimage.

It is a history the assembling of which – and hopefully the reading of which – is not unconnected with a great deal of pleasure. An abundance of material has been found, in a vast variety of scattered and isolated sources. The immense bibliography of the history of the Church has at times been more of a hindrance than a help, because most of it concerns the bishops and the diocese and not the influence of the Cathedral on the everyday life of the man on the farm and on the streets of St. David's. The feudal *Black Book of St. David's*, and a great local stock of wills, land and marriage settlements, indentures of all kinds, remain largely a mass of half-digested material, work for a life-time, not easily linked with the continuing life of the country. Great stretches of local history remain untouched – the history of some of the more notable of the historic farms; the story of the nineteenth century sea captains; and the family histories of the Vicars Choral, the Lower Chapter that became intimately connected with the farms. But there have been three sources of material that have been immediate and relevant to the straightforward social purpose. First, the Parish Chest, rich, although not so old, in content. Secondly, the newspaper, and more particularly what was once known as the Solva paper. *The Dewisland and Kemes Guardian* goes back no further than the middle of the nineteenth century, but an enlightened editor made its continuation, *The West Wales Guardian*, a rich source of information on the antiquities of the parish. Thirdly, there has been the fund of what is now called 'oral history' – the memories and reminiscences of old characters and the notebooks and writings of still older characters. They were well aware of the historical significance of the soil from which they sprang; they knew their family histories, stocks that had been here for centuries. As Gerald the Welshman said, they were knowledgeable to the seventh and eighth and ninth generations. They had cherished the remembrance of old customs; they were rich in what can be called a Celtic memory.

They understood the purpose of this book. People forget, and records get lost. George Owen of Henllys knew that it is wise to record and to assemble, and he told us why.

> Because that either the negligence of such as in elder times lived, or not weighing that time would consume the remembrance of things necessary or worthy to be known, have omitted to commit the same to writing, by means whereof many things worthy of remembrance are forgotten.

The story inevitably, and in defiance of 'Celtic continuity', has been one of change. Porth Glais is not the same as it was. Into this creek in their time came coracled Saints. The men of King Arthur, hunting the Twrch Trwyth (in the Mabinogion), landed in Porth Glais, and went on to Mynyw. Scandinavian raiders, settled in Dublin or the Isle of Man, came to Ramsey and Skomer and Skokolm and swept in to raid the valley and destroy the church. So did Anglo-Saxon raiders; and the Irish pillaged and struck terror and stayed. Gruffudd ap Cynan came into Porth Glais with a motley mob from Ireland and joined forces with Rhys ap Tewdwr, prince of Dyfed seeking sanctuary in St. David's, to fight for the recovery of their lands in the battle of Mynydd Carn. In 1880 Charles Brown of Solva, tidewaiter, saw boats coming in from Bideford and Barnstaple and Bristol, and fishermen from Penzance. The farmers of the hinterland kept their boats here, joint owners with captains and mariners and merchants. Richard Fenton came here, and climbed the highest point of Ramsey and looked at St. Bride's Bay, and saw that it was alive with small craft in all directions.

Today, Dean and Archdeacon and Minor Canon are the only clerics of the Close. Even fifty years ago there were many more; and there were fifty or more names on the electoral roll of the Close, which was a parish within the parish. How many there were when St. David's was in its heyday we do not know; but we are told that the jackdaws of the Close took no terror of crowds, as long as they were dressed in black.

The greatest change came within the last two centuries. The year 1750 was the beginning of a revival which was more than a Methodist Revival, and the Wales of today and the St. David's of today were fashioned, first by that religious awakening, then by its extra-religious, political, educational and social consequences. The initial crusade against spiritual and educational poverty became submerged in a vast complex of national upsurge that combined Nonconformity and Liberalism and changed attitudes and bases of power and methods of local government, and made inevitable the disestablishment of the Anglican Church in Wales. The independence which the Celtic Church had lost when Bernard became the first Norman bishop of St. David's had been recovered. And the Methodist clerics who began the long road to independence all belonged to the Diocese of St. David's.

The Church revived itself in answer to the Nonconformist charge. And the symbol of its regeneration in St. David's was the restoration of the Cathedral in the 1870s. Private enterprise and trade sprouted. Horizons were widened, not least by the great numbers of captains and master mariners. There was talk of the railway, and Captain John Rees built the City Hotel facing the station that was to be but never came. But the pilgrims came, in vast numbers to see the restored Cathedral, and that was the beginning of tourism in earnest and of the pilgrimage of this twentieth century.

Not all has changed. Coastline and cliff remain. And Carn Llidi, thanks to a strange amalgam of lights and levels, turns now and always its seven hundred feet into the dominance of a mountain. And when the thousands come to St. David's in 1980 and 1981 to witness the eight hundredth anniversary of the Norman Cathedral, they will look at a nave which, despite all the surrounding change, is the identical nave of Peter de Leia, Prior of Wenlock, the first builder. And while they think of Peter – most of the history of St. David's is that which links it with the Christian faith – they should remember that he built on a foundation laid by a Celtic missionary monk of a race which at one time were the sole inhabitants of all these western lands. This is Tyddewi, the House of David.

CHAPTER ONE

In the Beginning

In 1915 H. J. Fleure, Professor of Geography and Anthropology at the University College of Wales, Aberystwyth, published in *Archaeologia Cambrensis* a paper on the distribution and spread of Stone Age monuments in Britain. Having considered their distribution patterns, he stressed the importance of the seaways that connected them. In 1925 he contributed an article entitled 'Pembrokeshire: An Essay in Human Geography' to a booklet produced to celebrate Elementary Education in Pembrokeshire, fifty-five years after the Elementary Education Act of 1870. He emphasised the peculiar geographical position of Pembrokeshire, its climate and cultivation, and the remarkable story of its life 'which makes it stand out so separately from the remainder of Wales.' He emphasised in particular the position and history of St. David's (appropriately the booklet carried a photograph of boys and girls studying practical geography outside the new County School built in 1902). He emphasised the importance of the sea in its history – it was a tiny settlement that had grown as a focus behind the great number of little landing places. He noted the strange fate that had transformed an old centre of intercourse with Ireland into a quiet little city. He ended with a reference to a developing tourist trade, to a rural life that was undergoing a great change, and to an isolation that was fast disappearing.

In 1932 the first edition of Sir Cyril Fox's *The Personality of Britain* appeared. In it he studied the sites of monuments and archaeological finds throughout the whole range of British pre- and protohistory, related them to the physical geography of the country, and then went on to plot and identify for the first time the patterns of ancient sea routes that had fed and linked them.

In 1941 E. G. Bowen, now Emeritus Professor of Geography and Anthropology at the University College of Wales, Aberystwyth, published *Wales: A Study in Geography and History*. This was a study in historical geography, of the relations that geography and history bear to each other. He, too, paid special attention to the cultural landscape of St. David's, its scattered farms and lanes and hedgerows, its arable and pasture lands, and its memorials of the past – Cathedral and Bishop's Palace, and St. Mary's College, and the medieval chapels; its hills and promontory forts, and the standing stones and dolmens whose origins lie in the megalithic civilisation of three thousand years before the birth of Christ. To understand the cultural landscape of St. David's, he implied, is to grasp the social and economic history of its past, to relate these to the characteristics of its physical geography, and to see them all in the wider context of the people who settled here and contributed their share to its landscape.

These studies in human geography, of movements and settlements in history, led their authors to certain conclusions. Using all available evidence from history, geography, geology and archaeology, and the results of modern methods of carbon dating, they classified and grouped their findings, plotted them on maps, and looked for patterns. They saw first that movements of people in ancient times had depended on sea routes, because it was easier to travel over water than through rough untamed country. They saw, secondly, that waves of new and civilising influences coming to northern Europe from the Mediterranean and the Middle-East had perforce used sea routes, past Spain and France, and in a great sweep into the Irish Channel, into Ireland, and into the South West through the Bristol Channel, and along the southern coastal plain into Wales. Archaeological finds and datings proved that these successive newcomers, looking for breaks in long voyages, and for short land crossings, had used promontories to good effect, and crossed them to avoid dangerous headlands and currents, and had built and settled on them. Finally, they saw that there had been times when a common western civilisation pattern had embraced Brittany, Cornwall, Wales, Ireland, the Isle of Man, and the Western Isles of Scotland, whose lifeline reached across peninsulas and the sea. Ireland, in particular, had been significant in this pattern. So had the St. David's headland.

One other major conclusion emerged from *The Personality of Britain*, based on the geographical differences between Eastern and Western Britain. Eastern Britain is flat and low, easy to communicate over, open to overland influences crossing the narrow Channel which separates it from the Continent. The west is mountainous, inaccessible, and difficult in communications, more open to influences coming in through the western sea routes. It has a heavily indented coastline and inviting sheltered coves. Because it is further away from the Continent it has been later in receiving continental influences, and has run the risk of being cut off whenever wars or confusions have disturbed the east. Whenever that happened the west fell back on and fed itself along old and familiar seaways. The growth of the Celtic Church depended on this western nourishment, and the historical significance of St. David's rests entirely on it.

In 1954 Professor Bowen published the first of three books on this theme, *The Settlements of the Celtic Saints in Wales*, which was followed in 1969 by *Saints, Seaways and Settlements in the Celtic Lands*, and in 1972 by *Britain and the Western Seas*. In the first he traced the history and travels of the Celtic Saints and the locations of their churches. In the second he demonstrated 'how the great activity known to be associated with the seas of the Atlantic margins of Europe in prehistoric times continued to be of outstanding significance in the diffusion of Christianity in proto-historic times.' The substance of these conclusions he gave in his lecture on 'The Importance of St. David's in Early Times', delivered to the Friends of the Cathedral and printed in their Report in 1955.

Fleure's little city is still little – its population remains under two thousand. Nowadays city and parish rely for their prosperity on agriculture and tourism. There is little to do with the sea, except that holidaymakers crowd the beaches, and Porth Glais and Porth Stinan thrive on holiday boating, and that boatmen fish and take tourists round the islands. The Cathedral is the biggest draw, as always, and the Cathedral is here because of one fact: that the Normans, when history brought them here, realised the religious and political significance of this place in the cradle lands of Celtic Christianity in Wales, and that significance rested in turn on the strange workings of history and geography in early and pre-historic times.

It is the custom of all geographers to begin their account of the land by considering the geology and then the history of how the land was shaped. It is a science which has become embellished with names that are familiar to the people of St. David's, terms like Demetian and Pebidiog rock, Caerfai red conglomerate and Llanfirn shale, and Caerbwdi sandstone, the sandstone out of which most of the Cathedral and many of the buildings and houses of the City have been built. One of the most distinguished of geologists, twice President of the Geological Society, was Dr Henry Hicks. He was born in St. David's.

The foundation of this headland is pre-Cambrian, the oldest of all rocks and the most enduring – the rock of Carn Llidi, Carn Treliwyd, Clegyrfwya, Carn Rhosson and Carn Biri. Around and lying on this pre-Cambrian base, 3000 million years of age, are the younger Cambrian sedimentary rocks of sandy stony soil: they form the plateau below Carn Llidi and Pen Biri; they are the cornlands of historic times.

Around Porth Lisgi and Caerfai stand rocks that are twisted, and folded and faulted in a giant grotesque posture which reveals the contortions of thousands of millions of years ago, when rigid masses of the earth's crust settled down to form the pre-Cambrian base and the spine of high land to the north. Thenceforward it was a matter of constant earth movements, of faulting and thrusting and deposition, of moving glaciers, of erosion and melting and rising and sinking of sea levels, which ultimately formed the peninsulated and intricate coastal patterns of today. In 1188 Gerald the Welshman, coming to St. David's with Archbishop Baldwin to preach the Third Crusade, stopped at Newgale and inspected there a wonderful sunken forest which was then to be seen. Nearly eight hundred years later the citizens of St. David's and curious thousands from far and near flocked to Whitesands Bay to see the revealed stumps of another sunken forest. Once Carn Llidi was an island in a molten sea of lava; now Ramsey is an island in rough waters, with Skomer and Skokolm, and little Green Scar off Solva. Green Scar was isolated by the erosion that made the fiord. Ramsey on the contrary was split from the mainland by the blow of a vicious axe (so the legend says), and the jagged edges of the wound are still there to see.

It was this turmoil of water and rock, of heat and cold, that made this headland, its defensive north wall of granite, its hard rock coast, its creeks and coves, its softer slopes, its islands, and its climate. Neither in earliest times nor now could it offer an easy life. Archaeological remains tell us that earliest man preferred the less cold and softer rock formations in the south of the county for his home and shelter. He settled in the caves of carboniferous limestone in Caldy and Hoyle's Mouth.

The first men who settled around St. David's, and who left their marks behind them, did not live in caves. They came, short, dark haired and dark eyed, from the Mediterranean, from southern France and Spain, and probably originally from the Bible lands of the East. They were men of the New Stone Age.

This Neolithic Man left the warmer shores of the Middle Sea for reasons we do not know, and moved west and north, four thousand or more years ago. In his dug-out tree trunks of boats he carried with him his family, the animals he had tamed, and the grain and the flint implements he had collected, followed the coasts of Western Europe, found the promontories, and settled on their higher slopes around the northern coasts of our peninsula. With him he brought elements of the culture of his lands of origin, some knowledge of farming, a familiarity with boats and the ways of the sea, an inclination towards some kind of settled life now that he did not have to hunt for his food, and an awareness of a more stable society and strong family kinship. It was a slow, steady, peaceful occupation, a migration in family units rather than in the mass, and he found the coastal northern European lands, on the edge of the habitable world, to his liking. We know that he settled on higher slopes within reach of creek or cove because it was there that he built his monuments, his cromlechau, his burial places of the dead. We know therefore that he brought with him a respect for the dead and an awareness of something beyond the animality of life. He was the first settled occupant of the St. David's peninsula, the first farmer, the first builder of huts. He had found what he wanted, land to cultivate, sea, stone, huge masses of stone and the outstanding feature of the land, and flint for stone axes. He showed his skill in the use of dry-walling. He laid a double row of larger stones for foundation, filled in, and built on them, the kind of foundation that *The Black Book of St. David's* tells us was used for building medieval mills, centuries later. The same skill made dry stone walls around little fields. Men build their hedges today on the same plan.

His greatest skill he showed in the building of cromlechau, the three or more massive standing stones on which rested a delicately balanced massive capstone, which in his time he covered with a mound of earth and under which he buried his dead. Time and man have removed the mounds, and now we see the stone frames in their naked grey stark strength. He built them on the Atlantic coast of Europe, in Spain and Brittany, on the promontories of western Britain, and in Ireland and Scotland, and in doing so forged a cultural link of massive and baffling architecture which was to be absorbed later into another and vaster and more colourful Celtic culture in these northern lands. There was no uniform type of cromlech: Capel Ifan, overlooking Newport and Nevern, was chambered and had a kind of portal to be found also in Ireland; Carreg Samson at Longhouse, overlooking Abercastell, was a long barrow with seven uprights and a through passage. Coetan Arthur is within the parish of St. David's. It is badly broken, but archaeologists say that it would be the most distinctive of all were it complete. And high up on Carn Llidi, and above Coetan Arthur, are two small burial chambers, simple capstone boxes using the rock face that was at hand. No one knows whether their cromlechau were simply temple burial places, or ritualistic centres which drew together the members of a family or a tribe. We do not know whether the builders were ordinary settled farming folk or a group of skilled elite, educated priests, the pre-Druid owners of the Old Wisdom. Was this culture diffused and spread steadily from its origins in the eastern Mediterranean, or did it develop spontaneously as groups of migrants settled into a stable agricultural community? We do not know.

Standing stones belong to the end of the Neolithic Age. Like the one at Trecenny, a massive erect stone with a square head, they present their own problems. There is little certainty about either their date or their purpose. They may mark burial places, although there is no great evidence for this. They could be signposts to ancient tracks, or observation posts of the sun or moon. The largest and most impressive in the parish is Maen Dewi, which stands in Dowrog Moor, the two hundred acres of lowland heath in the middle of which is a now silted twenty acre pool and around which is a complex of ancient tracks, from Treiago to the old settlement of Treteio, from Dowrog Bridge to Waun Beddau, from Hendre to Drws Gobaith. The longest of them all, running north and south from Ogof y Ffos on St. Bride's Bay to Rhyd y Cleifion and across country to the slopes behind Penbiri, is Ffos y Mynach or the Monk's Dyke. Archdeacon Payne wrote about it in 1816. Jones and Freeman investigated it, and quoted Archdeacon Payne. Richard Fenton explored it and failed, like all the others, to explain it. Baring-Gould (*In Dewisland*) had his own explanation and related it to Christian times: after Cynyr of Caer Gawch had made over his possessions to the Church the monks of St. David's dug a trench and threw up a bank to cut off their land from that which was secular, and to form all that part which they had enclosed into a refuge and a sanctuary for all who fled from misrule, or from the consequences of their crimes. All that can be said is that it is or appears to be a system, now a broken system, of sunken track and raised pathway across the peninsula. Was the standing stone of Maen Dewi a signpost pointing to an ancient track across the moor? On the available evidence it stood alone and apart and solitary until about 1860, when the cottages were built. If the monks put up that stone, it would have been a thousand years earlier. A Neolithic menhir, the single standing stone, would have been older by another two thousand years.

Westwards, between Maen Dewi and Ramsey Island, is the flat-topped mass of Clegyrfwya. When Baring-Gould excavated its summit in 1902 he thought he was excavating a post-Roman Iron Age fort that had been occupied by the Iron Age Irish Celt who figures in the Life of St. David, the Boia after whom the rock is named. Instead, he found polished stone axes and scrapers and pottery which could be identified, not with the Iron Age, but with a much earlier Stone Age. He did not then realise that Clegyrfwya had been twice occupied, that Boia had re-occupied what was an old Neolithic settlement, had fortified the outside, and for some reason had ultimately to escape from it so scurriedly that he left nothing more than some wood ash behind. Further excavations in 1943 revealed what Baring-Gould had never dreamed of, that below the ruins of the late Iron Age occupation where Boia had lived were foundations of two Neolithic buildings, one of them a rectangular house. In the rock floor were found two rows of four sockets into which the first occupants had fixed the timber posts that supported their roof. *Archaeologia Cambrensis* printed a full report in 1952, and an analysis of the two excavations, one of which belonged to the cromlechau and the menhirs of the Stone Age.

Neolithic Man, farmer and craftsman in stone, survived the coming of new cultures. He stayed (his descendants are still around) and picked up from newcomers something of the arts of metalworking while retaining his Stone Age craft. He may have learnt something of the gold craft of Ireland, but his home on the Headland was far away from the gold route between Wicklow and southern England, and of that little connects with St. David's except the legend of the Dewisland boy who found traders playing with pellets of gold on St. David's Head. There have been very few archaeological finds in metal in the parish, very few Bronze Age finds, and indeed there has been very little planned excavation of any kind to find them. The most recent discovery came by accident. A bulldozer disturbed a tumulus (due south of Cruglas Bridge) on the St. David's to Fishguard road which was mentioned by Jones and Freeman and is marked on the Ordnance Survey map. The Dyfed Archaeological Trust Report of 1975/76 confirmed that it was an earthen round barrow of the Bronze Age containing 'two central human cremation deposits with associated pottery built over another site associated with the Beaker (early Bronze Age) culture.' The sherds or fragments of broken pottery that were found were evidence of the Beaker people who buried their beakers with their dead and who migrated from Central Europe some three thousand years before the birth of Christ. They mixed and married with Neolithic Man. And it was this ethnic mixture that awaited the next arrivals from Europe to these shores. They were our Celtic ancestors.

The Celts, a race of fiercely independent and tribally organised peoples, came out of Central Europe about 1000 BC, overran northern Europe south to the Mediterranean and west to the Atlantic, and became the dominating race in Europe until they met the Romans. They had been in our islands for five hundred years before Julius Caesar came to investigate in 55 and 54 BC, and had come over, it is now believed, not in mass migrations but in smaller groups of tribal settlers each with its own individual cultural characteristics. The last wave was that of the Belgae, who settled in south-east England towards the end of the second century BC. The

Demetae had already settled in south west Wales, and from them is derived the name of Dyfed.

When this migration of tribal units spread into northern Europe and into Britain, they brought with them an Indo-European language, a common language which later developed into two main dialects in these islands, the Goidelic, which included Irish and (following the spread of Irish tribes) Gaelic and Manx; and the Brythonic, which included Welsh and Cornish and Breton. They were a quarrelsome and independent people, but they had this bond of a common language; and later, after their conversion to Christianity, they retained the *cyfathrach*, the kinship of Wales, Ireland, Scotland, Cornwall and Brittany which was the unity of the Celtic Church.

In terms of archaeology they have left us the impression that they were a people intensely concerned with matters of warfare and defence. The Iron Age Irishmen who had re-occupied the Neolithic fort of Clegyrfwya had fortified it, built ramparts to link with natural walls of rock, and had made ditches and banks as secondary defences lower down the slope. They turned a natural rock mass into a fortress camp; they revealed their concern with defence; and they proved that they were builders and engineers. A similar but less obvious skill can be seen in the string of coastal forts around St. David's Head. Castell Coch, north of Longhouse, and Porth y Rhaw, west of Solva, are distinctive and coastal forts on the fringes of the parish. Inside are Penpleidiau, between Caerfai and Caerbwdi, the two protecting 'caers', Castell Heinif, and Caerau, north of Pwllcaerog. All have their similarities; they are called *cestyll* (castles) or *caerau* (forts), and may have affinities with the coastal forts or raths of Ireland; and they are all defensive earthworks, built across the natural advantages of a promontory, and depending on banks and ditches with sometimes a stiffening of stone. Although generally classified as pre-Roman Iron Age, they may well have been built and used at much later dates. What their exact purpose was is another matter. Obviously, they were built in times of uncertainty and danger. The field names around them to this day suggest violence and defence: near Castell Heinif is Parc y Daran, field of thunder, and the clash of iron swords. This is the land of *castell* and *caer* and *milwr*. Were they emergency defences behind which families and cattle could be hurriedly moved in time of sudden danger? They seem safe from the sea: who were the enemies from behind? Were they symptoms of man's growing love for better settlement, and his growing awareness that family and property were worth preparing defences for? In any case, they were the handiwork of the Celt, not impossibly defending himself from another Celt, and it is obvious that he had an eye for country, and the imagination to look for protection in the lie of his land. Grass grown banks of earth and linked walls of stone and rock have now been smoothed by two thousand years of wind and weather; time has moulded them into our landscape. But they remain a significant feature of our pastoral background.

The most notable of these Iron Age remains are on St. David's Head, where there are the remains of a promontory fort which was a complete pastoral settlement, our closest and earliest link with the basic craft of communal farming. The headland is isolated from the land mass by a rampart, Ffos y Milwr, the Warrior's Dyke, a massive dry stone wall which could in its heyday have been fifteen feet high. Supporting it on the eastern or landward side are breastworks and ditches, and an enclosed area that would have been a corral or cattle fold. Small rectangular enclosures lie outside the barrier – these are the Celtic fields, looking like many of the local fields of today and like most of the fields of the parish before the economics of mechanisation compelled the levelling of hedges and a certain loss of character. The tip of the headland has its own natural protection of cliff and rock; and in between the tip and the rampart are the sites of these people's homes, the hut circles, Cytiau'r Gwyddelod (the legendary huts of the Irish), sheltered from the north. These circles and the ancient track over the causeway were excavated in 1902, but very little was found beyond spindlewhorls, rubbing and pounding stones and scrapers, and hardly anything that could be called a weapon or utensil in iron. Small agricultural settlements and small hill and coastal forts, we must assume, made up the pattern in the centuries before the Roman occupation of south eastern Britain and the entry into the proto-age, which means the threshold of recorded history.

The Romans had conquered the Celts in Europe. They were also to subject the Celtic settlers in these islands, swelled by Celtic refugees from Gaul, to Roman order and discipline in a system of government that allowed Celt and Roman to live together in comparative peace, and allowed the Celt to absorb some of the discipline and skills of the Roman mind and exercise some measure of self-rule. The Romans never conquered, or tried to conquer, the Welsh. There was only a military occupation based on a rectangular system of roads and fortifications – the four Cs of Caerleon, Carmarthen, Caernarfon and Chester – and it is doubtful whether their physical presence was ever felt beyond that rectangle. The language of their culture and learning, the language of the Church throughout medieval Europe, and their cultural influence, on the other hand, must have spread further afield. All that can be said is that no fact or find has so far been produced to prove that they ever came to the St. David's peninsula, or to Ireland, or that the Roman road came any further than Carmarthen.

The old writers believed otherwise, and the old guide books advertised an unquestioned and accepted Roman presence. The Ordnance Survey map SM 72 of St. David's shows four stretches of Roman road, two between Penarthur and Waunbeddau, two between Penarthur and Whitesands, and the Roman station on the dunes. But Sheet 138/151 of 1965 has no Roman markings, and the OS Map of Roman Britain is (except for Castle Flemish, which is now taken to be a native homestead built under Roman influence, and Octopitarium, St. David's Head) a total blank west of Carmarthen. This is a situation that must be accepted until archaeological finds prove otherwise. However, these assumed locations and destinations of Roman roads shown on older maps may have a special and different significance, an element of truth hidden in a clutter of old assumptions. There is, for instance, the old belief, remnant of traditional academic and classical education, that a straight road is always a Roman road. And again, as churches in medieval times collected and advertised relics of the Saints for the sake of pilgrimage and profit, so tourist literature of a later age advertised bits of catching history, such as assumed Roman sites, for the sake of tourism and profit. And there is the story of Richard of Cirencester, chronicler monk of the fourteenth century.

Richard of Cirencester wrote a history of Roman Britain and said that the Via Julia, the great Roman road into South Wales, carried on from Muridunum (Carmarthen) to 'a point on the western coast', thirty short miles to the coast of Ireland. And there, he said, was a Roman station called Menapia. Fenton thought he had found it. Jones and Freeman decided that if it ever existed it was buried under the Burrows. And during the Second World War an enormous quantity of sand was carted away from this area for the construction of St. David's and Brawdy airfields, and Evan Evans, who drew the parish map for Henry Evans's second edition of *The Twr y Felin Guide*, kept those diggings under constant supervision. Nothing to suggest a Roman camp was seen, nor has anything been seen since.

We must assume that the monk of Cirencester knew of the importance of Carmarthen, of the historical and geographical significance of Ireland, and of the link by road and sea between Carmarthen and Ireland. That was the whole purpose of his argument. He erred on distance – it is over forty miles – but he was right in that Porth-mawr is the nearest crossing point to Ireland. Legend – Rhygyfarch's *Life of St. David* – says that St. Patrick prepared a ship in Porth-mawr and sailed for Ireland. The *Lives* tell us that Aeddan, Declan, Findian of Clonard, Gildas, David himself, crossed between Ireland and St. David's. It has been said that Irish Saints and medieval pilgrims on their way to one of the most famous shrines in Europe, St. James of Compostella, passed through St. David's. Henry II, on the expedition to Ireland in 1171 that stilled his conscience after the murder of Thomas Becket, and on the return journey, passed through St. David's; and a twelfth-century manuscript, *De Situ Brecheniauc*, records the journey from Llanfaes in Brecon to Ireland of Marchell, mother of Brychan Brycheiniog. She was returning to the country of her father to marry an Irish prince, and took a road that could well have been used by her father on one of those raiding parties which were the regular excursions of the Irish. The manuscript tells us that she sailed from Porth-mawr. Whether it was she who gave its name to the little village of Caerfarchell is another story. Richard of Cirencester knew of the old Roman road from Brecon to Carmarthen, and he knew of Porth-mawr as an embarkation point to Ireland. Between Carmarthen and Porth-mawr were two ancient tracks. One was a road used by raiders and pilgrims and saints, and on it was the church of Clydau, with its three Celtic crosses; and Nevern, full of Celtic crosses and burials, cromlechau and standing stones and circles, and the bilingual Vitaliani and Maglocunus stones – this was and still is the shortest road from Carmarthen to the west, the road to Porth-mawr over Dowrog Moor, Tir y Pererinion (Pilgrim Land), to Feidr Dywyll and Bonyng's Gate and the Cathedral Close. The other road came from Carmarthen through Whitland and Spittal, Llawhaden and Whitchurch and Llandridian, pilgrim resting places, past Dwr Cleifion (the old way from Haverfordwest) to the City and the Tower Gate. These were the ancient tracks which the monk of Cirencester called Roman roads. On a much larger scale, in the seventeenth century, and in the strip map style used in guides to our modern motorways, John Ogilby traced the ancient roads to St. David's, one from Holywell in North Wales, the other from London.

Christianity reached south-eastern England some two hundred years before the departure of the Roman legions between 410 and 415 AD. There is very little evidence that it spread beyond the towns and the villas of the wealthy, nor that it departed from the normal Roman pattern which was a diocesan urban church where each city had its bishop. There is no evidence that this type of Christianity spread into Wales except possibly into the south-eastern quarter where there is a questionable Christian church at Caerwent. What is important however is that there is growing evidence that some form of 'diocesan' Christianity of Roman type survived the final withdrawal of Roman troops from Wales. It could not be the same as the diocesan Christianity in south-eastern Britain and we think that it was organised in the West in Ireland and Wales on 'tribal' lines. That is that some Christian teachers either continued alongside of the Druids or replaced them at the court of the local chieftain whose headquarters would be in a hill fort. The head of these Christian teachers would be the equivalent of a bishop wandering about the tribe's territory, which would be his diocese. Into such a situation either just before or immediately after the Roman withdrawal came a number of Christian missionaries from the Eastern Mediterranean who introduced a type of monastic Christianity like that of the Egyptian Desert. On the one hand there is now abundant archaeological evidence to prove that the western shores of Britain and especially the Severn Sea were in direct contact by trade with the Eastern Mediterranean, and that this monastic type of Christianity came along these trade routes, possibly directly to St. David's Head and to Llanbadarn and elsewhere. On the other hand, we think that this new type of eremitical Christianity fused with what remained of the now weak and older Roman pattern and that of this fusion and revival of energy the Celtic Church with its Celtic Saints (St. David included) emerged. In whatever way modern evidence is considered it makes it abundantly clear that there was Christianity (largely Eastern in form) in western Wales, including the St. David's area and the coast of the Severn Sea, at least three hundred years before St. Augustine came to Canterbury.

It is likely that St. David's, centrally placed between Christian settlements on the Severn and Christian settlements in south-east Ireland established in the same way, made its first Christian contacts through the movements of missionaries and refugees moving from Gaul to Ireland. The Roman occupation in Britain, molested in the south by the Anglo-Saxons, in the north by the Picts, and increasingly from the west by the Irish, was further imperilled by the withdrawal of the legions to defend the main body of the Empire. As a direct consequence there were movements of people in Gaul and in Wales itself. In the last days of the Roman occupation Cunedag (or Cunedda) was sent from Manaw Gododdin, north of the Forth in Scotland, into North Wales to expel the Scots (the Irish) from these regions, and he did so with a very great slaughter. And in the fourth century AD a tribe from Waterford in Ireland, called the Deisi, came over and made settlements in Dyfed, and further complicated the mixture of bloods on the St. David's headland. The generally accepted explanation for these movements of people is that they were associated with invitations from the Romans, and especially from Maxen Wledig (Magnus Maximus), to protect Wales and the fringes of the Empire against further incursions by the pagan Irish. The ultimate kingdom of the Sons of Cunedda stretched from the Dee to the Teifi, and the adjacent kingdom of the Deisi in Dyfed stretched eastward into Gower. The Deisi ruled this kingdom up to the tenth century. The ogham inscribed stones of the fifth and sixth centuries derive from this Irish invasion. On these inscribed stones were funerary and commemorative messages, written in the Ogham alphabet which originated in southern Ireland, or in Latin, the language of the Roman Church and reaching these parts from western Gaul, or in both.

The settlements of the Celtic Saints eventually moved hand in hand with the growth of the Celtic kingdoms. The first step was the conversion of the princely families of those kingdoms, and the Saints themselves, as the history of David shows, were members of those princely families.

CHAPTER TWO

The Coming of Dewi Sant

About 1090 Rhygyfarch of Llanbadarn Fawr wrote his *Life of St. David*. The 1963 Report of the Friends of the Cathedral contains a lecture by Professor D. Simon Evans on 'An Approach to the Historical Dewi', and his introduction refers to and quotes from an article (in *Studia Hibernica*) on St. Patrick and his biographers. There is a problem here which the writings of Nora Chadwick have done their best to explain. It concerns the accumulation over the centuries of legends around the names of both Patrick and David, and other Saints, the scarcity of historical fact, the almost complete lack of contemporary witness, and the difficulties involved in the interpretation of *Lives* of Saints which were written after a lapse of centuries by medieval clerics. We all know that Patrick belonged to the fifth and David to the sixth century. We know that both became great missionaries and founders of monasteries and the patron saints of their respective countries. When we begin to look for biographical and historical details of either, they are very hard to find.

Stripped of its legendary trappings, the story of Patrick is that he was born in western Britain (one legend mentions the Severn area, another Dumbarton in Scotland) into a family connected with the Church. His father was a deacon, and he was the grandson of a presbyter or priest. Captured by Irish pirates, he was taken to Ireland as a slave, escaped, and ultimately returned to Ireland to work as a missionary. He became based on Armagh, where he built his monastery and did his greatest work.

David on the other hand was sprung from a princely class. His mother was Non, daughter of Cynyr of Caer Gawch, descended from Brychan Brycheiniog, the legendary father of a brood of Saints called the Children of Brychan. Brychan's mother was the Marchell who sailed for Ireland from Porth-mawr. David's father was Sandde or Sant, son of Ceredig, founder of the kingdom of Ceredigion, who was the son of Cunedda Wledig, the man who led his tribe into North Wales from Gododdin in Scotland. This son of Ceredigion, David, was born, according to the *Life*, in the time of Triphunus, grandfather of Voteporix, King of Dyfed, whose name appears in Latin and in Ogham on a famous inscribed stone at Castell Dwyran. A son of Triphunus (whose name may well be remembered in the name of a farm, Lochtwrffin, in the parish of Llanrheithan) was Aercol Lawhir, Agricola the Generous, who gave to St. Teilo the land on which Llanhowel Church was built. They were all kings of the Deisi.

That is the genealogy of St. David as it is given in *Bonedd y Saint*, the Descent of the Saints, compiled in the twelfth century, and as it is given at the end of Rhygyfarch's *Life of St. David*. There are, however, some records in manuscript and in stone that belong to the intervening centuries, and they tell us something about his reputation and his work.

The first is to be found, appropriately, in Llanddewibrefi, the second most important of the churches of St. David. Built into the wall of the church is a broken piece of memorial stone whose message was recorded by Edward Lluyd in 1699. Here, it says, lies Idnert, the son of Jacobus, killed . . . and the message ends with *Sancti Davvid*. That stone contains an almost contemporary reference to the Saint. It is in Latin, the language of Roman learning and of the Celtic Church, and it uses a type of phrasing – *Hic jacet* – which was brought into Wales by missionaries from Gaul and initially from North Africa. It appears to record the death of a Christian who belonged to the cult of David, victim of the violence against man and church which was by no means absent in the Age of the Saints.

The name of David is to be found in Irish manuscripts, in the *Catalogue of the Saints of Ireland* and in the *Martyrology of Oengus*. He is referred to as *David Cille Muni*, David of the Church of Mynyw (a phrase familiar in the Irish Lives) and, for the first time, he is linked with the first day of March.

In the *Life of St. Paul Aurelian*, written in Brittany in the early years of the ninth century, we have the first reference to the ascetism of the Saint. He is called David Aquaticus, *Y Dyfrwr*, The Waterman.

At the end of the ninth century, Asser, cleric and member of the *clas* or community in St. David's, wrote his *Life of Alfred*. In it he refers to the *parochia Degui*, the territory of David – a statement of the continuing influence of the Saint, two hundred years later, expressed in terms of the power and territorial extent of his church. According to the Laws of Hywel Dda there were in the kingdom of Dyfed seven houses – St. David's, St. Ishmael, Llandegfan, St. Issel's, Llandeilo, Llandeulyddog and Llangeneu – which belonged to the bishop of St. David's.

'Armes Prydein Fawr' is a Welsh poem contained in a manuscript called *Llyfr Taliesin*. This poem, written in the early years of the tenth century makes five references to David, and its chosen language makes clear that David at this time was regarded as patron saint and standard bearer of the Welsh; to him and to God alone was obedience to be rendered. Although Sir Ifor Williams was of the opinion that the writer was a cleric rather than a bard, the poem seems to have had an implicit aim, a political aim also implicit in the three variants of the *Life of St. David.*

The last of the 'David' references comes in *Annales Cambriae*, the Welsh Chronicles. These are brief historical notes extracted from the Easter Tables and compiled towards the end of the tenth century. They are so involved in the affairs of St. David's that it must be assumed the manuscript was written in the scriptorium of the monastery. For the year 601 is entered *David episcopus moni ieudorum.* The date of entry and the last two words of the record are controversial. It may, however, be a reference to the death of St. David.

About the year 1090 Rhygyfarch wrote his *Life of St. David*, and although he claimed to have collected together some very old writings of the country and especially of the monastery which had survived the constant devouring of moths, it is obvious from the first few paragraphs that he was not writing a documentary history. He had no contemporary records, and the writing of a documentary history was never, in any case, the aim of the clerics of the twelfth and later centuries who were responsible for the *Lives*.

Divine oracles foretold the birth of David. Sant, prince of Ceredigion, was told thirty years earlier that he was to be the father. In the fullness of time he came to a community of the people of Dyfed, and met Non. Gildas, struck dumb while preaching in a certain church, found that Non was hiding in the church, and then realised that the child she was carrying was destined to be a saint of grace and power and rank. Patrick, after his escape and wanderings, came to Ceredigion, then to Dyfed, and then to Vallis Rosina in the Alun Valley, and perceiving that the place was pleasant vowed to serve God faithfully there. He was stopped by an angelic voice and told that Ireland, not Vallis Rosina, was to be his mission field, and sailed from Porth-mawr. Miracles came before and after the birth on the serene spot surrounded by lightning and thunder and floods, and the stone split at the place where a church of St. Non now stands with that stone lying covered in the foundation of its altar. At the baptism a fountain of clearest water, bursting forth, suddenly appeared for the administration of the rite, and the blind monk who was holding the babe received his sight. And all that were present glorified the Lord and holy David on that day. The child was educated, and grew up full of grace and lovely to behold, first at Hen

Fynyw, then with Paulinus. Then David at the command of an angel went out into the world, and founded monasteries, returned to Hen Fynyw, and came in the end to Vallis Rosina (the Valley of the Close) which the Britons commonly call Hodnant, and kindled there his first fire in the name of the Lord. The smoke from that fire aroused the anger of a druid and chieftain called Boia, who was prevented from killing David and his attendants by a miracle, and in repentance gave the whole of Vallis Rosina to David for a perpetual possession. There was founded the notable monastic community that laboured in increasing zeal with hand and foot, that regarded possessions with disdain, that when outside labour was finished read and wrote and prayed, and that adopted voluntary poverty and humility and obedience, 'imitating the monks of Egypt'. Meanwhile the report of holy David's good name grew, and the reputation of his monastery. His disciples went forth to preach and to found churches. He himself, with his companions, Padarn and Teilo, went to Jerusalem, and returned bearing gifts, one of them a portable altar. Miracles increased, and then came the 'poisonous serpent', the heresy of Pelagius (that man can gain salvation without the means of grace), and the synod of Llanddewibrefi, and the Saint's greatest sermon, preached on a pile of garments that later swelled into a hill. Thereafter the brethren continued to build churches and monasteries, and David the bishop was made the chief overseer of all, and the other bishops surrendered to him both monarchy and primacy. On the third day of the week on the first of March, having preached to his brethren that they should persevere in the things they had seen and learnt from him, he died, and was buried in his own monastery.

That is the legend according to Rhygyfarch, the monk who wrote a magnification of the Saint and his work, the austere goodness of his character, the extent of his missionary work, the hardworking strictness of his rule, the austerity of character and power of preaching that had made him eminent above all other Saints.

It all began in the Valley. Inside, we imagine, a wattled circular palisade surrounding the wattled huts of monks was a wooden church, small as Celtic churches were, which housed the altar rather than the community at worship. Around was the land this community farmed, and the district they accepted into their spiritual care. Our knowledge of the *clas*, the term given to this community, is fragmentary. It was a community of clerics whose head was prince or chief, and therefore hereditary. Obviously, the early missionaries had taken for granted that to convert the prince was also to convert his tribe. The characteristics of the *clas* were tribal: the clerics were leading members of the tribe, assisted by lay members of the tribe;

their church stood on tribal land; they educated the children of the tribe. This is the explanation of the correlation that seems to have existed between the settlements of the Saints and the old Celtic kingdoms, and why the influence of the Saint expanded with the growth of the kingdom. According to Rhygyfarch, Boia gave Vallis Rosina to David. We learn that Cynyr of Caer Gawch in Mynyw gave his land to David. In 1082 Rhys ap Tewdwr, king of Deheubarth, the man who took refuge in David's sanctuary, gave the land of Pebidiog which he had recovered from his enemies to the bishops of St. David's, in gratitude, or in hope of salvation. The bishop, himself a member of the princely class, worked in co-operation with the tribal prince and became quite naturally the bishop of a kingdom. There are 53 dedications to David, churches stretching from South Cardigan, the kingdom of his father, right across south west Wales (and in addition churches in Ireland and Brittany and elsewhere), all sprung, as it were, from the mother church in St. David's. Some he had himself dedicated; others were dedicated by his disciples and believers in his cult; and there were later rededications. In total they reflect the influence of the man and the spread of his cult in a clearly defined area of South Wales. This was the background to the immensity of the medieval diocese. Hywel Dda said that Mynyw was 'a principal seat in Dyfed'; he had inherited Ceredigion and Ystrad Tywi; Dyfed came to him through marriage; and when he came to rule Deheubarth his kingdom and the vast medieval diocese were co-extensive; by 720 St. David's had absorbed the diocese of Llanbadarn and was later to solve some controversial boundary problems with Llandaff. Ecclesiastical and political boundaries agreed.

It was this diocese as it was in his day that was uppermost in Rhygyfarch's mind when he settled down to write the first *Life of Saint David.* His father was its bishop; his brothers were all clerics in its service. Hywel Dda was dead. William the Conqueror had already paid his dark shadow of a visit to St. David's. Rhygyfarch began to write the Life of the Saint whom he regarded as superior to all others. He had before him a few manuscripts written some time or other during the five hundred years that had passed since the Saint's death. He knew that the diocese of St. David's, and the prestige and authority of his own family, lay under threat from a Norman sword.

How did Rhygyfarch see the situation ? In the west was the tribal and independent Celtic Church to which he belonged. In the east was an Anglo–Saxon–Norman diocesan church, centred on Canterbury and strongly linked with the main stream of continental Christianity. They were two streams that over five hundred years had developed their own peculiarities in ritual and organisation. There was in addition a continuing Celtic hatred of the Anglo-Saxon people, a political gap which religion could not bridge. The Celtic church differed in its dating of Easter; it differed in matters of tonsure and baptism; Celtic priests were not celibate; their church lacked diocesan or metropolitan authority. The Celts above all were strongly independent and would never have allowed the development of a church united and orthodox in all things: they were united only when face to face with a hated Anglo-Saxon Church represented by Canterbury. In the sixth century Augustine had hoped to reconcile them; he had been commissioned that the ignorance of the west should be taught; its weakness strengthened by persuasion; its perversity corrected by authority. They came face to face when, about 603, he met the British bishops. Hopes of some understanding and co-operation rose after 768, when the Church in Wales finally adopted the Roman method of calculating Easter. And some hope of peace and security must have dawned after the establishment of a political boundary between Celt and Anglo-Saxon in Offa's Dyke. When Pope Leo III spoke to all the people of Britain in 789 he included Wales, but he was very careful to limit the jurisdiction of Canterbury to England. A Celtic understanding with Rome, possibly. With Canterbury, no.

It was the onset of the Viking invasions in the ninth and tenth centuries that began to alter things. Danes and Norsemen began to harry and loot the western coasts, concentrating particularly on the mother churches, and Anglo-Saxon raids added to the devastation. *The Welsh Annals* tell the brutal tale of St. David's.

810 Y llosges y Saeson Mynyw
906 Miniw fracta est (dilewyt)
975 Gothrit et haraldus vastaverunt Meneviam
987 Gentiles vastaverunt Meneviam
993 Tertio Menevia vastata est
998 Menevia vastata est (diboblet) a gentilibus et Morganau Episcopus occisus est
1012 Menevia a Saxonibus vastata est
1022 Eilaf vastavit Demetam, Menevia fracta est. Y torret Mynyw
1071 Menevia vastata est a gentilibus
1078 Menevia a gentilibus vastata est (diffeithwyt yn druan) et Abraham a gentilibus occiditur
1088 Archa s. David ab ecclesia furata est, et auro argentque quibus tegenature spoliata est. Ducpwyt ysgrin Dewi yn lledrat or Eglwys ac yspeilwyt yn ymyl y ddinas
1089 Menevia fracta est a gentilibus insularum

And then the devastation stopped, presumably because by now the hated enemies had been converted to Christianity. How complete the devastation was there is no means of knowing. It is generally believed that the Danish raids, the raids of 'the black pagans', were small and carried out by groups of two or three ships. The fact remains that gold and silver were taken, and stock, and probably men and women as slaves. Two bishops were killed, and the shrine, the reliquary of St. David, taken outside of the City and desecrated. The raids may have been small; the victims were defenceless; and the raiders had no mercy.

There was no hope of concerted resistance against these attacks because there was disunity amongst the Welsh princes, and in desperate bids for help against the aggressors some of them engineered unholy alliances with Anglo-Saxon kings. Asser of St. David's went to work with King Alfred the Great, and to plead for aid. Hywel Dda turned east and entered into alliance first with Edward the Elder and later with Athelstan. His kingdom of Deheubarth paid homage and tributes in gold and silver, in cattle and hunting dogs and hawks. These alliances aroused fear and opposition, and the greatest fear as always was that a proud and independent Celtic Church should fall into the hands of Canterbury. Religious unease turned against political expediency, and it was this, according to Melville Richards, that led to the writing of the prophetic poem called 'Armes Prydein Fawr'. It was a poetic cry for unity, a plea that the Celtic people should come together to push the Anglo-Saxons, the usurpers of Brythonic land, into the sea. In this poem Dewi, David, appeared as a symbolic leader, and it was his unsullied banner – *lluman glân Dewi* – that they were asked to raise aloft. The Patron Saint had become a rallying point of patriotism.

A hundred years after that poetic protest against Hywel Dda's political entanglements Rhygyfarch began to write his *Life of St. David*. Dangerous times called for a leader. His father, the learned cleric who had to rush flabbergasted from Llanbadarn Fawr to meet none other than William the Conqueror in the church in St. David's, had been recalled as bishop. The peacemaking of Hywel Dda was falling apart. Rhygyfarch knew that the Norman French were advancing in Wales, and he knew that the church of his father was in peril. He wrote, therefore, in praise of David, of his monastery in the Valley, of his missionary work and the strict austerity of his cult, and of the vast area of country that now nurtured that cult. Rhygyfarch magnified his subject. That is why modern scholarship, and Nora Chadwick in particular, looks on this *Life* as a document that tells us more about the time of Rhygyfarch than about the time of David. Nora Chadwick considered it as our earliest and most authoritative surviving Welsh contribution to the last phase of the controversy about the independence of the Celtic Church, its last defensive cry. In 1115, fifteen years after Rhygyfarch's death, Bernard the Norman was elected bishop of St. David's, a deliberately blunt and political choice. He was not even priest: on the Saturday he was ordained, and consecrated bishop on the following day. Rhys ap Tewdwr, patron prince of the church in his day, who had paid his rent to the Conqueror, had been killed fifteen years earlier by the Normans, and it was Caradog, monk-confessor, harpist at the court of Rhys, who described the seven years of desolation, of defencelessness, before the Norman Conquest, before the danger became imminent. The tomb of the Saint, he said, was masked in briars, and the place a ruin.

Gerald the Welshman, about 1200, rewrote Rhygyfarch's *Life*. He had tried and failed to become bishop of St. David's, which is why the modern figure of Gerald in Holy Trinity Chapel shows the mitre, not in his hands but lying at his feet. Gerald had Norman blood in his veins, but he had little love for Norman ways with church property. His mother, however, was Welsh, and as canon and archdeacon he spent the prime of his life and energy in trying to keep St. David's independent of Canterbury. There is much in his writing to suggest that he saw in St. David's what his maturer years wanted to see: a remote and solitary place, a place ideal for contemplation and scholarship. He spent the last fifteen years of his life here, and was buried here. It is no wonder, therefore, that the legendary events of David's early life are localised in his work. Rhygyfarch made Sant and Non to meet in Dyfed. Gerald made them meet in Pebidiog. And it was he who tied the details of David's birth and baptism to Porth Glais, and by so doing encouraged to grow and cling around the place the legends which the people of St. David's and all Welshmen have cherished ever since.

In 1326 a Welsh version of Rhygyfarch's Latin *Life* was written by the Anchorite of Llanddewibrefi. He cut out the Irish elements that were in Rhygyfarch, and the journey to Jerusalem, and made the aim and purpose of the Synod of Llanddewibrefi, not the removal of the Pelagian heresy, but the election and proclamation of David as head of the Saints, as 'pennadur ar seint ynys Prydein'. When the Anchorite was writing, Wales had been deprived of its independence for sixty years, but Dafydd ap Gwilym was writing, the Mabinogion were being compiled in the Red Book of Hergest, and there was a sudden spurt of the national spirit in Wales. Owain Glyndwr's uprising came eighty years later.

Rhygyfarch said that David was educated at Hen Fynyw. Mynyw (in Latin, *Menevia*) is the accepted old name for St. David's, and *Mynyw* is related to the Irish word *mwni*. Local people call the old farm of Tremynydd Tremwni, and the Irish Saints came from Ireland to Cell Muine (*The Life of Findian*) or Chell Muny (*The Life of Declan*) or as in the Latin *Life of St. Finnian* to *civitas Kellmunnensis*, the monastery of the wooded valley or the grove. But if Mynyw is St. David's Hen Fynyw was and still is on the west coast of Ceredigion.

Below Carn Llidi and overlooking St. Patrick's Chapel (or the reputed site of it on the dunes of Porth Mawr) is Ty-gwyn Farm. Legend persists that here was once a monastery of the same name. Richard Fenton had no doubt of it. Jones and Freeman referred to faint traditions and ruins of uncertain date. Baring Gould, writing on Celtic monasteries in *Archaeologia Cambrensis* (1900) mentioned the white-washed stone-built monastery, the Candida Casa of Ty Gwyn. There is so far little archaeological proof. Graves have been uncovered. The Penarthur inscribed crosses, now in the west end of the Cathedral, including the Gurmarc stone, are said to have come from there. Some say that David was educated in this monastery, and that Non retired to it. Some go further and say that the conflict between David and Boia arose because the Saint wanted this monastery (it was a remarkably exposed site for a monastery) moved to Vallis Rosina and Boia objected. So be it, but modern scholarship will not accept that Rhygyfarch's Vetus Rubus or Hen Fynyw was in St. David's at all.

Let us go to Ceredigion, to the land of Ceredig who was David's father. In Ceredigion was one of the most famous of monasteries, the monastery of St. Padarn in Llanbadarn Fawr, famous for its learning, the monastery of Sulien and his four sons. Some miles further south was another, on the coast south west of Aberaeron, and around it to this day is an indisputable cluster of 'David' names. In the cantref of Anhuniog is Hen Vynyw itself, the parish church of which is now St. David's, and nearby is a Ffynnon Dewi. On the coast is Llan Ina, and St. Ina was David's aunt; and Llangrannog, the monastery of St. Carannog, who was David's uncle; and nearby again is Llannon, the church of St. Non, David's mother. Here, it is said, David received his early education. And here, some say, he was born.

There is no disputing where David built his monastery. That crowning glory belongs to St. David's. In an article in *Antiquity* (1945) Professor E. G. Bowen detailed three phases in the settlements of the Saints in South Wales. The earliest settlements, highly Romanised, affected the eastern districts. The second, the 'Irish' phase, influenced both the eastern Romanised area and the St. David's peninsula and the extreme western region which the Romans had but lightly touched. This was the Brynach phase. The last was the phase of St. Teilo and St. David. They, with Padarn, were second generation Saints. The older generation, Cadog and Dyfrig and Illtud, had laboured in the south-eastern parts of Wales, and the great monasteries they had founded had grown into centres of scholarship and of seclusion at the expense of missionary work. David and Teilo came as revivers, a puritan cleansing force whose rule was austerity, obedience and hard labour, and a force overwhelmingly eager for missionary preaching. They were the makers of a revitalised Celtic Church, inspired by Mediterranean monastic ideals and by the founder of strict monasticism in Gaul, Martin de Tours. They had the enthusiasm to convert and preach. The dedications to St. David are evidence of the spread of his cult into areas that had already known Christianity and into areas that were newly converted. That this austere and revivalist monasticism spread further afield than Wales can also be accepted: that is the most logical explanation for the inclusion of St. David amongst the list of Irish Saints in the *Martyrology of Oengus*.

The Celtic Saints were great travellers. They believed that 'it was good and godly to go on pilgrimage to holy places', and, as Gildas the Wise put it, 'to voyage over seas and to pass over broad tracts of land was to them not so much a weariness as a delight'. They did it all for the love of God. According to Rhygyfarch, David, having completed his education, went forth to start his missionary work, by amassing bundles of souls for the heavenly barns of eternal blessedness. He started from Hen Fynyw across South Wales to Glastonbury, the oldest Christian foundation in England, and across the country to the ancient kingdom of Mercia, back through Glascwm in Radnorshire and Erging (or Archenfield) in Hereford, and to Hen Fynyw again. On that journey, according to legend, he founded twelve monasteries. There followed the momentous journey from Ceredigion to settle in Vallis Rosina, where he kindled his first hearth in the name of the Lord. The smoke from that fire, forecasting greatness to come, filled the whole of the island, and Ireland besides. Rhygyfarch makes David go later, accompanied by Padarn and Teilo, to Jerusalem to be consecrated Archbishop. In those desperate days of the Celtic Church Rhygyfarch wanted to show that David's authority came from here and not from Rome or Canterbury. This was the last stand of the Celtic Church.

The most distinctive mark of David's monastery was its ascetism, its strict rule which was 'the rule and model of right living'. Men submitted themselves to a life of austerity and strict discipline (excessively so, according to Gildas), to toil with their bodies to pull the plough, to live on bread and water and the herbs of the countryside, to immerse their naked flesh in the cold waters of the stream, to banish luxury and all riches. The paragraphs describing the strict 'Waterman' rule of David's notable monastery, which included caring for the traveller, the sick and the old, are among the most interesting paragraphs in the *Life*. They bear the mark of a rare authenticity, which suggests that they could well have come from those very old writings, survivors of the constant devouring of moths and the borings of ages, which Rhygyfarch said he had found in the monastery.

Water was important to the Saints, and Rhygyfarch knew the significance of holy wells, the springs of living water worshipped by pre-Christian Celts, and later sanctified by the Saints, or started by them. Through wells they performed miracles, and alongside them they built their chapels. Of these wells, sacred and otherwise, St. David's has been blessed with an abundance. Every farm, the older houses in the City, each has its well. Penlan Farm has three. There are necklaces of them from the Square to Porth Glais, in Naw Ffynnon (the place of nine wells), even on the high ground of Maesymynydd. Rhygyfarch mentions at least four: the fountain of clearest water that gushed forth for the administration of baptism of the infant David (which according to local tradition was in Porth Glais, but not according to Rhygyfarch); the well of Merthyr Dunod which sprang from the spot where Boia's wife killed her step-daughter as a sacrifice to pagan gods; the well which sprang in answer to David's prayer and the complaints of the brethren, the water of which turned into sacramental wine, St. Mary's Well; and the well started by David in answer to the prayer of a rustic whose land was drained dry.

Francis Jones's *Holy Wells of Wales* lists 236 wells in Pembrokeshire, of which twelve belonged to St. David's. Ffynnon Gweslan and Ffynnon Eluid are no longer identifiable. Ffynnon Faeddog is on the road to Porth-mawr: Maeddog is St. Aeddan (St. Aidan of Ferns in Ireland) whose name remains in the name of Trefaeddan Farm. There is Ffynnon Penarthur. And Brorghys or Burghers' Well, the Ffynnon Cwcwll of Quickwell Hill (*cwcwll* comes from the Latin *cucullus*, the cowl of a monk which was similar in shape to the covering of the well). Whit – or Whitewell is the well on the site of the priory or hospitium, a sanctuary for the sick and old established by Adam Beck, bishop from 1280 to 1293; it once supplied the Deanery with water. And the strange Ffynnon Lygad, high on the west side of the rock face of Clegyrfwya, a basin of a well which tradition says ebbs and flows with the tide. Each of these wells had its tale to tell, enchanting if not credible. It is a pity that some have now been lost.

The well, the spring of clear water, symbol of life and purity, was of great importance in the mind of the Celtic Christian, and in particular to the cult of David. Around the well the Saint met his people, and alongside it he built his church. The river, the Alun, was equally significant. So was the surrounding sea, and the coastline and the little landing places. All played their part in the establishment of the monastery in the Valley. The place became a crossroads, a meeting place for those intrepid wanderers who carried their merchandise of the Word to all the countries around the Irish Sea. As Nora Chadwick has emphasised, the early Celtic Church was a church of seafarers; like St. Brendan, they were the navigators of Christ. And because David had built his monastery in the Valley and through it had spread his influence far and wide, the Normans, when they came, had enough political tact and religious respect to grasp the significance of St. David's in the Celtic Christian mind, and they built their cathedral on the foundations that he had laid.

It was Gerald the Welshman who thought that remoteness from the bustle of the world, a seclusion apt for meditation, had persuaded David to choose this site. No one can say that he was wrong. That stillness can be met to this day on the coastal path, in the Cathedral Close, on the cliffs below Treginnis and on the cobbled pathway that leads to Cloister Bridge and the Great West Door. And one can hear it in mid-winter, time of evensong, when in the company of the buried Saints one monkish voice intones words some two thousand years of age.

To some of the Saints in the Age of Saints solitude, a self-imposed withdrawal, was the golden dream, the ultimate discipline. After having submitted themselves to the austerity and discipline of monastic rule, and after having toiled and prayed and watched, and quelled the fires of lust and banished luxury and riches, some wanted to practise greater abstinence and lead a more spiritual life as hermits and anchorites. They looked for caves and the loneliness of islands. Some, we know, went to Caldy. St. Govan found his well of fresh water and built his little two-celled chapel in a desolation of rocks within a stone's throw of the sea. And to Ramsey, Ynys Dewi, the island across the water, came St. Justinan in a vessel of woven osiers and hides tanned in oak bark and rubbed with grease from sheep's wool, praying continually to God that He might convey him to a land where he could lead a solitary life. On this island of Ramsey, said George Owen, were two chapels – they are not there any more, although inscribed stones and graves have been uncovered – one belonged to Dyfanog, the other to Stinan, the St. Justinan of the coastal chapel and the Lifeboat Station. Both were Saints of Brittany and great friends. St. Justinan was, like St. David, a strict ascetic. The legend goes that he was excessively so and for that reason was murdered by some monks on the island, and swam over to the mainland, through the 'Watrin', carrying his severed head in his hands. His murderers were struck with leprosy and were sent to work their penance on Ynys y Gwahan, the Leper's Island which is north of the Sound.

St. David was the great missionary of the Celtic Church. The Normans who were to take charge of St. Davids in 1115 knew the significance. They wrenched the Celtic Church eastwards towards Canterbury and overland towards Europe, and away from Ireland and the western seas. They built a Norman cathedral, turned the old Celtic tribal diocese into a Norman feudal diocese, and through Pope Calixtus II canonised the Saint and put his name on the Calendar of Saints. Kings of England and archbishops of Canterbury ordained that his Day should be celebrated with a service of nine lessons. It is regrettable that sometimes, when we look at their great edifice in the Valley, we forget that they would never have done what they did without a Celtic base on which to build.

They did not kill the dream of Celtic independence. In 1406 Owain, Prince of Wales, Owain Glyndwr, wrote a letter to Charles VI, King of France, in which he promised obedience to Pope Benedict XIII. Dreaming of an independent Wales, he asked two things:

> That the church of St. Davids shall be restored to its original dignity, which from the time of St. David, archbishop and confessor, was a metropolitan church.
>
> Again, that the same lord Benedict shall provide for the church of St. Davids and the other cathedral churches of our principality, prelates, dignitaries, and beneficed clergy and curates who know our language.

That was five hundred years after the time of Rhygyfarch. Five hundred years after the time of Owain Glyndwr came Disestablishment.

Owain Glyndwr was a man of the fourteenth century. He stood midway. But there is another and not inappropriate context. His dream of an independent and metropolitan St. David's looked back to Rhys ap Tewdwr, the arms of whose house was the yellow lion rampant. North and south of the Choir in the Cathedral which the Normans built are two effigies each bearing the royal arms of Deheubarth. These two effigies are said to represent the Lord Rhys and his son Rhys Grug, both of whom lie buried in the Cathedral. 'Y vlwyddyn honno,' says *Brut y Tywysogion*, 'y bu varw Rys Gryc yn llan Deilaw vawr, ac y cladwyt yn Mynyw yn ymyl bed y dat.' The grandfather of the Lord Rhys was Rhys ap Tewdwr, patron prince of the Cathedral. The mother of the Lord Rhys was Gwenllian, daughter of Gruffydd ap Cynan, who once sought refuge in

St. David's, and Owain Glyndwr's mother claimed descent from her.

Welsh prince and Norman lord and bishop; and the females of princely Welsh families who married Norman barons: there somewhere is the historic background of St. David's Cathedral.

CHAPTER THREE

The Cathedral Church

The Normans took over the old Celtic Church by means of two acts of staggering effrontery and practical directness, and then reorganised it out of all recognition.

The first was the visit of William the Conqueror to St. David's in 1081. He came, it is said, in the guise of a pilgrim, but looked between his fingers at the fair land beyond. He assessed the situation on this Headland, looked directly towards Ireland from this oldest and nearest of crossing points, and saw to it that the Welsh princes knew where they stood. Roger of Montgomery, Earl of Shrewsbury, was consolidating behind him. Sulien, the bishop, rushed unceremoniously from Llanbadarn to St. David's to meet him. We do not know what impression Sulien and his church made on William, nor can we assess the effect of Rhygyfarch's *Life* in praise of the Saint, written about ten years after William's visit. What we do know is the perhaps very significant fact that there was no further interference in St. David's for another twenty-five years. By 1115, however, disastrous changes had overtaken the country. William's first visit coincided approximately with the battle of Mynydd Carn, which confirmed Welsh princely dynasties in their kingdoms in north, south and mid-Wales. After William's visit, Rhys ap Tewdwr paid rent to the Conqueror. But in 1093 Rhys was killed fighting the Normans in Brycheiniog, six years after William's death, and it was then that the confusion arose which led Rhygyfarch to write his sorrowful *Lament* over a country now mutilated and enslaved and stupified by the Normans. When Wilfred, last of the Welsh bishops, died in 1115, there was no Welsh prince to exert his influence, and the Normans moved in to St. David's for the second time.

In that year they made Bernard, chaplain to Matilda, wife of Henry I, bishop of St. David's. He was appointed by the exercise of royal power, against his wishes, and, according to the Llanbadarn chronicler, 'o anuod holl yscoleigion y brytanyeit gan eu tremygu', against the will and in contempt of all the clerics of the Britons. 'No bishop of alien race,' said Gerald the Welshman, 'will ever be accepted either by the Irish or the Welsh except by compulsion and the exercise of royal power.' The Normans had made their own choice, and appointed the first of a long line of alien bishops.

What did Bernard find here? According to Archdeacon Payne in *Collectanea Menevensis*, the Welshman Wilfred lived with his clerics or *eglwyswyr* in their church in the Valley, and sent out missionary monks to administer the sacraments and preach in various parts of the diocese and to collect offerings and oblations. These they divided into four parts, one for the clergy, one to maintain the fabric, one for the poor, the fourth for the bishop himself. There was no diocese in the strict meaning of the word, only an ill-defined area which varied with the changing fortunes of the kingdoms of Dyfed and Deheubarth. The only church was the Celtic monastic settlement in the Valley, and that had nothing in common with the monasticism of the Normans. It had its secular community of *claswyr*, and was the mother church, the senior of the Celtic churches in the west. The Normans, in other words, found an ill-defined authority in which discipline and central organisation, as they knew them, were completely lacking. The first task of a Norman bishop was obviously one of definition.

It is said that Bernard established and defined the archdeaconries, although opinions differ on whether he was the first to create them, and for this purpose he used the demarcations of the ancient Welsh kingdoms as guides. Two only of the residences of the archdeacons, St. David's and Brecon, remain in the Close; those of Cardigan and Carmarthen have long disappeared, although Joseph Lord's map of the Close of 1720 tells us where they were.

The body of the *clas*, 'the learned ecclesiastics', Bernard made into the chapter of canons, the community of the Close, binding them by a strict system of rules and dividing the parish and its tithes into 'prebends' or 'shares' of the profits to be divided amongst them. And he used for this purpose a method distinctive to St. David's, the division of the parish originally into three and later into four areas, with in each case the addition of Whitchurch. These were the 'Cylchs', which in some form or other persisted in the vocabulary of the parish up to the twenties and thirties of the present century, and in one instance till today, as bases for civil administration, for electoral lists, rate collections, and for charity collections. Some of the 'Cylchs' were unequal in their revenues, a problem which Norman efficiency solved by making them circulate, which explains 'cursal' prebends. And it was this comparative poverty that led the bishop to look for revenue from other areas and churches outside the parish, which is why, for example, the prebend of Mathry, prebend of the golden corn, came into the coffers of St. David's. Gerald the

Welshman was well acquainted with this greed of the Normans: Bernard, he said, panted after riches, and at the same time alienated many of the lands of his church without advantage or profit and disposed of others indiscreetly and improvidently. The Normans took, and the Normans gave away. The demesne of Fishguard was given to the lords of Cemaes, as Francis Jones noted in his too brief essay on the history of Fishguard in the 1977 Jubilee booklet. As part of Cemaes, Fishguard was ruled by Welsh chieftains, overrun by Normans, and endured a disturbingly rough history. The neighbouring parish of Llanwnda remained part of Pebidiog under the bishop and, like St. David's, remained at peace, unravaged by Norman arms.

Bernard was determined to keep a tight grip on the canons and their activities, with himself as imposed and not elected head. This explains why there was no office of dean in St. David's (the bishop was the dean) until the time of Queen Victoria, when it was enacted that the Chapter should consist of dean (taking over the old office of precentor, leader of the choir) and canons, two in number. The Welsh Cathedral Act changed Victoria's statute of 1842 by instituting four canonries residentiary, each residing for three months of the year. Nowadays the demands of parochial work and economics have established that there should be twelve canons, residing during their term of duty in the Canonry, which was once the Chancellor's house.

Bernard also appointed a corresponding number of subordinate officers, which in effect gave each canon his deputy. The establishment of the Church had to be maintained, and the canons, with other duties on their hands, were absent at times. These subordinate officers, partly clerical, partly lay, assisted in the ordinary services of the choir, and were called Vicars Choral. Incorporated, they later became the Lower Chapter.

This first Norman bishop, appointed by an alien king against the wishes of the Welsh bishops, became the founder organiser of the See of St. David's as history has known it. He was consecrated (echoing Rhygyfarch) as 'archbishop of the first and greatest province of the whole island' and enlarged and defined it accordingly. Having defined, he organised and systematised the community of the Cathedral, and established an organisation that stayed largely unaltered for eight hundred years. That was not all. Ironically, like Gerald the Welshman but for very different reasons, he became a great defender of the See, claiming for it a metropolitan status and independence from Canterbury.

Lastly, when he became bishop he also became Norman lord marcher, and was confirmed in this by Henry I in 1115 and by Pope

Calixtus III in 1123. Church property was now held under the system of feudal tenure. This was of especial significance in St. David's. David and his successors as bishops had been given lands by the princes: Aircol Lawhir and Rhys ap Tewdwr by conferring Pebidiog to the bishop had made it into an independent episcopal kingdom; 'the whole cantref,' as Gerald said, 'was conferred on St. David's by the pious bounty of the princes of South Wales.' Bernard, by confirmation of Henry I, now inherited this independence. Mishaps and offences, alienations of lands, cashing in on church properties, nepotism, and the involvement of canons and vicars choral in land deals and leases: these were later developments and confusions that remained until Disestablishment cleared all away. Equally important is the fact that episcopal independence gave Dewisland its unique inviolability. It kept the land at peace and allowed old traditions and customs to continue undisturbed.

After Bernard came David Fitzgerald, and after him Peter de Leia, Prior of Wenlock, the man who built the cathedral to house the community. In 1215 Iorwerth (or Gervase) became bishop, a Welshman chosen by Welsh clergy and not by the king. He instituted the office of precentor, and with Anselm and Richard de Carew strengthened the financial position of the chapter. When Thomas Wallensis (1248–1256), Richard's predecessor, founded the treasurership, all the additions had been made that gave St. David's a constitution similar to those of the great English cathedrals. Architecturally, though, all that had been achieved by that time was far from what we see today, and the great years of medieval worship through pilgrimage and the building of churches had still to come.

The four bishops, Beck (1280), Martyn (1296), Gower (1328), and Houghton (1361), have their own special distinctions as builders and organisers. They were in addition great officers of the crown. Beck was Lord Treasurer and Chancellor of the University of Oxford; David Martyn was Chancellor of Oxford; Gower was Chancellor of Oxford and Lord High Chancellor of England; and Houghton, a man appointed because he was regarded as a safe appointment from amongst men of greater ability, was also Lord Chancellor. Three had had previous connection with the Cathedral, Gower as archdeacon, Houghton (born in Caerforiog) as precentor, and David Martyn as canon. The growing community of the Close knew beforehand what kind of men they were.

Beck established the collegiate churches of Abergwili and Llanddewibrefi, the hospitals for the reception of pilgrims at Llawhaden and Whitewell, and created the office of chancellor and those of bishop's vicar and sub-chanter. And he forced the canons to reside within the community.

Henry Gower is best remembered as builder of the Bishop's Palace and as builder, or rebuilder, of the Close Wall. It was inevitable that the Wall must have consolidated the feeling of oneness within the community, and given a feeling of security, although it was not a strong military defence. Strangely, there came a time when that Wall meant the isolation of the chapter from the City and the flock.

Adam Houghton, most diligent of legislators, brought some order into the trade, wages and markets of the City. He (according to Jones and Freeman) established the Cathedral School and a body of choristers. When he found that the hospice at Whitewell was neither fulfilling its functions nor living up to its spiritual ideals, that it 'gave no alms, did no work of piety, celebrated no divine office, and spent (its) emoluments on profane uses', he promptly took away all its resources for the benefit of his College of St. Mary, his greatest work. For better or worse he also ordered that the vicars choral and the choristers should live together.

These were the Cathedral's greatest days, time of its greatest bishops and time of its greatest building. These men built to last, and there is no question that what they built – and the same applied to the craftsmen who took and figuratively blessed and cut the stone and timber and gave them to the building – they regarded as the outward and visible sign of their worship. Their church was the sacred reliquary which held the body, the relics of the Saint, and those presumably of Caradog and Justinan, within its walls.

The last of the great bishop builders, on the eve of the Reformation, was Henry Vaughan (1509–1523), who gave us the exquisite beauty of Holy Trinity Chapel, St. Justinan's Chapel which is now a ruin, and the third storey of the Tower. This was a period of some revival in the history of the Cathedral after a spell of too many and too indifferent bishops, and it was not inappropriate that in these earlier years of the Tudor dynasty a Welsh bishop, Vaughan, should be responsible for the beautifying of the Cathedral, only a few years after Owen Pole, Treasurer, had completed the exquisite ceilings of nave and choir, and only a few years before the break with Rome. After that break came the dissolution of religious houses (including St. Mary's College), the bringing from Greyfriars Church in Carmarthen of the tomb of Edmund Tudor, father and brother of kings, to rest in the centre of the presbytery. And the end of shrines and pilgrimages around which so much of medieval piety and splendid worship had revolved.

Today we can look up at the richly decorated ceilings and the newly gilded coats of arms in the Lady Chapel, and look around at the pure austerity of stone. There is little or nothing else to indicate the rich pre-Reformation colours of monuments and pillars and walls. One cannot find in a contemporary ground plan of the Cathedral the colours and medieval services of the Chapels: the Chapel of St. Andrew in the north transept (to whom jointly with St. David, some say, the original dedication was made) which is one arm of the cruciform; the Chapel of the St. Thomas who was murdered in Canterbury; the Chapel of St. Nicholas, sometimes called the Wogan Chapel; the Lady Chapel or Chapel of St. Mary, the traditional east end of a cathedral; St. Edward's Chapel; Holy Trinity Chapel; and in the south transept, the other arm of the cruciform, the Chapel of the Patron Saint, sometimes called the Chanter's Chapel. Each Chapel had its altar – the altar of St. Stephen in St. Andrew's Chapel; St. David's altar and that of the Holy Innocents in his south transept; the altar of the Holy Cross in front of the Rood Screen; and the altar of the Chapel of St. John which, it is said, was at the southern end of the Screen.

Masses were said daily or at appropriate times at all of these. In 1302 a chantry was established by Sir John Wogan, Knight, and the first link forged between Cathedral and Picton Castle, which demanded that three chaplains were to celebrate daily at the altar of St. Nicholas for his soul, for the souls of King Edward I (who had made him Chief Justiciary of Ireland) and his heirs, and for the souls of Bishop David Martyn and his successors. What the cross-legged Knight Templar's tomb is doing in St. Nicholas's Chapel is another story. Sir John Wogan was a lawyer, not a soldier, and never a Crusader.

Another indication of the number of priests needed to administer and to serve at these altars and to maintain the services of the Cathedral can be gathered from the Return for South Wales under the Chantry Act of Edward VI (1548): St. Mary's College, it said, had a master, 7 fellows and 2 queristers, a staff that had been 'united (about 60 yeres past) to the cathedrall church of Saynt Davis, to the intent to have a master of the same colledge founde and 27 vicars corall, 8 queristers and other servants.'

The medieval significance of St. David's as one of the great shrines of Christendom ended abruptly when Henry VIII broke with Rome in 1534. Two years later William Barlow was elected bishop. Barlow was a violent Protestant, a member of a family famous in the history of Slebech, gifted as the sparks fly upward to incite trouble, an acrimonious and controversial character. He saw at least three problems facing him. He ruled over a vast and unwieldy diocese difficult to administer at the best of times from remote St. David's, and now, in times of far-reaching change, more so. In pre-Reformation days bishops had helped themselves to revenues from outside: Beck to maintain his collegiate churches, Gower to maintain the Bishop's Palace and the Close Wall, Houghton to maintain St. Mary's College. Now the Reformation changed the pattern of ecclesiastical revenues and Barlow had to maintain his medieval inheritance on a reduced income. His Protestant fervour looked out on a St. David's still steeped in medieval traditions, in his own words, an antique gargle of idolatry. There is no proof that he stripped the lead from his Bishop's Palace to provide dowries for his daughters (he had left St. David's before they were born), but he began the disintegration of the Palace by neglecting it, and he certainly curbed the popularity of St. David's as a place of pilgrimage and made himself unpopular with the canons who saw the shrine being deprived of pilgrims and themselves of their gifts. The Welsh people, said Gerald the Welshman, venerated relics, and Barlow dismissed them as 'rotten skulls stuffed with petrified clouts'. He was realist enough to see that the Palace was far too big a place to maintain (its purpose was gone, although it continued to be occupied for another fifty years and it was 1633 when the last Chapter was held within its walls); realist enough to know that the end of medieval religious fervour was at hand; and realist enough to anticipate history in a way, to end his problems by moving to Carmarthen. Thomas Cromwell, his patron, was executed, the plan fell through, and local history seems never to have forgiven him for having tried. With him came to an end the great medieval reputation of the Cathedral.

Richard Davies (1561–1582) was a Welsh-speaking Welsh scholar, a member of the Council of the Marches, a Justice of the Peace, a resident and participating bishop. He is accredited with an earnest endeavour to search 'for the chiefest means' of improving the Church. As a leader in the implementation of the Elizabethan settlement he had to carry out the orders of Elizabeth I that the church services should be rendered in the vernacular, which meant the substitution of English for Latin and, carried to its logical conclusion in Wales, the introduction of Welsh. Elizabeth ordered that the Bible should be translated into Welsh, the essential preliminary, and it was Richard Davies, with the co-operation of his precentor in St. David's, Thomas Huett, and William Salesbury, who began the task by translating the New Testament and the Prayer Book. We are reminded of Owain Glyndwr's dream that the church of St. David's should be restored to its original dignity and that it be provided with priests 'who know our language'. Richard Davies began the process of fulfilment; he could hardly have foreseen the consequences, the spiritual, moral, educational and national consequences of the nineteenth century, nor the coming of Disestablishment.

That was a long time ahead. From the latter half of the sixteenth century down to 1874 there was no Welsh bishop. It was a period of dilapidation and loss. The Reformation closed St. Mary's College and destroyed pre-Reformation records and treasures that were held to be 'ungodly'. Richard Davies himself and his precentor are held responsible for the fact that there is no longer available a Register of the Chapter Acts of St. David's prior to 1560. The Commonwealth had little mercy on the internal beauty of the Cathedral. Cromwell left the chapels roofless, ivy-garbed and mouldy. The lead from the roof, it is said, was given by him to a Swansea gentleman and used to cover the old Swansea market. Business men took over the revenues of the Church; tithes were alienated. By the eighteenth century two hundred and fifty parishes out of the three hundred in the diocese had been taken over by lay people and country squires. This loss of revenue led to the pluralism and absenteeism and spiritual poverty which was the main grievance of Erasmus Saunders's *A View of the State of Religion in the Diocese*, published in 1721.

Bishops meantime indifferently came and went. Marmaduke Middleton, a Welshman, was bishop from 1582 to 1594. From that time to 1803 there were twenty-eight bishops. Some of them, George Bull and Adam Ottley notably, were men of character and idealism: George Bull was old when elected, a man who showed enormous sympathy with the young clergymen who started the revival within the church which led to the Methodist Revival. Generally it was a time of low ebb, characterised by Thomas Burgess as the period of 'declension and dilapidation'. Yet it contained within itself the seeds of one of the greatest periods in the history of the diocese.

The greatest misfortune lay in the parish church where priest and people found it difficult to participate. The parishioners were credulous and uneducated, and unable to read Welsh, and remained unable till Griffith Jones started his Circulating Schools. Services in English and the preaching in English which had so embittered John Penry meant nothing to them. Some churches were totally neglected, others held services very rarely, some served for the solitary habitations of owls and jackdaws. The priests and curates who were supposed to minister to the parishes were fettered by their own difficulties. Poorly paid, faced with areas that were far too large for them to manage, ill-educated, discouraged and therefore feckless, they too had a language difficulty. Although most were Welsh, they found it difficult to communicate in Welsh, to preach and minister the sacraments in Welsh, because their training had been in English. Difficulties of communication on both sides, therefore, were responsible for the lack of what Griffith Jones called 'friendly access to advise on their spiritual state', and this in his view was one of the two reasons for the rise of Nonconformity. The other was 'want of plain, practical and zealous preaching in a language and dialect which they (the ordinary people) were able to understand'.

Howel Harris, speaking like Griffith Jones from within the church, found another reason: the remoteness and materialism of the higher clergy, and the feeling that the Anglican Church had very little to offer to the ordinary parishioner. Two unrelated diaries of the time provide their own silent comment on the perils of the priest isolated from his flock. In 1871 Francis Kilvert of Clyro, a poor but cultured and compassionate curate, came to St. David's. Those who have read his diaries remember his ability to 'connect' with the lives of his parishioners in Clyro, his compassion for those who were sick and poor. A century earlier, James Woodforde was writing his *Diary of a Country Parson*, the diary of the life of a country gentleman parson, cushioned in his own comfort and good eating, in Norwich. James Woodforde's boon companion and neighbour in Norwich was another parson. The remarkable thing is that this companion, Thomas Roger du Quesne, often mentioned in the *Diary*, happened to be Chancellor of St. David's Cathedral from 1776 to 1793. He lived in very great comfort in Norwich, and made, as far as is known, only one journey to St. David's. After that one awful journey, he found he could not sleep on his first night because of cold and the snores of a neighbouring canon, and then forgot everything in the feastings and the grand company assembled at St. James's Tide in the Close. One wonders how much he gathered of the life and religion of the ordinary people of St. David's.

Further evidence of isolation and lack of communication can be found in an article called 'The Vicars of St. David's in the Distant and Recent Past', published in the 1953 Report of the Friends of the Cathedral. In it is this sentence – 'though the curtain wall was down and its gateway ruined, both might have been intact for all the traffic we had with the outside world.' That broken and ruined wall of the Close, and the experience behind it, can be taken as symbolic of the isolation of the eighteenth century Anglican Church from the Welsh people. From those ruins arose the revival within the church and the Methodist Revival that followed it.

In 1803 Thomas Burgess was elected bishop, and after him Connop Thirlwall. It was a time of strong Nonconformist challenge, and these were the men who reformed the administration of the Cathedral and diocese and regenerated the spiritual life to meet the challenge. In 1839 Llewellyn Lewellin was precentor, and in 1840 he became the first of the deans of St. David's. Connop Thirlwall in 1870 made James Allen canon residentiary and Chancellor. The man who had been vicar of Castlemartin for thirty-three years moved to St. David's, became dean, and spent the rest of his life and money in the great tasks of reformation and the restoration of the Cathedral. These were the first of a succession of deans, men of great character and influence, who became leaders of the church and the community at large, and automatic chairmen of local committees. Undoubtedly, they all built on the foundations laid by Thomas Burgess. It was under his leadership that administration and organisation improved, that Welsh bishops were elected, bishops chosen to suit the needs of their territory and time, that archdeacons and rural deans were energised into getting things done, that extra moneys and extra clergy became available, and that educational standards were improved. Lampeter College was established to become the first college in Wales to supplement the older universities in the training of priests.

As things happened, it was not enough. These bishops and deans were men of intellect and administrative power, ready to immerse themselves in Welsh life. Burgess took great interest in the Welsh Eisteddfod, and many of the *personiaid llengar* followed his example. But they were English, and Lady Llanover, 'the violent Welshwoman', said of Connop Thirlwall that, whatever his qualities, as a 'Welsh bishop he might as well be in New Zealand'. And then, by a strange quirk of history, there came the re-emergence of what has been called the 'Celtic Pool'. The Irish Sea, which in pre-history had carried megalithic ideas of architecture and the Ogham script, and, in the sixth century, the early Christians into Wales and St. David's, now busied itself with passing across new ideas of law and legislation, of politics and freedom and nationalism. The result of the consequent upsurge of national emotion was the call to 'get rid of Eglwys Lloegr'.

In his book, *Wales in British Politics 1868–1922*, Kenneth Morgan states that 'every major social and cultural movement in Wales derived its impetus from nonconformist leadership and that it was disestablishment which symbolised the nonconformist campaign for social equality'. Then he lists the Irish parallels that inspired nineteenth century Wales: the Irish Land Act of 1881 which opened the eyes of the Welsh to a fuller realisation of their own land problems and which led to the Welsh Land Commission of 1896; the disestablishment of the Irish Church which became law in 1869 and led to the call for disestablishment as a major claim in Welsh demands for self-government. The Act for the Disestablishment and Disendowment of the Church in Wales was passed in 1914, after long controversy, but because of the First World War it was 1922 before it was implemented. By this time the bishops themselves were ready to see an end to a long drawn battle. Edwards of St. Asaph, destined to be the first Archbishop of the Church in Wales, was reconciled to it. John Owen, bishop of St. David's, who at the beginning had fought bitterly against it, in the end fought hard for better terms. The great nationalistic aims of three generations, and one of the dreams of Owain Glyndwr, had been realised.

A History of the Church in Wales, edited by David Walker and published in 1976, ends with the basic question, has the Welsh Church after disestablishment achieved integration within Welsh society? What, it could be asked, is the meaning of integration? And what is one's interpretation of a Welsh society? The Cathedral Church of St. David's, whose historical base is the Celtic and Welsh Church of St. David, is now part of the Church in Wales, with clergymen who are Welsh-speaking and capable of carrying out all its services in the Welsh language. Congregations are part bilingual, part English-speaking. Ever since the Reformation there has been compromise in language, as nonconformist chapels deeply rooted in the Welsh tradition are now impelled to compromise. And the fact that never in the parish of St. David's has there been a parish church apart from the Cathedral has never helped matters. The Parish Magazines of a century ago show how Welsh and English services alternated between nave and chapel. Indeed, in the 1880s there was a strange adaptation. The south transept, which in its time has been called the Chanter's Chapel and St. David's Chapel, was walled off and used for services in Welsh. Today Welsh speaking worshippers in the Cathedral are in a minority, and Sunday services in Welsh are held in one of the chapels.

By Disendowment all the ancient endowments given to the Church prior to the Act of Uniformity of 1662 were confiscated and given to secular use. This secularised property was divided into two parts. One, the sum paid by the Ecclesiastical Commissioners to Welsh bishoprics and cathedral chapters, estimated at an annual income of £27,000, was to be paid to the University of Wales and the National Library. The other was to be divided amongst the various County Councils, each receiving the parochial endowments existing in its own county. The amount received by the then County of Pembrokeshire was £229,576.5.3. The disendowments clauses left to the church its cathedrals and churches, its glebe houses, and property worth £102,000 per annum, while secularising property worth £158,000.

Surprisingly, there were no serious after-effects: the new Church flourished in an atmosphere of improved relations and greater freedom. Parish and Cathedral were affected in two ways. The parish lost its vicar. The Church could not maintain both a dean and a vicar, and the dean, whose duties previously had been confined to the Cathedral, became the incumbent of the parish as well as dean. And the old system of residentiary canons who kept residence each for three months had to be abandoned for the present system whereby a canon leaves his parish and keeps residence for a month. The ancient glebe surrounding the Cathedral was re-purchased from the Welsh Church Commissioners into whose possession it had passed by the terms of the Act. The Friends of the Cathedral provided the money. The remainder of the glebe was handed over by the Commissioners to the University of Wales, as required by the Act.

D. J. Jones, assistant missioner, became vicar choral in 1903, bishop's vicar in 1907, and later subchanter and vicar of the parish. He was the last. After his departure the Vicarage at Penrhiw became a guest house until, in 1952, it became the mother house of the fourteen sisters of the Community of St. John the Evangelist.

St. Non's House was built by Morgan Griffiths as a summer house. In the grounds is a chapel to St. Non built in the style of Celtic churches, built by Morgan Griffiths in co-operation with David Thomas of the Cloisters. Inside are windows dedicated to St. David, St. Non, St. Brynach and St. Winifred and St. Bride. The altar is built of relics from the chapels of the coast, stones, it is said, from the hospital of Whitwell, a white stone from St. Patrick's Chapel, a piscina from the one-time chapel at Caerforiog, and a holy water stoup reputedly from the Chapel of the Fathom at Gwrhyd. In 1939 the house ceased to be a private residence and was taken over by the Passionist Fathers as a retreat and a training school for Catholic priests. Westward of the house is the sacred well of St. Non, whose waters are gifted to heal the ailments of afflicted eyes. It is one of the oldest centres of pilgrimage.

In these concluding items of a less momentous recent history can be found some signs of the changes that have taken place, and some reflections of a more ancient background. A replica of a Celtic chapel; a vicarage becoming the home of an order of Anglican nuns whose first mother house (now closed) was in Ireland; a summer house becoming a Catholic seminary; the Close becoming less of a community of clerics, and that community smaller than ever before; old homes of the vicars choral in the City (they complained bitterly at one time that the Cathedral chapter made no attempt to provide them with homes) now in private hands and in the tourist trade – there has been secularisation and almost an obliteration of a clerical presence in the City; and there has been expansion, because the invading waves of pilgrim tourists are becoming ever and ever larger, and they, as through the ages, come to see the great centre of our history, which is the Cathedral itself.

CHAPTER FOUR

Rural Life

The Farm and the Farmer

Before we can discuss the farms and the farmers of the Dewisland area we need to know something of the origins of Welsh society generally, as we shall find that the pattern of rural settlement is closely related to the evolution of Welsh society over the ages.

First of all, we can take a brief look at the settlement pattern as it is today. The older farms in the parish are on high ground on the south-facing slopes of Carn Llidi and Penbiri and around the coast to Porth Glais. The others are on the flat land and invariably on the fringes of moor and common land. Because of consolidation there are fewer farmers and occupiers today, but the identity of old farms absorbed into newer units remains clear, and the old homestead may no longer be a farmhouse. Most of the farms are scattered, but in some cases farms or farmhouses are huddled together – Trelerw, Portheiddi, Treleddid Fawr, Tretio – as they were in the Irish 'clachans'. Around these are or were little groups of cottages, as in Fachelich, Rhodiad and Caerfarchell. On other sites little clusters of cottages have almost or completely disappeared, with only a garden hedge or collapsing wall as reminders of former human habitation.

The farm names are interesting. Many were mentioned in, and are older than, *The Black Book of St. David's*. With the exception of one small mixed group they fall into well-defined families, similar to the Cornwall patterns of Tre- and Pol- and Pen-. In the south west of the parish are the Porth- farms, their names commemorating the ancient link with harbour and sea and between the farmer and his boat. It is impossible to think of the Caer- farms without thinking of the Celtic forts. The Llan- farms are a reminder of the fact that the original meaning of *llan* was 'enclosure'; it meant a graveyard wall long before it came to mean the church as well. In the same way, 'Close' in Close Wall is the same word as *clôs*, or *buarth*, the enclosure of the farmyard. The last of these prefixed farm groups is the Tre-family. It is the most numerous, and the most significant. *Tre* or *tref* in Welsh means 'home'.

The first man to write authoritatively on the Celtic tribal system was Frederick Seebohm (1904). He believed that human society in general had progressed from the primitive hunter stage, where man had to hunt for his food to survive and live, to a nomadic and pastoral stage, where man had to be endlessly on the move to find pasture for his flock, and ultimately to a settled stage, where man cultivated the soil and began to gather the attributes of a stable society. Seebohm found ample evidence of the second stage, where communities of free men led a pastoral nomadic life, and very little evidence in Wales of communities of bondmen who, as their name implies, were tied to the soil and on whose labours the settled freemen depended for cultivation of the soil. He therefore regarded Celtic tribalism as predominantly pastoral and nomadic. Researches of the last forty years by Professors Bowen, T. Jones Pierce and G. R. J. Jones have corrected this view. In 'The Tribal System in Wales: A Re-assessment in the Light of Settlement Studies' (*Welsh History Review*, Volume 1, 1961) G. R. J. Jones develops the general theory that there were two distinct settlement forms in the Celtic Middle Ages: one of related clans of freemen who lived in dispersed or scattered homesteads, the other of communities of bondmen who lived in small hamlets. Furthermore, they had a social organisation strictly related to land holdings and dependent on blood kinship: they were related to the lord of the *cwmwd* (administratively equivalent to the modern community council area), paid rents and services to him, and in return had rights to arable and common pasture land. The holdings of all members of the clan in both kinds of land made up their *gwely*, their 'resting place'. It was the custom of 'gavelkind', the custom that a dead man's land be divided equally amongst his male heirs, that led eventually to a situation where land continually subdivided became too small to be profitable. This and growth in population inevitably in time compelled younger members of the clan to move outwards and build their homes on the fringes of rougher pasture land. As a consequence, and when the limits of expansion were reached, the old custom broke down, and a process began which continued in Norman times and has continued ever since – the stronger members of the clan bought out the weaker and undivided rough pasture land had to be brought under cultivation and enclosed. That was the beginning of growth, in farms and in estates.

The bondmen also had their land rights, both arable and pasture. They paid their services and rents communally to the lord, and helped one another in the cultivation of their plots. In course of time they escaped from their bond or claimed the status of freemen. In both cases, land became available for appropriation or consolidation, and this too helped in the break up of the old system.

The names of the farms are provocative enough to encourage the interesting but dangerous exercise of hunting for origins that M. L. Dawson undertook in the *Pembroke Guardian* at the end of the last century. Prefix joins with the name of a geographical feature or, more especially in the case of Tref- with the name of a Celtic or Irish Saint or chieftain. Tref- meant a clearing or settlement and then the homestead inside it; and always there is the implicit meaning of 'home', as in *adref* (towards home) or *gartre* (at home). Later it became the name for a collection of homes, a hamlet or village, and still later it came to indicate an administrative unit, as in Tref Abergwaun.

Two farm names are of particular interest. It must be assumed that *gwely*, the 'resting place', the stake in the soil, derived from a first award of land to an ancestral head of a tribe or clan. That original award was called Old Settlement, and the two farms in mind are called by the Welsh original of that term. On one side of Dowrog is Hendre Eynon. On the other is Hendre. Once we assume that Hendre represents an original settlement, other characteristics of the ancient *gwely* and of the parish as it is today fall into place. G. R. J. Jones explains that eventually an Old Settlement, because of the old Welsh laws of inheritance, became a shared open field, and there is evidence of open field and individual plot cultivation in the history of Hendre. The growth of population demanded that rough ground on the fringes had to be brought into use, and all the farms, the homesteads, the *tyddynod*, would then develop along the edges of the moorland. Constant forays into rough land searched for cultivable soil; little units would come into use, and be enclosed. Most of the fields of the parish have traditionally been small, and many of them carry names which express this extension into the rough. Enclosures of this kind and the growth of scattered farms continued, helped by the abolition of gavelkind in the Act of Union in 1536, but it is probable that in the parish of St. David's the process was slower than elsewhere. The parish was isolated; its 'old pastoral and tribal traditions died hard'; and it suffered under one great impediment, the intermixture of Church lands that remained until the days of Disestablishment. Lack of good land exerted a constant pressure; and the value of owned and inherited land has never been far from the minds of the farmers of the parish; and this explains why, in poorer times, the younger sons had no choice but to become servants to other farmers, or migrate into the industrial areas or overseas. The search for recoverable land went on meantime, as it does today.

Alongside Maen Dewi are two cottages that are examples of this urge to find land. They belong to the legendary *tai un nos*. A squatter on waste land, said the legend, had the traditional right of claiming as his own the land under whatever rough erection of a shanty home he could put up in one night. Smoke from the chimney in the morning gave him the right to claim a circle of land around his makeshift home, and the privilege of building a permanent home in his own time.

All this pressure for land, and constant wrestling for waste ground, this emphasis on the value of a precious commodity, meant that land had to be guarded and safely handed on. An old tribal solidarity made for stability and strength. Even today a meshwork of family kinships of farms and people in the parish is proof that an awareness of the Celtic *gwely* is still strong.

We can now look at the great manorial lordship of the Bishop and its lands which, after the Reformation, were split up into vast estates. The story begins in 1082 when Rhys ap Tewdwr gave the cantref (the hundred homes) of Pebidiog to the Bishop of St. David's, who at that time was Sulien. By the end of the eleventh century (according to Francis Jones in *The Journal of the Historical Society of the Church in Wales*) the whole of that cantref was the property of the church, and, with the exception of some losses, it was comparatively intact when Wilfred, last of the Welsh bishops, died, and when Bernard, first of the Normans, was elected. Bernard made it into a feudal barony; he himself held full authority as lord marcher. Seventy-eight years later David Martyn became bishop, and it was for him that *The Black Book of St. David's*, inventory of his lands and rents, was first compiled in 1326.

This book is our guide to Norman St. David's. The City itself was feudalised in strict Norman style, but in the country subtle Norman ingenuity had combined Norman feudal holdings with a continuation of traditional Welsh land holding. The *gwely* was in these farmlands, the Welsheries, where tribal holdings sometimes contained widely separate pieces of land, a disadvantage that can still be found today. All landholders paid dues to the lord bishop, as they had formerly done to a Celtic tribal chief, but there was a difference between privately held and common land. Most awkward of all was the way in which church lands became mixed with others in an uneconomic pattern. In much later times this pattern became even more irritable, because the church held on to its lands for the sake of profits and in disregard of agricultural progress.

The Black Book, having listed its jury whose job it was to collect the facts, begins with 'They say', *dicitur* – the age-old way of establishing rights in the country, from *Domesday Book* to *Black Book* and to the establishment of rights of common land in the 1960s. The evidence of the spoken word ('It is said') is older than what can be found in books and holds more than is ever found in document or coded law.

They beat the bounds of the parish in the old days, when there was neither map nor book; and the boundary was confirmed because that was where people through the generations had always said it was.

'They say that the Lord has there three water mills, that is the mill outside the town of St. David's, the mill at Saluach, and the mill at Poultcauok, and they are worth yearly according to their true value £20.' That is how the *Black Book* starts.

Y Felin, Dewston or Dewiston or Lower Mill, was until fairly recently in good working order, fed by a mill race from inside the walls of the Close. In 1490 John the plumber and his associate received 1/8d for two days' work on 'the aqueduct'; during the Second World War it was cleared by German prisoners of war. The mill at Felinganol is now disintegrating, its channel clogged. There was once a corn grist mill at Caerforiog at a meeting place of three parishes. There was another in Caerbwdi, below the massive four-square lime kiln, once in the occupation of Abram Rees and owned by the bishop; and one at Abereiddi; another in Trefin, mill of the manor by the edge of the sea, immortalised in Crwys's poem in North Pembrokeshire dialect, now with a mill wheel lying on its back in the middle of the floor; a corn grist mill of considerable importance in Pwllcaerog (the Poultcauok of *Black Book*), occupied by Ebenezer Rees and owned by William Perkins; and two others on the outside of the parish, Abercastell and Llanrhian. Like the chapels of old they encircled the parish church of St. David's and indicated that the major industry was and always had been agriculture, and that the major element in that industry was the growing of corn. All have now come to their end.

The Black Book tells us how they were built, great stones for the bed, walls of stone or clay and wattle carried by the tenants at their own cost – 'they make the sluices and repair the mill dam.' On the roof, thatch; the straw of oats and barley was no good; that of rye and wheat was good. All in all, the mill, as a piece of architecture, as part of economic life, was important, an essential part of the economy. It ground the corn for all the people to eat, and it had a close link with the church. In an English charter granted to Thurgarton priory about 1150, a mill was given to the brethren as a priority, 'until I shall give them a church or something else which could be more useful to them'.

The only alternative to the mill was the quern, the bowl for handgrinding. But to the lord of the manor the mill was a means of controlling people and of revenue and he did his best to ban the quern. The small stone basin found in Gwrhyd Bach, once thought of as a font, then more probably as a stoup, was finally considered by the Ancient Monuments Commissioners to be one of these ancient handmills, used in a Celtic home to dodge a Norman imposition.

What does the 1326 *Black Book* say about St. David's? In the first place, it was a town, a borough, not a city, and was called Menevia. It was the oldest of settlements because of the monastery in the Valley; there was no other church, and no mention of a parish. It had a population of about a thousand, and one hundred and forty of these were burgesses. On the outside was the Cantref of Dewisland, the Welsh Hundred. The rural hinterland had retained much by way of old Welsh customs, but the town, according to Willis Bund, was thoroughly anglicised, no different in its set-up from any town in England. This distinction between town and country remained over the centuries: when the manorial courts met for the last time at the Grove Hotel in the early years of this century, they met in two sessions. The Court Leet for the Manor of the City and Suburbs met in the morning, the Court Leet for the Manor of Dewsland in the afternoon.

The bishop himself held, in addition to the mills, a town 'long house', land attached to Whitwell, a demesne of 73 acres and 60 acres of pasture among the sands and other pieces of land, including the island of Ramsey. These he rented out. A large number of burgesses held burgages or parts of burgages, paying rents at various rates. Sometimes these were joint holdings. Some held burgages or tenements with rent, some land without houses. All did service to the lord, attending to the mills, guarding fugitives to the church, guarding the shrine and the town. Some paid rent in kind, capons and gloves; and in wax and needles, not impossibly for candles and the repair of vestments in the church. The tenants harvested crops of barley, beans, buck wheat, oats, peas, vetches and wheat, and kept horses, cattle and sheep.

The people of the Welsh Hundred were co-owners, holding their land on the basis of tribe and family. They paid 'heriot' (dues of the best of whatever was stipulated, payable on the death of a member), carried heavy materials to the mills, kept and escorted prisoners, paid rent in fowls and toll on the buying and selling of horses, did their turn in reaping corn, normally for three days each, watched for wrecks, and guarded the market which was a valuable source of revenue to the lord.

The Tydwaldy tenants, probably a class of tenant rather than people from any precise areas, paid a very large range of services and specialised in cartage, the carrying of foodstuffs from manor to manor. They also held their bovates and carucates of land, paid rent yearly in fowls, and immemorially in flour and cheese. But, said the

Black Book, in the time of Bishop Gervase that rent was commuted in money for the convenience of the church.

Commuting of services for money became a key element in the developing history of feudalism and became prominent in the affairs of the feudal church in St. David's. The Celtic monks had done their own farming, even to the extent of using their bodies to pull their ploughs because the use of animals was forbidden. As bishop and monastery gathered possessions and were given land they had to get extra labour. The land that was given to the Saint for the salvation of the soul of the giver eventually became a commodity. Then the bishop found it was easier to get workmen for pay, and old workers commuted their services for money. The Normans were accustomed to giving away land to favourites or relatives in exchange for or as reward for services. In course of time money payments became easier than two days' service on the lord's farm; obligations were turned into cash payments; and land was leased out for money. Then there came a time when land that was on long lease became freehold through long forgetfulness; manorial courts became neglected; tithes became rents; and the hard task of regular collecting was forgotten in a cash payment once or twice a year. These changes led eventually to a subtle change of climate; lay and ecclesiastical landlords lost personal contact with their tenants, and close relationships were traded for rent. The church still owned the land; but control, through renting and leasing, had passed on to lay hands.

The church of the *Black Book* was heavily involved in land holdings. According to Willis Bund, of the 67 places mentioned, 27 concerned persons in orders. In 63 cases out of the 67 the persons described were landlords, tenants of the bishop. They were a fourteenth-century well-to-do and independent clerical landed class holding possessions that were substantial if not large, and they were married and therefore saw to it that their children were involved in their leases. In much later times the vicars choral were equally involved in the farms of the parish. This involvement is a part of history that has never been adequately traced. Over two hundred years after the *Black Book*, in the time of the Commonwealth, lands belonging to the bishop were sequestrated and sold to Humphrey Hill, citizen and mercer of London, for £2,496.15.11¼. It involved over two thousand five hundred acres in the old Norman manors of Brawdy, Pointz Castle, farms like Treleidir, Carnwchwrn, Treswni, Emlych, Tremynydd and Trelerw, Ramsey Island and Middle Mill, and many smaller parcels of land in and around St. David's. Most if not all of it was leased by the bishop to many families some of whose names – Angell,

Pardoe, Ryman and Hargest – figured prominently in the lists of canons and vicars choral of the Cathedral.

Lastly, the *Black Book* distinguished very carefully between demesne and common land. In English law the king owned all the land. His representative in St. David's, the bishop, had his own lands, but he had only a share and a right in the common lands – they belonged to all and he could do no more and no less than the other tenants, a reminder that once all land in Wales belonged to the tribe and could not be disposed of without the consent of the tribe. It is not surprising, therefore, that the people of St. David's have always watched carefully over their common land, and never more so than when the new Parish Council began its precarious life in 1894.

The chain allegiance of the feudal system eventually had to break up. The Reformation came, and with the enterprise of the age of Elizabeth landlordism and private trading were bound to flourish. In Pembrokeshire the Barlows and the Perrotts became prominent. Their time ran out and the Wogans and the Philippses took their place. All these were great landlords and all had some contact with St. David's. Caerforiog, for instance, was at the beginning of the sixteenth century the property of one of the Perrott family; in 1738 it passed from one of the Wogans to Samuel Harries, whose family were related to the Wogans by marriage. By 1836 and the time of the Tithe Act the largest landowners in the parish, besides the Church and the Lort Philippses, were two members of the Harries family, John Harding and John Hill Harries, both linked with Cruglas. It is only natural, therefore, coming as we are to the larger and more recent estates, to begin with this estate which St. David's knows best as the Trevacoon estate. It began early, and it was nearly the last of the larger private estates to sell out.

Some fifty years after George Owen had written his *Description of Pembrokeshire*, a man in the parish of St. David's began to make his mark in the world, with the help of the Church. The Archdeacon of Carmarthen had since the Norman Conquest owned the tithes of Llanrhian, the manor of 'Clegyrvoia', and a tenement called 'Crukeluse', for which he was paid the annual rent of £3.13.4. This tenement of Cruglas had by 1650 been granted on lease to George Harry, ancestor of the Harrieses of Trevacoon. His eldest son, John, obtained a lease on the property in turn from Thomas Staynoe, Archdeacon of Carmarthen, in July, 1681, and that lease was regularly renewed till it terminated in the death of George Harries of Rickeston in 1897. It was Samuel Harries, second son of John Harries, who was the real founder of the Trevacoon estate. In 1727 he held messuages and lands in Porth-mawr, Treleidir, Tre-hysbys,

Trehenlliw, Trefarchan and Trevinert; he had already (in 1719) acquired a lease on the tithes of the parishes of St. David's and Whitchurch, and it was in 1721 that he had a famous row over tithes (and corn) with William Bowen of Llan-ferran. He was just about the biggest holder of land in the parish.

The Harries family played a remarkable role in the history of parish and county for two hundred years. There were two branches, one in Haverfordwest, one in Tregwynt, and between them they were connected with a host of old country houses – Cruglas, Caerforiog, Hilton (in Roch), Trevacoon, Priskilly, Llandigige Fawr, Portheiddi, Llanfirn Eynon and Trecadwgan. They were related by marriage to many of the old county families: the Foleys (Dr Samuel Foley lived in Glasfryn); the Voyles of St. Elvis, an old merchant family of Haverfordwest that made its fortune in Elizabethan times and later started mining in St. Elvis; Scourfields of Williamston and the Philippses; and earlier the Perrotts. A Francis Green in 1852 married one of the Harries daughters of Trevacoon. A Samuel Harries married the widow of Thomas Williams of Cwmwdig, daughter of John Harries of Portheiddi. A John Harries was in the early days of Nonconformity involved in the establishment of Trefgarn Owen chapel and Albany Chapel in Haverfordwest. John Harding Harries married Martha, daughter of William Williams of Llandigige, one of the early pioneers of Methodism. One at least of the Harrieses was a vicar choral: Samuel Harries (1759) has his monumental plaque in the Cathedral. His brother, Dr George Harries gave a new front to Cruglas; Samuel gave a new front to Trevacoon. Samuel Harries, 'the Major', ran a famous pack of hounds, and was in the habit of sending his coach and horses over to Treleddin for the use of the famous actress, Mrs Jordan. The Harrieses were trustees of Dr Jones's Charity, substantial landowners, High Sheriffs of the County, Justices of the Peace. They maintained the law and signed papers and checked the accounts of the overseers of the poor and the parish vestry. They were representatives of the country class which was responsible for local government until the institution of parish and county councils. They may have been anglicised in that they mixed and married with English county families, but it is said that they spoke Welsh. Each was a farmer-squire-churchman, and they lived in substantial farmhouses, Cruglas or Llanunwas or Priskilly. It is these farmhouses that are typical of a parish which has no great country houses like the south of the county or the Teifi Valley or the Vale of Aeron. And it had no dominating 'South Wales Squire' of the type described by Herbert Vaughan. The only notables of St. David's that Lewis Dwnn could find were Thomas Hargest and Francis Perry of Trecadwgan, gentleman. Howel Lloyd's *The Gentry in South West Wales*, which deals with the position and influence of the gentry in their greatest periods in history, Elizabethan and Stuart times, passed St. David's by without a single reference, except, that is, to some of its bishops and chancellors.

Surprisingly, there are no records of tithe barns, either, in sharp contrast, for instance, with Llandaf, where according to *Archaeologia Cambrensis* (1902) there were nine at the beginning of the nineteenth century. One can only surmise. The Harrieses rented the tithes of St. David's and Whitchurch; other members of the family rented those of Mathry and Trefin. The church collected the rents. The Harrieses collected the corn and kept it in their own barns.

In 1696 another important estate, known ever since as Dr Jones's Charity, was established through an indenture of release between William Jones of the Parish of St. Gregories in the City of London clerk, executor of the last will and testament of John Jones then late of the County of the Borough of Carmarthen Doctor of Physic deceased, and on the other part certain Trustees, among whom were members of the old landed gentry of the county, Sir John Philipps of Picton Castle, John Laugharne of St. Bride's, John Barlow of Lawrenny, George Lort of Pembroke, Charles Philipps of Sandy Haven, and Thomas Williams of Caerforiog. By 1825 there were the inevitable changes, and Samuel Harries of Cruglas appeared on the list. The wishes of the will were that the real estate, lands, tenements and hereditaments as well as the appurtenances thereunto belonging with the issue and profits thereof should be used to set out and train apprentices of poor families and also towards the maintenance of such poor families. The Charity was to apply in particular to the parishes of St. David's (through the Subchanter and Vicars Choral), Lawrenny, Cosheston and Lampeter, and the trustees were empowered to do all they could to maintain and enlarge the scope and income of the Charity by exchanges and sales of land. In 1825 the estate included 129 acres (in the occupation of William Harries) of the manor of the lordship of Hendre; 33 acres of 'Gwrid Mawr', occupied by William Raymond; townred and fields of 'Gwrid Mawr and Gwrid Bach', 21 acres in the occupation of Thomas Martin; 10 acres in Llandridian; the water grist mill called 'Gwrid Mill'; houses and strips of land in St. David's, Tretio Mawr and Caerfarchell and Clegyr; slangs in Skyfog; cottages and gardens in Trefarchan, Treginnis and Fachelich; 24 slangs in Tremynydd and in Porth Lisgi.

An article on 'Pembrokeshire Antiquities' in the *County (West Wales) Guardian* in 1931 says that John Jones was born in 1650 near St. David's, where his father had considerable property. His father became rector of Lawrenny, where he and his wife and his son John (who had qualified as a doctor and settled down in Carmarthen and died in January 1698) lie buried. Nothing else is known about his father, except a statement in the *Royal Commission on Ancient and Historic Monuments of Pembrokeshire* (1925) that he had lived in an ancient and historic house in Llandridian, but a biographical cutting from 'Pembrokeshire Antiquities' (in Volume 16 of Francis Green's scrapbooks in the Library in Haverfordwest) gives one other and most important item of information. John Jones's mother, wife of the rector of Lawrenny, was a Hargest, one of the vicar choral land-leasing families of St. David's.

Dr Jones's Charity is still operative after four hundred years, and the Minor Canon of the Cathedral still issues his annual announcement that funds are available on application. In 1808 its rent roll in St. David's amounted to £169. By 1930 it had grown to £492, and formed towards the end of the nineteenth and the beginning of this century one of the most contentious sources of argument in the Parish Council. Its first impact on the question of land came in 1856. Some five years after the parish had reached the peak of its population, 2,513 in 1851, Dr Jones's Charity sold some of its St. David's estate, lands, cottages and gardens in the City, fields and lands from Treginnis to Llaethty and Clegyr, Gwrhyd Mill, various fields, cottages in the townred of Hendre, and parts of Harglodd, Tretio, Caerfarchell, and Skyfog. This was not insignificant, even in comparison with the larger sales to come, and it formed part of a considerable change of pattern in the fifty years up to 1880, when many of the larger farms, Hendre Eynon, Penbiri, Treiago, Trecenny and Pwllcaerog were advertised for sale, some more than once. Some larger sales from the Picton and Dale estates were to follow, probably motivated by the desire to invest the proceeds in the Industrial Revolution. These sales offered opportunities for improving holdings that were uneconomic and disjointed, and nothing proves how awkward land holdings were more than the catalogues of the Charity Sale issued by Messrs. Goode and Owen of Haverfordwest and the maps they supplied with their catalogue. Hendre was advertised as 'a very valuable and improvable farm and lands, with valuable rights appurtenant to the Manor of Hendre', but the maps of Hendre and Gwrhyd show confusion, multiple ownership, bittiness of fields broken by intrusive church holdings, odd slangs of one acre or less, and waste land. The Tithe Commutation volume had reckoned that the parish contained 16,000 acres of land statute measure, 4,000 of arable and 8,000 of meadow or pasture; 3,983 acres were common or waste. Land, as always, was scarce, and life was restless. The log book of the Board School in

1874 made many references to upsets in the school population because of movements of families. The Poor Law was facing its greatest problems, and the lists of the poor and vagrant were the largest in the county. The small farm worker was giving up his cottage and few acres, soon to move in to the City, or emigrate to mines and ironworks, or be tempted to migrate over the water. The deserted villages were not far off.

Characteristically, the fields in the parish have traditionally been small, of the Celtic type. They still are, except where modern machinery and modern farming have compelled change. The broken nature of the land forced fields to be small. But there is evidence that not all were so. What Gerald the Welshman called stony, barren, unimprovable territory had not all been enclosed. Travellers' tales tell of environs having no hedges to divide the property of farmers, where the sheep and even the geese were tethered together. Malkin in 1804 saw tethering only after he had crossed Gwrhyd Bridge. The famous Harries row with Thomas Bowen, one hundred years earlier, had proved that corn lands in the parish lay in open fields; farmers literally and deliberately trod on their neighbours' corn. But the troubles that followed enclosures in England never happened in Wales, probably because the open field system was not so common in Wales. Enclosure in the parish was a long slow plodding process of sub-dividing large open fields where they occurred, of bringing poorly drained land into cultivation, and of trimming waste land on higher ground. The little diary of John Williams of Trearched (1720) demonstrated how one young enterprising farmer got down to hedging and walling. William Watts Harries, vicar of Prendergast who held large holdings in the parish, co-operated with his tenants. In 1845 he leased some land to Bowen of Tremwni for seven years: Bowen had to erect a hedge at 5/-per perch and cart stones at his own expense, for which he got fifty per cent rebate on rent day.

Field names tell the story of this claiming and clearing. The developing history of Hendre can be read in the field names listed in the sales catalogue – Gwndwn Gwyn – pasture land made arable; Foes Hir – land drained (*foes* meaning ditch or fosse); Gwaun Rydynog – meadow or moor where the bracken (*rhedyn*) had to be kept down by the plough; Llain yn Roft Ucha – a strip of land recovered from the wild in the croft or small field on high ground; and Parc Llwyd and Parc Llwyd Newydd, and Parc Newydd and Parc Newydd Isha – extensions from land already cleared, so that a 'new new' field had been made. The process is visible today – the edges of bad land are ploughed; pieces of cultivated land stick into moors like fingers; or creep up craggy slopes.

This was the method of recovery and enclosure in St. David's. In fact, the only formal Enclosure document relating to the parish, it seems, is that of Thomas Tamlyn, land surveyor, of 4 Castle Terrace, Haverfordwest, who in 1864–68 dealt with 'The Inclosure of Waste Lands on the Manor of Dewsland duly authorised under the Acts for the Inclosure, Exchange and Improvement of Land.' This document is in the Record Office in Haverfordwest. Bishop Connop Thirlwall, and overseers and churchwardens, Ebenezer Rees of Tremwni, Ebenezer Williams of Penarthur, William Rees of Croeswdig, George Llewhellin and Arthur James are the personalities involved; Treswni Common the area. Allotments are fixed, one recreational for the people of the parish, another for building. The bishop was awarded a piece of land of sixteen acres in lieu of and in full compensation for his right and interest in the soil of the sand lands. Roads were re-adjusted: a public highway leading from Treleddin to Fishguard, and from St. David's to Porth-mawr; and all changes confined to the area between Porth-mawr and Treleddin.

The end of the nineteenth century found parish and country in the middle of religious, political, social turmoil: church and Liberalism and land were involved. Then came World War One and Disestablishment, and within a few years two of the larger and older landlords vanished from the scene.

The first change came in 1918, when the Trevacoon estate was sold. Farms from Croesgoch down to St. David's, towards Skyfog and Solva and Brawdy; dwelling houses in the City, chiefly around Goat Street and Catherine Street (this was Harries territory as Priskilly Terrace shows); pockets of land; Prospect Hotel and one of the old granaries; Llanoy, Penysgwarne, Trefeigan, Trefochlyd, Carnhedryn, Skyfog, Caerforiog Mill and farm, Llandigige, Tretio, Tremynydd, Treleddid, Trefelly, Porthmawr, Rhosson, Trelerw, Llanfirn and many more: well over three thousand acres were involved, and more than £140,000 realised. Here was a much larger force for change and economic adjustment than the earlier sales. Men changed their farms, and men who had never known anything but tenancies and landlord and agent found themselves for the first time owners and men of property, at a price. Freehold had arrived. Unfortunately, it brought with it freedom and an ill wind. In less than ten years economic collapse had struck the country and many farms were sold at a loss. When agriculture began again to improve and prosper the mid-thirties had come, and very soon another World War. It was at the end of this that the Milk Marketing Board and the Potato Board, and increased tourism, began to give the parish the prosperity it now enjoys.

The second catalyst, following Disestablishment, was the steady selling off and still continuing sale of the properties of the Church by the Commissioners, traditionally the most tolerant of landlords, and by the University College of Wales, Aberystwyth. There are very few landlords now, with the exception of the National Trust.

Before describing how the Dewisland farmer and his family lived we should take a glimpse at one or two of the more interesting farm houses where once the freemen lived. Amongst them are some of the houses which Henry Goffe called 'Trefs or Towns, though consisting of but one house and most of them but two'. They are slung along the valley of the Alun and above it, from Clegyrfwya to Pwllcaerog, and all are solid, thick-walled and distinctive. But some, like all human life, are more distinctive than others. The January 1902 edition of *Archaeologia Cambrensis* contained a long, detailed and illustrated article on some of these distinctive homes, Llaethty, Porthmawr, Clegyr Foia (sic), Rhosson Uchaf, Trefeiddan, Gwrhyd Bach, Hendre Eynon (known as Tre Eynon about 1800), and Pwllcaerog. There is a certain uniqueness that belongs to them and to their siting. Llaethty is on the southern slope of Carn Llidi, Porthmawr on a southfacing slope above Porth-mawr, and there were and are three houses in the shelter of the rock mass of Clegyrfwya. Others, Penbiri, Llanferran, Trellwyd, and the ruins of the old Hendre farmhouse – they creep up and cling to the rising ground or the protecting rock. Others, the minority, cling to the edge of the moor.

The article of 1902 was written by Romilly Allen: he had made notes on and sketched these houses in 1883 and now felt compelled to draft these into a 'recording angel' of an article because in the meantime the process of demolition had practically removed their distinction as a style of domestic architecture. Today all except Rhosson Uchaf and to some degree Hendre Eynon have been modernised. On Romilly Allen's evidence all of these old farm-houses had a rectangular main building, divided into two large living areas by a wide passageway. This main building, thatch-roofed, on either or both of its long sides had lean-to additions, invariably slated, which Peter Smith in *Houses of the Welsh Countryside* calls lateral offshuts; with access from the inside they provided privacy and warmth, and a considerable area of extra space without adding to the weight of the roof span. In almost all cases one of these recesses formed a heavily protected porch to the front door, often framed by a pointed arch, and inside which was a stone bench of the kind that Rachel Allen saw in a house on the slope of Carn Llidi. Another of these recesses formed the ingle nook, the *simdde fawr*, underneath a massive rounded chimney sometimes wrongly called a Flemish chimney. Others functioned as working areas, kitchens or dairies, bedrooms or parlours. All shelves and benches were of stone, the primary building material in an area short of wood. And under these stone benches were often cubby holes, furnished with what the Welsh called *torch*, a wreathed or woven nest of straw. In these the ducks and geese, granted immemorially their right of way, laid their eggs. Now with modernisation the old flag floors have given way, but there is one very old floor in the Mathry area which is still cleaned, as old St. David's floors were, with sand.

Some say that these houses, estimated to belong to the sixteenth century, were planned in imitation of church architecture, nave and aisles, and not impossibly by some of the master masons who had finished their work in the Cathedral Close. There are other explanations. The Laws of Hywel Dda tell us that in the old Welsh houses of the tenth or twelfth century six pillars or roof trees supported the roof, placed in two rows of three, facing one another, and having branches which crossed at the roof pitch to form a nave in the middle of which was the hearth. Outside these columns were aisles, in which the *gwely* or common couch of rushes was laid. There is no great difference here from the old house of Rhosson Uchaf, and no great difference either from the suggestion of the ground plan uncovered in the Iron Age remains on Clegyrfwya.

In these houses, old and not so old (Sir Cyril Fox in later years added another two to the Romilly Allen list, Croftufty and the old Lleithir), lived the most significant stability of the population, the farmers, growers of barley, men of the most ancient craft. And it is not unlikely that the Romilly Allen houses belonged to the more prosperous, the stronger people, who wanted to demonstrate their strength, seniority, or superiority in a style of house that spoke of their substance. Among them were the Arnolds of Penarthur, the Beynons of Harglodd, Penbiri, Porth Lisgi and Treiago; Bowen of Trefadog and Treleddin, Carnwchwrn and Treswni; the Griffithses of Pointz Castle and Priskilly and Trellwyd; Grinnis of Porthmawr; the Harrieses of Porth Lisgi, Heathfield, Tregwynt, Portheiddi, Cruglas, Granston, Trevacoon, Treginnis, Rickeston; Davieses of Penbiri, Treiago and Rhosycribed; Hicks of Porth Lisgi and Rhosson; Martin of Gwrhyd and Trehenlliw; Meyler of Tremynydd; Mortimer of Hendre Eynon, Treginnis and Trewellwell; Owen of Harglodd and Llanferran; Perkins of Porth Lisgi, Llanfirn and Pwllcaerog, and of Trefelin and Longhouse; Properts of Hendre Eynon and Penbiri; Rees of Llandigige Fach and Ramsey and Tremynydd; Reynolds of Treglemais; Raymond of Solva and St. Elvis; Williamses of Hendre, of Hendre Eynon, Treginnis, Penlan and Llandigige, Llanrhian and Trearched, of Croeswdig, of the Commercial and Grove House and Ramsey. Some of these names do not appear on the roster of today: the Meylers and the Mortimers are no longer farmers. But if we select the most prominent and oldest of the parish farms – a list of forty-six, most of them mentioned in *The Black Book* – we find that in only six cases are the occupiers of today, husband or wife, not related to the old stock. The Welsh Land Commission of 1896 commented that it would be difficult to find any other equal area in the United Kingdom where there had been less severance of the old families of owners and occupiers of land. That is still true. Their long associations with these farms – they have played their musical chairs with them – and their blood connections and intermarriages are reflected in massive deeds and indentures of contracts. The stranger never fully realises (neither, it is said sometimes, do they) the extent of the network until the assemblage of relatives come face to face in a funeral. This is the essence of the *llwyth*, the tribal strength, based on land, and in which marriage came naturally by arrangement of family and kindred.

The registers prove that there were also marriages into the families of nonconformist ministers as had happened of old into the vicar choral families (or would that be better stated the other way round?), and prominently into the families of master mariners. The old farmers, in any case, were themselves mariners and owners of boats.

We can now look at a close-up of rural life in Dewisland – the farmer and his family at home: first, on the island of Ramsey; then in a farm at Pwllcawrog in the mid-nineteenth century; and finally at Treginnis Isa farm in the early years of the present century.

Ramsey Island is physically, clearly, a detached portion of the mainland, sharing with it sea mists and windswept clouds followed at intervals by periods of glass-like clarity between the rain storms, even in winter. The atmosphere, however, is laden with legends from the people who inhabited it in the past. We are told of those who met here the fairies, *Y Tylwyth Teg* and *Plant Rhys Dwfn*, and of many more who claimed to have heard the sound of bells from beneath the sea. Leaving the mists of time we come to a clearer atmosphere in the Middle Ages when the island was in the possession of the Bishop and its farmland was for long a valued part of his vast estate. The inventory of the possessions of Bishop Thomas Beck, made in the year 1280, indicated that seventy goats and forty-four horned cattle were kept on the island and that seventeen acres were devoted to oats, ten to wheat and three to barley. It is clear therefore that the land on the island was fully fertile and that a wide range of mixed farming was practiced. Farming continued well into modern times, certainly into the middle of the present century, and, in fact, it was not until 1905 that the island and the Chapel of St. Justinan on the mainland, continuing an ancient connection, were sold into private hands by the Ecclesiastical Commissioners, thereby breaking a link in the historical association of the island with St. David's that reached back to Norman times.

We are fortunate in being able to obtain a vivid account of farming on the island from the Diary of Ivor Arnold, who with his brother Adrian farmed here in the first decade of this century. It is a record of nine months of tough, rough day-by-day farming, a weather beaten life, ploughing, sowing and planting, reaping, threshing and winnowing, and rowing stocks of oats over to Porth Glais. Barley, potatoes, turnips and peas were grown, sheep were reared and their wool taken over to the mainland by boat. Rickety buildings had to be repaired, and stones were gathered (as by Wordsworth's Michael) to build a sheepfold. A hard life, hard wind, hard soil, boisterous winds and rain. We know that there was a corn mill on the island and that modern machinery had been taken over. The island also had its lime kiln, which implied the ferrying across of coal and lime. Pigs were kept here, fed on skimmed milk, and horses bred here. And last of all, even in Ivor Arnold's day, there came the cultivation of tourists, who flocked to Dewisland in summer in their hundreds. Ivor Arnold was a farmer, and a labouring farmer, but he was not R. S. Thomas's Dai Puw, docking swedes; nor Llew Pugh the plowman, nor Huw Puw, whistling in the hedgerows in an eternal winter; nor Iago Prydderch, whose dark figure marred the simple geometry of square fields. Besides earth, there were two other dimensions always in the awareness of Ivor Arnold. In every one of his 270 entries (hardly a word when he was on the mainland) he noted the direction of the wind. And he had a strange affinity with the birds of the air. 'April 8 – the birds came here today.' 'April 12 – the birds went away yesterday.' He and Adrian collected their eggs by the hundreds, especially the precious eggs of the guillemot. 'Adrian and I went to Justinian. We went with 500 guillemots' eggs with us.' We know that birds' eggs were sent off to Bristol to refine wine for the wealthy. The poorer people of the City risked their limbs to get them, lowering one another over the cliffs with ropes, the gash of a swirling Sound below, and on the way back they picked samphire for salads and pickles. More often than not Ivor Arnold was alone on the island, but even then he never seemed to be alone when the birds were there. Sometimes he had his signalled conversations with men of the Bishop's Lighthouse. Some of the old St. David's characters came across. Eli James brought parties over in summertime. And Henry Owen – 'out gathering fossils and flowers and taking snapshots of the birds. He was driving the rats out of the parlour with his stick before going in there.' And always, even when ploughing in the foulest weather, he had his eyes – Ivor Arnold, that is – on the other and third element, the Sound and the sea. He never missed a boat in the Sound, knew many of them by name. His own boat was always near, tied up on the handy sea, ready when the wind blew or in the still moonlight to take him over to Carnarwig or back to the Island. And he loved wrecking. As a mountain is always a challenge to a climber, so any sight of wreckage – 'we had a pitch pine baulk under the Bitches' – drew him out. He farmed, but, like so many of his fellows, he loved his boat and the sea.

Ramsey, however, had a grimmer history of the sea. More than most parts of this coastline it has been the scene of wrecks and disasters. When Ivor Arnold came to the last full stop in his Diary, he drew a neat line across the page. On 28 September 1908 he began to write again. The wind was blowing south and it was thick with fog. He was alone in his farm on the Island. 'I was chopping up sticks in the house when three men came to the door at 7 o'clock a.m. They had a hatchet and a long knife in their hands which I couldn't help keeping my eye on.' They were the crew, wet, bedraggled, barefoot, of the steam ship *Szent Istvan* of Fiume, wrecked on the south west of the island 'in a place called slippery hill'. Ivor Arnold piloted them over to St. Justinan's in their own boats, and there Miss Baker received them on the lifeboat slip and showed them every kindness. Ivor Arnold knew well George Owen's immortal phrase about Ramsey's 'deadliest doctrine'. It never showed kindness to the slogging farmer who tried to cultivate its soil. And its teeth had no mercy for the drifting ship.

Pwllcaerog in 1850. 'Mishtir'

In the County Library in Haverfordwest is a typewritten transcript of a lecture given in 1908 by Edward Perkins of Pwllcaerog (1838–1918). The first page, perhaps more than one, of the original cannot be found, and the narrative begins on the hearth of the farm that locals call Pwllcawrog on a long winter's night, and with the bachelor living-in male workers of the farm. There were three or four, and an equal number of female servants, thrown together under this patriarchal Welsh farmhouse roof. The language of the hearth was Welsh; the darlith had been in Welsh, although there is extant a copy of the same lecture in English, dated 1910 and adapted to Penysgwarne. Edward Perkins said it was a happy household, and there is ample proof that he was right. The day's work started early, long before dawn, and stretched, with an hour or two for dinner, over as much as sixteen hours. Supper was at eight, and there were four hours of winter dark before that. This was the time of laughter, of the waggish story teller, and talk and homecraft: always plenty of time, and few entertainments that were not common to all. The young men had their crafts: they made *costrennau*, straw bags or baskets used for carrying all kinds of dry stuff, corn for the horses, potato peelings, ashes from cleaned fires. Every thrifty housewife had dozens of *costrennau* in the lumber room: they were suitable presents for young couples at the start of their married life. Others of the male servants made sheepskin riddles, and chairs, and carved pieces of wood for their sweethearts, love spoons, and *pren gwast*, thin slivers of smoothed and polished wood for making corsets. There was much weaving of rushes and straw, for ropes, and collars for horses and oxen. Some, covered with horse hide or that of seals (*morloi*), were reserved for special occasions, and for trips to market. These articles of daily use, of straw and rushes and skin, could be depended upon to last for a year; and of them, as with basic foods, there was a year's stock in hand. Little was bought for money, and everything that was useful and wanted was made. It was a quiet life, thrifty, happy, industrious, hard, careful of tomorrow, geared to the cycles and seasons of the year.

All this industriousness of winter nights came to an end at eight o'clock. After supper time, the servants went out to feed the animals and put them right for the night. Thereafter, the long day's night drifted into sleep, or into *caru*, the courting and bundling about which the *Blue Books* made so much fuss. Whatever were the consequences of *caru*, as Henry Richard said, there was no other time.

Arthur Young's instructional articles in the eighteenth century had encouraged some improvement, but in basic agricultural practice and in implements – cart, harrow, harness, plough – there had been little change for centuries, little perhaps since Roman times. When Edward Perkins was born, there was only one threshing machine in the parish of St. David's and around. The Biblical flails thumped the corn from morning to night, and from Michaelmas to Calan Mai (May Day). The man who thought of cutting and binding his corn with a machine was mad, and a sinner against God and his fellow-men; to run the risk of wasting his corn was to challenge the Almighty, for corn was God's direct gift to man. Sickle and scythe cut the corn and every straw was gleaned.

The days of oxen as working animals were rapidly coming to an end. But the harness, the yoke, their straw links and loops, were carefully maintained. When a schoolboy in St. David's Edward Perkins had seen oxen being led on their way to Porth Glais to fetch loads of lime, and, rarely, he had seen them pulling the plough in the fields. It was commoner to see a leading horse with a bull in the shafts. Harries of Trefacwn had worked a bull and a horse to pull cart or plough without any trouble for forty years. To make oxen into working animals was easy; once the yoke had been placed on the two bullocks they were left alone for a while, and when they were placed in the shafts an old horse was harnessed to them. More difficult was the task of the *cathrenwr* or the *cathrenwraig*, the man or woman whose job it was to lead, carting or ploughing, this team of two oxen and a horse or two. Ploughing with an antiquated plough, a team of four oxen and two horses, ploughman, cathrenwr, and one man sitting on the 'arnodd' or plough beam to keep it down, was the hardest job of all. The land was hard and rocky; the field burnt and ploughed for wheat, and sown year after year until in the end, emasculated of growth, it would be left for grassland, unseeded except for what had dropped from the hay.

Animals got the same rough treatment, for the treatment of animals and animal diseases was marked by cruelty and ignorance. Every year one or two or more of the dairy cows died from *pŵd* or tuberculosis; fifty per cent of the yearlings from 'warren' or black leg. Eight or ten horses on a single farm could be wind-broken, or suffer from *rhwstigo* or 'jibbers'. And all these losses were taken philosophically, as acts of Providence.

It was later, towards the end of the century and with the oxen now gone, that the horse became the prime beast of the farm, the pride of the ploughman. There is a marvellous passage in Ronald Blythe's *Akenfield* where old John Grout talks of horses and himself as head horseman, and how the ploughmen talked to them 'and you could see the horses listening.' Ivor Arnold on Ramsey, from Congrwn Bach, could hear Wil Morris in Pencarnan talking to his horses all day long.

Life was hard, and man earned his bread with the hard labour of the nails on his fingers, *wrth ei ddeng ewin*. Edward Perkins was reared on *bara haidd* which was barley bread, and darker, he thought, than *bara rhyg*, which was rye bread – tough stuff that made bone and muscle. The load of grain, sufficient for twelve or thirteen months, ten to fifteen *têl*, according to the number of mouths to feed, was sent to the mill to be dried and ground, and with it went the senior servant girl or an old and reliable dependent of the farm. Those days at the mill were great events, and the evenings of the drying and roasting days were great occasions (the news having gone abroad) for gatherings of farmer and wife, sons and servants. The young danced and revelled and flirted; the more serious male adults debated on the eternal questions of their religion, on the 'elect', and the problems of sin and man in face of the sovereignty of God. Ultimately, the miller's work done, tolls paid and all flour sacked, the load came home, to be stored in scrupulously cleaned bins and packed down so tight that not even one *gwyddonin* or weevil could find its way in. There at last was food for one year, for bread, cawl or soup, uwd, bwdram; wheat and barley first, oats about Lady Day (Gwyl Fair, 25 March) or St. David's Day.

The meat supply was controlled by the same factors, the size of the family and the need to provide for a whole year. Beef and bacon – some was pickled, some suspended from the beams to smoke and dry. No pig under twenty or thirty score was considered worth slaughtering. Here was meat, and lard which was often used instead of butter, and fat for cooking and for making candles. Edward Perkins failed to mention that the enormous amount of fat off these animals was also eaten in enormous quantities: it fortified against bad weather, made up for poor clothing, was insulation in cold and draughty houses. Every farm, big and small, kept its flock of geese, and hardly a Sunday at Pwllcaerog from Michaelmas to St. David's Day passed without its roasted goose in the oven. Feathers and wings had a variety of uses, and goose grease in those simple days of 1850 was the one and only embrocation: it cured the 'warren' in cows' udders; it cured bruises and the crick in the neck; with the help of red flannel it cured sore throat.

Edward Perkins went on to describe a typical Sunday in Pwllcaerog. The country was deeply under the influence of the Methodist Revival: Sunday was a day of rest and chapel going; whatever was necessary had been done on Saturday. A winter's breakfast, milk being scarce, was rye tea sweetened with honey along with a *halsten* or two of brown bread. The head maid had long been attending to the culm fire and had filled the great boiler or *crochan* before 7 a.m. After breakfast, a great commotion: chapel services began between 9 a.m. and 9.30 a.m., and there were many miles to walk. People washed and put on their Sunday best, and between 8 a.m. and half past all had cleared out with the exception of the younger children and the maid whose duty turn it was. She, dressed and pinked, put on a clean apron, and polished clogs and boots, and prepared to cook the dinner. All had been put ready beforehand: the great chunk of beef or bacon; the potatoes cleaned and the leeks chopped up; the goose in the oven. Believe it or not, in that relatively quiet cooking period between 8 a.m. and 10 a.m., she would sit down and read her Bible. At 10 o'clock she would sprinkle flour into the soup, and later cut slices from the breast of the goose for the children's lunch, served on wooden trenchers with goose grease and barley bread. By noon the meat had boiled and been transferred to a smaller *crochan* with the soup. It was now the turn of potatoes and cabbages. Around 1 p.m. the family were safely home, each enjoying a bowl of this nutritious *cawl*, followed by meat and vegetables. Then, as later, the meals of the next two days would be warmed up soup and cold meat and cheese and gruel. Wednesday would see the great boiler again at work, preparing for Thursday and Friday. Friday was baking day, and dinner was home brewed and warm bread straight from the oven. Saturday was 'remainders' day, the day of *lapscows*. In summer milk dishes replaced the *bwdram*, and butter from the milk of sheep, notoriously hard to spread, replaced cheese. There was but little variation in these meals, day after day, week after week. 'God,' said Edward Perkins, quoting, 'gives the food, the devil provides the cook'.

We can look at this picture set within the wider social context of the time. Edward Perkins was born some twenty-three years after the guns of Waterloo were silenced. He knew the second half of the nineteenth century, and he remembered what his father and grandfather had told him, which meant the first half of the century: wars in Europe, the hungry forties, the influence of the Methodist Revival, depressions and recoveries in agriculture, migrations to the industrial areas, the Poor Law changes, the beginnings of modern transport which changed the pattern of society and the way of life of the countryside, and the beginning of an intellectual revival, as if, as he put it, the age of faith was giving way to a new age of enquiry.

First, the worker and his state of poverty. The poor of 1908 were still poor, possibly fewer, and less poor, than in the hungry forties, when England's wealth and prospects were drained by the European wars. There was one change. Now the Relieving Officer and the Workhouse (he used these English terms because they belonged to English institutions which he obviously detested) were the responsible authorities, officials taking over the burden traditionally carried by the charity which was the Welshman's readiness to bear the burden of his neighbour. There had been another change. Ever since the time of Elizabeth the First the Welsh married farm labourer had had his land, four or five acres, on which he kept his cow or two. He earned his wage on the big farm, his wife earned the *enllin*, the little extra, from those few acres. By 1908, nineteen out of every twenty of these little holdings, attached to each of the larger farms, had disappeared. Edward Perkins had his own explanations, which pointed at neither the greed of the farmer nor the oppression of the landlord. It was the labourer's wife who led a hard life, got up early, had all the work to do on the small holding, fed the animals, cleaned the stalls, took care of house and family. The sudden rise in her husband's wages in the 1860s and particularly the 1870s enabled her to free herself from this bondage. The Pwllcaerog farmer was obviously a praiser of time past, and he defended the tied tenancy. Contract between farmer and labourer might well have been for a year, more often it went on for a lifetime, and from father to son. It was a close relationship, patriarchal, and profitable to the good servant: no labourer went home in threshing time without his bonus of a half-bushel of wheat per day.

Not all accepted this hard life, whatever its advantages. Many, tempted, went to Glamorgan. Edward Perkins had met one such from St. David's who had gone off twice, starting very early and reaching Carmarthen by the end of the first day, Neath at the end of the second, and Hirwaun and work at the end of the third. His wages were sometimes fifteen shillings weekly, more often ten shillings. And out of that at least seven shillings went on bed and board. Edward Perkins did not blame the man for going away, although he might have doubted his wisdom, remembering when wages in terms of money were boosted by wages in kind.

Generally, said Edward Perkins, it was a time of improvement, especially from the poverty-stricken inept standards of the small farmer. The 1850s saw, with the establishment of the British Schools, a considerable spurt in education. The better-off farmers took their sons on horseback to Carmarthen and to Brecon. Others from St. David's went by boat to schools in Bristol, the greatest city in the west. In spite of an elemental monotony of work and food it was not too bad a life.

The Farm Worker of the 1800s

Black's *Guide to St. David's* of 1856 said that the City was made up of the clergy, and of the labourers who worked on the farms outside. Historically they have always formed the largest element in the population. During the first half of the nineteenth century there was an enormous national increase in their numbers, some sixty-four per cent in some areas, and then there was a very sharp drop, for a wide variety of reasons, towards the end of the century. This decrease was accompanied by changes within the farm servant class, and, significantly, in the relationship between servant and master. At one time there had been little difference between the farmer and his worker, and Edward Perkins's reminiscences of his life in Pwllcaerog do not conflict with this impression. Further confirmation can be found in Eiluned Lewis's novel, *The Captain's Wife*, which is as much a social document of this parish as a novel of Dickens is of London. 'Family and farm hands, in her childhood, were bound by their common tasks and shared a common leisure . . .' It was a coherent society, despite or because of the hardness and poverty of life. Younger sons and daughters of farmers found themselves servants in other people's farms. And maids and men servants lived in, the men servants sleeping above the stables or in the upper *storws* or storehouse, reached by the outside stone stairs of which hardly an example remains. The married labourer lived in his cottage, tied to the farm; he had his few acres, cared for by his wife, who also worked on the farm in busy seasons. *The Royal Agricultural Society of England Journal* of 1887 reported that for hoeing turnips labourers' wives were paid one shilling per day, and for harvest work and haymaking one shilling per day and their food. Meagre wages were supplemented in kind, and, as Edward Perkins was proud to say, the relationship between farmer and labourer was long lasting with son following father as a matter of course. The children also had to work: their pennies paid for their boots.

Things changed. The 1873 Act made it illegal to employ children under eight; three years later the limit was raised to ten; then came compulsory education and still tougher measures to compel attendance. The costs of running a farm increased; with a dwindling labour force the farmer had to do with old men and *crwts* and imported labour from the Reform Schools. Arable gave way to pasture, and thistles grew in the fields. By 1890 the agricultural labourer in the tied cottage had practically disappeared. Improvements in education and a greater awareness of things made people conscious of their circumstances and of the need for betterment. Religious awakening, a growing sense of personal values, universal suffrage, aroused a revulsion from the older poverty and mean cottages and hunger, the hunger that made men pray

O Heavenly Father bless us,
And keep us all alive,
There are ten of us for dinner
And food for only five.

Money, the actual value of money, was changing. Newspaper reports on 'The Agricultural Depression in Pembrokeshire' commented on the situation. Farmers wanted an abatement in rent because of falling values, rising wages and bad seasons. Wages and farm expenses doubled. There was no profit in corn. Animals fetched low prices. Tithes had come down but rents had not. The agricultural labourer was no better off for his higher wages. As far back as 1873 *The Dewisland and Kemes Guardian* had carried a leader and a headline – 'The High Price of Provisions'. In December of the same year the paper announced that 'during the past half century almost every article had nearly doubled in price and wages have increased in the same ratio. Money is worth only half of what it was fifty years ago'. For this and for other reasons the old paternalism of the farm disappeared. The Land Commission of 1895 noted that 'the servants are gradually losing their character as members of the family and do not remain much in the kitchen. They have little or no domestic life'. A very ancient pattern of society was breaking up.

Six years earlier the *Dewisland and Kemes Guardian* had printed a letter, ostensibly (but one never knew for certain in St. David's: most letters to the press were anonymous) from 'One of the Working Men'. The matter in hand was poverty. Parents complained that they had to pay a penny per week for each of their children attending school. In November 1889 Mortimer Propert explained that the School Board had the right to excuse payment when a family could not afford the charge. The Working Man replied:

> We do not want uncertain charity. I remember the time when scarcely a farmer in St. David's kept a carriage, when all lived on the homeliest fare, dressed in the plainest style. But at the present time most farmers have carriages, and they have given up the homely manners of forty years ago, because, I suppose, they have gone on with the time. So have we their servants gone on with the times . . . Farmers have been able to get allowances on their rents and tithes, but we their servants have no like means to better our condition. We must pay mostly, or allow, rack rents for cottages, and we cannot force shopkeepers or others to make us allowances. We are carefully registered as voters, and we are promised much in election times, but changes have generally brought a balance of benefit for employers . . .

This matter of carriages had obviously developed into a social symbol. Carriage or no carriage meant the difference between being somebody and being nobody. When Queen Victoria came to the throne in 1837 there were less than three wheeled vehicles in the parish. Mrs Williams of Maendewi and Mr Roch of Lleithyr (this is from a newspaper cutting in one of Francis Green's scrapbooks) owned wagonettes, and Henry Harris of Treginnis owned a carriage which looked like a box on two wheels and was called 'dwmbwr dwmbar'. George Williams of Gospel Lane had a carrier's van, and Thomas Martin, a local joiner, had a tricycle with low wheels to carry his tools from farm to farm. In 1847, ten years later, nearly every farmer had his dogcart.

Craftsmen – blacksmith, carpenter, joiner, mason – worked at their trade, and farmed their few acres. Sometimes there were men engaged by farmers as dual purpose farm labourers, doing the ordinary work of the farm only when their craft skills were not needed. Many old crafts had died out, and two of these had very strong links with the farm.

There was a time when most of the little bays around the coast, the little landing places, had a corn mill or a lime kiln. In those lime-kilns limestone from Pembroke and West Williamston was burnt and used to counteract the acidity of the soil. Solva had more than eight kilns; a ruin of a magnificent square one stands in Caerbwdi, deserted but not collapsed above the badly ruined corn mill; there were two in Abereiddi; Porth Glais had four, now reconstructed by the National Trust, and, according to a sale catalogue of 1871 confirming what is recorded on the Tithe Map, a fifth on Rhosycribed land. Liming the soil was a hard job – there is some evidence that small fields were skimmed of soil, limed, and then re-covered. The job of burning was equally laborious. In 1930 the Pembrokeshire County Council discussed the re-introduction of liming, to revitalise a deteriorated soil and to reduce an equally serious unemployment. Owen Williams from St. David's spoke from experience as an old limeburner, one of the last, who used to burn four hundred tons a year. He condemned the proposed re-introduction as too expensive and too laborious: men, he said, would not work at limeburning any more. But men had worked on limeburning for centuries and limed their land. George Owen of Henllys praised its value, not so much for the farmer as for the farmer's son. John Williams of Trearched, a century later, had had his doubts. In the end, around the end of the nineteenth century, the kilns began to run cold. But the use of lime continued, and the older citizens of St. David's can remember long queues of carts going on a day-long journey to fetch lime from Haverfordwest, until the railway and Mathry Road Halt brought the distribution centre nearer, and brought competition from artificial fertilisers. Lime was still used in building construction, and in the old, old habit of whitewashing cottages and farmhouses, outbuildings and walls, and roofs. It was an old Welsh custom, for Dafydd ap Gwilym and Ieuan Gwynedd had praised in poetry the 'white houses' and '*bythynod gwyngalch Cymru*'. Francis Kilvert must have seen it elsewhere, but when he came to St. David's with his father he was dazzled with white – St. David's, he said, looked like a town under snow. Some of the other nineteenth century tourist pilgrims were ruder. Edward Walford, writing of *Pleasant Days in Pleasant Places* in 1878, saw rows of cottages and third and fourth rate houses daubed crudely with whitewash. Even worse had been the defacement of Reformation days, when in 1630 the whole of the inside of the Cathedral was whitewashed. James Baker, who wrote an article on a visit to St. David's (A Dead City', printed in the *London Magazine* in 1889) was taken round by an old clerk, a quiet placid old man, who did not look above sixty, but who said he had been sexton for fifty-eight years. 'Many a time had he seen the whole of the beautiful building daubed with whitewash: but now the whitewash and desecration days were over, and slowly the building was being reclaimed from the ruins of its former glory.'

Some of the old people say that the limekilns in Porth Glais were handy in another way – the lads of the City, after a night's carousing, would sleep it out close to their warmth. And there are true tales of the limekiln that stood once in Jubilee Gardens in Haverfordwest. Tramps gathered there on cold winter nights. Next morning, still unsobered, they had to be taken to hospital and treated for burns.

There were other kilns in the old farming days, now remembered only in the names of fields. Kiln in Welsh is *odyn* and the field kiln called *odyn fwni* was used to dry corn. There is still a *parc yr odyn* on many farms. It was a long trench with a fireplace at one end and a wide opening at the other. Over all was erected a flat pitched timber roof, over which was spread a haircloth, *brethyn rhawn*, and on this the corn was spread: the will of John Harries of Cruglas (1701) mentioned 'bags and sacks two dozen, half a dozen winnowing sheets, 2 old hair cloths, and 12 sieves for winnowing'. Heath or furze or fern, *ffagl rhedyn*, was burnt in the fireplace and the smoke of the furze was thought to add a pleasant flavour to the grain. There was a *melin eithin*, a furze mill, below Treginnis: a mill and malting and drying floors (essential elements in home brewing) and kilns were mentioned in a sale catalogue of 1885. There was a gorse mill, forerunner of the chaffcutter, in Rhosycribed: here and in Lower Treginnis, on the steep slope of land above the sea and Ogof Mrs Morgan, are green tufts of grass and masses of gorse that once fed the mills. Many a time, we remember reading, Adrian and Ivor Arnold went out to gather furze on Ramsey; and they must have seen the Treginnis mill. The structure is still there, but the wheel is gone, and some years back an enterprising farmer converted the whole thing into a highly efficient sheep dip. Not far away are the ruined shafts of the old copper mines.

According to David Williams's *The Rebecca Riots*, there were in 1831 two hundred and forty weavers in Cardiganshire, two hundred and sixty in Carmarthenshire, and one hundred and thirty in Pembrokeshire. They were widely scattered, but the largest return for any one district was seventeen for the neighbourhood of St. David's. These men, and the women who must have helped them, were part of a strong subsistence economy, producing for the needs of their community. The only two woollen mills that have survived,

Middle Mill and Tregwynt, are now busier than ever because, as it is the way of progress, they have extended their trade beyond their community. The wool trade, which according to George Owen, was the third most important in export terms at one time, closed during the early eighteenth century; and there is only one record of wool export from St. David's – sixty stone from Porth Glais to Bristol. What continuing woollen trade there was was local and self-supporting. The old people say that every farm at the beginning of this century grazed its flock of sheep, of fifty more or less, and that the wool was taken to the mill to be washed and carded and turned into cloth for the farmer, his family, and his labourer. Some say that what actually damaged the industry was an invasion of commercial buyers from England. They came to Haverfordwest, made a day of it at the Grove (so, it is said, did the farmers) – the transport was there, the price was tempting, the wool was away.

In 1606 Richard Owen willed to his sister 'a pair of walls and ground thereto belonging, called Tucker's Land situate in St. Nun's Street'. There had been therefore a tucking mill within the City, as there was another much later, Y Pandy, not far from the corn mill in Caerforiog, and another, later, in Porth y Rhaw, which ceased working about 1915. *Slater's Directory* of 1880 mentioned a carding mill in Nun Street in the occupation of Benjamin Price, who eight years earlier had been advertising in the *Dewisland and Kemes Guardian* for 'a person who thoroughly understands the spinning and weaving'. A gravestone in the Cathedral Yard commemorates the death of seventeen-year-old Elias Morris, of The Factory, St. David's. Samuel Williams's papers (in the National Library of Wales, Aberystwyth) refer to David Morris of the tucking mill (1886) and to the carding mill at Tan y Rhiw (1870). Tan y Rhiw is now a dwelling house converted from the old mill, a hundred yards north west of Penitents Bridge. *The Twr y Felin Guide* of 1923 called it Melin dan y Rhiw, the Mill below the Hill. Locals called it Felin Rollo.

Slater's Directory of 1880 mentions three woollen manufacturers in St. David's – George Thomas of High Street, John Jenkins of Nun Street, and William Thomas of High Street. By 1884 (*Kelly's Directory*) things had changed. James Griffiths was at the carding mill, and the weavers were Thomas George of Goat Street, John Jenkins, and Thomas Thomas of New Street. Benjamin Griffiths's name appears for the first time in 1891, and appears again in *Kelly's Directory* of 1906 – Benjamin Griffiths, woollen weaver, Nun Street and Carding Mills. His wife ran a sweet shop and sold clothing in Nun Street, and acted as agent for Commerce House in Haverford-west. The mill in Felin Ganol (Middle Mill) was established in 1907 by the same family under the name of Thomas Griffiths and Son, and for some time the two mills worked in partnership. It is said that Ben Griffiths used to carry his carded wool from Middle Mill to Dan y Rhiw for scouring, and carry it back again. The old records show that he sent his suitings and shirting material all over England and Wales, to individual customers, to institutions, and to at least one Prime Minister. Now Middle Mill specialises in making woollen carpets, and draws its customers – and hundreds of curious summer visitors – from very far afield.

It is easy for us in the year 1981 to understand how change, in economic facts of life, in market demand, in transport, in the viability of some of the country's basic industries, can alter a man's life and that of his family in a staggeringly short time. That is the burden of our present day. Rural peace and a traditionally more stable life, and remoteness from all industrial change: these cushioned the thrusts of change on St. David's. It is not easy to see how the face of the parish changes imperceptibly – the size and shape and number of houses and fields; and how our dunes and coastal paths are in a state of being constantly worn down. The great surprise is that the elemental moors and the common lands have changed. Over the centuries the farmers and their workers have looked across at them, have threaded them with pathways, have lived on the rim of them. Farmer and labourer have claimed and recovered from them; have trespassed on their boundaries, have filched from what historically had been everybody's grazing, filched, as Gerald the Welshman said they always did. At the same time they have guarded them and maintained their rights in them, rights of grazing, the right to dig for peat and to carry away timber. They did that after the Commons Registration Act of 1970 as conscientiously as the Courts Leet of the past and as the young Parish Council of 1895 had done. Nowadays the commons are neglected, although there is now a new committee to manage Dowrog's few hundred acres (and a notable orchid garden) as a nature reserve. No peat is now dug on Dowrog; it runs the risk of being overgrown. There was a time within living memory when twenty or thirty horses grazed Trefaeddan Moor in season and kept down the wildness so that the traversing paths, links between roads and farms and chapels and City, as they once were, were kept crisp and clean. John Miles Thomas, in his remarkably evocative *Looking Back*, reminisces on a childhood in St. David's around the turn of the century, and writes on the social significance of Trefaeddan Moor and Lower Moor, when the pools were solid sheets of ice 'and we played and frolicked in the light of the rising moon until hunger sent us home to supper'. There is no more grazing, no more playing, and old habits and old customs, and social patterns, were lost when the paths closed up. The moors have changed.

It was inevitable, and regrettable, that old customs should go, and particularly those of harvest. They were lively and communal and symbolic. One of these customs went by the name of *y Wrach. Gwrach*, according to the dictionary, means witch or old hag; in the old custom it was the name given to the last sheaf of corn in the field. In their excitement at 'harvest home' the harvesters threw their sickles wildly at this last sheaf, and the man who cut it had to move sharply out of harm's way. His reward was a jug of home brewed ale. Another version (described by D. Jenkin Evans) involved the clandestine transfer of the sheaf from field to farmhouse, safe and dry in face of all kinds of molestations and throwings of water, by one of the reapers. Safely home, the sheaf would hang on a beam for the rest of the year.

The very last ceremony was always the harvest supper, happily symbolic of the traditional communal nature of all harvest work. A community, said George Ewart Evans in *Ask the Fellows Who Cut the Hay*, is not formed by a number of people living together in chance association. The old village was integrated because its inhabitants had to work together within the framework laid down by the necessities of living and of time. A more or less common labour bound the people together; and out of this work grew the organism which was the old community. Agriculture remains the basic industry of the parish, but neither agriculture nor its fulfilment in harvesting is communal any more.

Treginnis Isha

In 1929, halfway between today and Edward Perkins's prime, a stripling of a lad began working in Treginnis. This is what he remembers of that time.

Lower Treginnis farm is two and a half miles from St. David's. It is situated on a peninsula and has two miles of coastline to be fenced to stop cattle falling over cliffs. The land is rocky, studded with fourteen hillocks, but is well watered with small springs and two ponds which used to feed the water mill at Porth-henllys. The farmhouse, stone built, has around it a generosity of farm buildings: an outside kitchen which was used for rearing chickens and for feathering at Christmas; stable; barn; culm shed; calves' cots with a loft overhead; cart house; and a large store where corn was kept; fat cattle sheds and a cowshed; and sheds for threshing machine and straw elevator. At Porth-henllys is an old dwelling house and ruins, now used to store seasonable machinery. Also on the yard is a round house with a pigeon loft – a blue flag floor with a well underneath and a hand pump to draw the water. In the adjoining field, walled like a pound or *ffald*, was once a slaughterhouse, three pigs' cots and a kiln house, relic of the good old days of barley malt, and now converted into a potato sprouting shed.

The family in 1929 were two bachelor brothers and a housekeeper who helped with the milking and churning, and looked after the poultry. One ploughman did all the field work, and a skilled craftsman, a carpenter, helped when required. I was seventeen years old in that year (said the new farm worker) and officially the cowman in charge of all the feeding of cows, calves and pigs. I also milked and helped with other jobs that came along – grinding corn, carting furze and chaffing for food for the horses, carting turnips and slicing them to be fed to the cattle. An oil engine drove the grinding mill, chaffed, sliced the turnips, and churned. Wages – the ploughman those days got eighteen shillings per week, and I as a cowboy got nine and six. I had in addition to mix the culm and carry it to the house. In summer, when there was not much yard work, I helped in the fields, weeding potatoes, hoeing turnips, harvesting hay and corn, manuring, pulling mangolds and turnips, and putting up fencing.

There were four horses, the one-eyed Boxer, a grey mare Scot, Bob, a light horse used to take pigs to market, and Rose, which won second prize in St. David's Horse Show in 1922.

The milk of twelve cows was carried to the dairy and separated, and the skim milk given to the calves. Twelve cattle were fattened and sold as beef – fattened on mixed corn meal with fattening cake and turnips and hay. There were sixteen store cattle, and if there were two or three heifers amongst them they were kept for milking. Another sixteen were reared on the bucket. And one Hereford bull was kept. Four sows brought two litters in the year, each litter averaging ten or eleven. Most of the pigs were reared as porkers of about five score, to be sold after fourteen weeks. Sometimes pigs were sold as weaners of eight or nine weeks old. Three pigs would be slaughtered for bacon. Seventy or more sheep produced an average of 110 lambs, to be sold in May or June – they were Ryeland and Kerry Hill – at an average weight of 70 to 80 pounds. Sheep were washed and sheared in June and dipped in August, in the presence of the police. Three geese and a gander for breeding produced about 25 goslings to be feathered at Christmas. In addition there were six ducks and 40 to 50 hens. During November and March the rabbit trapper visited the farm; he would catch about a thousand at the first trapping, each about 2½ pounds, and three hundred on the second.

One acre of potatoes were grown for use on the farm, with perhaps a ton or two – Majestic or King Edward – sold to the merchant. It was in this year that a few drills of early potatoes – Sharp's Express – were grown and sold to the City Bakery. Two acres of mangolds were carted in November and covered with straw as protection against frost. Three acres of turnips were carted in during the winter and fed as required. Twenty-five acres of hay were cut and harvested in June and July, to be followed by fourteen acres of Black Tartarian oats and twenty acres of barley. All corn was threshed in October and kept for feeding, and all straw was kept for feeding and for bedding.

How about prices in those days? A five-year-old mare, £30 to £35, a suckling colt, £10 to £12. Fat cattle were £2 per hundredweight, store cattle £11 to £12 each, sucking calves £2 each, and a cow or heifer in milk £20 to £25. Pigs were 8/- or 10/- a score for porkers, weaners 22/- to 26/- each. Seasonal prices ruled for lambs, 1/4 per pound and down to 1/- later. Geese were 2/6 per pound at Christmas, eggs nine pence per dozen, dressed chicken 1/6 per pound. Rabbits were 2½d a pound. Oats 2/- per bushel, barley 3/-, potatoes 5/- per hundredweight.

Before the General Election of the summer of 1929 the Conservatives were in power and they took off the rates from land and farmers rejoiced over it. But a cattle dealer who was a staunch Liberal commented that they had cut a cane to whip themselves. Prices slumped terribly in the following years.

The highlight of the year was the beginning of February when the fat cattle were sold. All would be up at 5.30 a.m., dogs and all – the greyhound, the sheepdog and the spaniel – to start walking the cattle to Mathry Road. The trap and pony would take a load of pigs.

Holidays for the year amounted to a few hours at Christmas and on New Year's Day, early milkings on Whit-Monday, Cymanfa Ganu, St. David's Fair, Mathry and Letterston Fairs, Rhosson's Sunday School party, and *cwrdd pishin* – the chapel meeting where everyone was expected to contribute his *pishin*, his piece. And every other Sunday was off.

The year 1929 saw a very heavy fall of snow and hard frost in February, followed by a very pleasant spring and summer. But the autumn was very rough: there were many storms and many ships lost, among them the *Moseley* in Jack Sound. There were no oilskins or wellingtons then – they were too expensive, and one had to make do with a sack or two to keep dry and warm. The only transport was a bicycle. And all were happy because it was the same for all.

That description of life on one of the historic farms of the parish was related by Dewi Rowlands, the junior farm worker cowman (*gwas bach*) of fifty years ago. He looked across then, as he looks across now, at Ramsey and the Sound, and has seen the changes on the island: Ramsey farmed, and Ramsey deserted, Ramsey the seal colony and bird sanctuary under the protection of the Royal Society for the Protection of Birds, Ramsey from 1978 to 1980 farmed, its buildings restored and part of its 625 acres stocked with a herd of red deer. Now Ramsey is on sale again, due to be left once more, one chapter closed and another for better or worse to be opened in a history that is full of chequered changes. But they are lesser changes than those that have fallen on farming in the last fifty years. Practically every detail in that description of Treginnis fifty years ago is now changed and out-dated – in the labour force, in the use of land and buildings, most of all because of mechanisation.

What, then, is the broad outline of farming in the parish today as we read in the annual summaries of the Ministry of Agriculture? Ninety-five people registered as farmers in Kelly's Directory of 1906. According to the Ministry figures of 1974 there were 83 holdings in the parish, and surprisingly, and very much more in accordance with the past than expected, 33 of them were classified as part-time, continuing the two-job tradition where the proceeds of farming were not completely the means of subsistence. Twelve were predominantly dairying (over seventy-five per cent of the outlay) and thirteen mainly dairying (over fifty per cent). Livestock, mainly cattle, accounted for another seven, continuing a tradition of centuries. George Owen had stressed the importance of cattle in the farming pattern; and in a meeting of the St. David's Farmers Club, held at the Grove Hotel in February, 1876, with Edward Perkins in the chair, it was claimed that 'the cattle of St. David's Parish were good enough to stand against all comers'. It is still accepted that a cow moved outside the parish will lose condition, and that a cow brought into the parish will show almost immediate improvement. Six of the parish farms were classed by the Ministry as 'mixed' and eleven as 'general cropping'. The greatest innovation has been early potato growing. Its small beginning was seen in the Treginnis record of 1929. Today it extends to between five hundred and seven hundred acres. Like tourism, it is a seasonal trade; and like tourism it depends heavily on casual and imported labour.

The spread of mechanisation into all aspects of farming has brought in all kinds of social change. Silage has changed the traditional hay harvest. The milking machine has changed dairying, and now bulk collecting has abolished the milk churn and the dialogues of the old familiar milk-stands. The combine harvester has dismissed the binder – in 1907 they were still cutting corn by scythe and binding sheaves by hand in Rhosson Ganol. The net result has been to increase efficiency, to reduce and change the function of the labour force, and to eliminate the physical and psychological togetherness that was once characteristic of farming in general and of harvesting in particular. Women, young and old, no longer work in the hayfield; straw-hatted and aproned, they raked every blade in field and hedgerow for the final harvest. The harvest thanksgiving festival is still held, but the old customs and festivities have gone, and those who now attend church and chapel to give their thanks have had very little to do with the act of harvesting, and no personal interest in it.

The nature of work has changed. The social pattern and the attitude of men and women – and their children – has changed in the way they approach their work and look at their surroundings. And the places where men once lived have changed. When they began to move from the farmlands into the City and away to the industrial areas, the men and women of the parish altered for good the human geography, the pattern of the community.

The Deserted Villages

The parish of St. David's is not unacquainted with the phenomenon of the deserted village made familiar in Goldsmith's description of the Irish village of Auburn. Around us are crumbling walls, a fallen cottage, piece of hedge, the overgrown tracery of a garden, a pine end. A changed map.

If we take a walk past the old farm of Treleddid Fawr and along the public pathway up to the high ground between Carn Llidi and Penbiri, we come to a rock called Trellwyd (Treliwyd to the locals) near a farm of the same name. From that high spot can be seen a magnificent sweep of coast, of gorse and cliff and sea. In a circle to the west are Carn Ffald and Carn Perfedd, Carn Lleithyr and Carneddgwion, with Carn Llidi in the background, and below Y Gesail Fawr, the steep-cliffed inlet, the *cesail* or 'armpit' where the seals live. In the centre of this circle is Maes-y-mynydd. There is nothing there now but ruins, walls of collapsed houses, remnants of gardens, strips of land marked as indelibly as they were on the 1840 Tithe Map. Once there were six or seven houses – Herbert Roach claims there were thirteen – and a community of families. A magnificent view, and remoteness. It is easier to understand, now, why they left than why they ever came. But they did live here; some of the older citizens of present day St. David's were born here, and as children walked all the way to school. Here their fathers had their boats, although it is impossible to explain how they ever launched them. To them, as to Neolithic Man, it was easier to launch a boat than to travel overland.

If we turn our backs on Maes-y-mynydd and look south, we find before us the sweeping plateau, the corn lands, the bowl of the valley that nurses the Cathedral, the little river, and the cornlands that stretch beyond the river to the edge of the cliffs of St. Brides Bay. There is the land of the deserted villages. The old documents make mention of the townreds of Skyfog, and Gwrhyd, 'Carvay', Treboeth, Trelerw, Portheiddi, Trefadog, Hendre, Llaethty. The census forms of 1841 and 1851 tell how many homes and people there were in each. According to Dr Jones's Charity sales catalogues there were a number of cottages around the old farmhouse of Hendre, not the imposing house built by Watts Williams, but its predecessor on another site, referred to now as 'the ruins'. Ysgeifiog (the Welsh original of the anglicised 'Skyfog') was a township. Now it is a little collection of farms and three homes. Once it had eight or nine, with large families in each. Thomas James, clogmaker and Methodist, a notable nonagenarian, is head of a family prominent in this community for generations. He remembers a village of three or four carpenters, a blacksmith, a thatcher, and clogmaker and cobbler in a society of perhaps fifty people. And always there was a foundation of three farmers. More surprising, the place in the last hundred years has produced five sea captains.

Old sales maps reveal the lay-out and size, the dimensions of the old village of Tretio which is known in the parish as Treteio. Around its central green are now two farms where once there were three. The Baptist chapel, revered and with its own special story, is no longer used, and crumbling. There are two restored cottages alongside it, and one house, now a holiday home, on the green. All around are the ruins of outhouses and cottages. Less than twenty-five years ago there were eight households, each with its large family. The old people died in the *bythynnod* where their families had reared their children for generations. No-one came to replace them. People moved away, some abroad, some to the industrial valleys. Small holdings were swallowed up by larger farms. The larger community has gone, and the village has lost not only a few human beings but a precious little pocket where men and women lived and bred and worked together, and where the Welsh language was alive and well.

The most interesting of the vanished villages is on the fringe of the parish. In 1974 and 1975, after a violent storm, a sea defence wall was built across the beach at Abereiddi. On the landward side is now a large open parking space of blue-black Llanfirn shale, ground fine, which nature may one day coddle again into grass. For grass it was not long ago. From the ruined lime kilns down to and beyond the wall, hardly more than thirty years back, was a garden for which

Henry Roach of Llanfyrn paid a rent of an ounce of tobacco (or was it half an ounce?) to the owner of the 'Morning Star'. The village of Abereiddi died from natural causes, three of them, and one was the sea. Surprisingly, when this little place was alive and well, hardly any holiday makers came to see it. Now, deserted, it is one of the most popular of beaches, hardly ever empty, full of grey-green peace.

On the high ground north of the bay, towards Trwyn Castell, they once dug for slate, and dug so deep and so near to the cliff edge that in the end it was easy for the locals to blast a gap of an outlet to the sea. That was how, long after the mining had ended, they made the Blue Lagoon into a harbour for their boats. On the headland is the tower landmark, a pillar and globe in slate, and the ruined offices, walls, pathways and entrances, all in blue-black. And on the terraced high ground, clear cut, is the line of tramway that took the shale down to the Slate Yard where it was processed. Half way down the slope to the valley and towards Porth-gain is the archaeological relict of the Powder House, a round house girded with a band of iron, and roofed once with earth. Lower down and near the floor of the valley are the larger ruins of the Manager's house, and below that the terrace of ruined cottages.

South of the bay, on the opposing high ground are two houses washed in pink. One is the home of Deraint Rees, sole survivor of the old Abereiddi families. The other, with its lean-to, pine-end-to-the-sea, was the Old Shop, where Ebenezer Rees sold his flour, groceries for the farms around, bean coffee, which he ground laboriously for his big customers, and sweets for the children. He never took cash on the nail from the big buyers, but once a month, before the 'wagin' came with fresh supplies, he collected his moneys to pay the carrier on delivery. There were two ways to that shop in the old days, the narrow ledge path which was narrow and dangerous enough to attract all children, even in the dark of winter, and the wide track used by the 'wagin' and today by Deraint Rees's tractor.

In the valley were three cottages, now summer homes, some of their old-time character gone. Alongside one is the coalyard mentioned in the Trevacoon sale catalogue. Inland is a ruin of a cottage, and further north was once a thatched cottage where lived Margaret and John Vaughan. One of the cottages was once the village pub, and alongside it was the unofficial pub, which sold the smuggled spirits brought in by Abereiddi's boatmen. They were skilful with boats, and to a man they loved poaching; some spent their life in that gentle art and in fishing. Counting the quarrymen, and Ebenezer Rees and Harri Ty-To, who went shopping to St. David's in pony and trap (all the others relied on donkeys), and William

Phillips, known as the doctor because once he effected some cures by means unknown to himself, and two carpenters – men, women and children, there were fifty in this close community less than fifty years ago. While the men worked or poached or idled, their womenfolk on a warm day sat outside the doorsteps of their terrace, darning and knitting, and around them were the fishing nets drying in the sun. It was a society happy within its means.

And so it remained until things happened, the Welshman's *tro ar fyd*, the turn of fortune. According to Barbara George's *Pembrokeshire Sea-Trading before 1900*, slates were exported from 1850 onwards from Abereiddi and Porth-gain up the Bristol Channel and to the south of England, but those quarries closed down in 1904, when the porous Abereiddi-Llanfirn slate failed to stand up to competition from the better quality slates of Caernarfon. The 'old chronicles' (the reminiscing elderly) say that the slate waste from the Yard in Porth-gain was mixed with clay and made into bricks in the Porth-gain kilns, originally set up to make bricks for building the stone-crushing plant that, derelict, now stands as the major archaeological remains, the 'atmosphere', of Porth-gain. The bricks also lost out eventually in competition with bricks of a smaller and more orthodox size, but the 1909 account books say that 47,000 and 66,000 tons of bricks were sent to Llanelli between June and August of that year, and that a cargo of 37,000 'seconds' were sent to Dublin. Local people still say that Dublin's slums, the dingy-fronted Sean O'Casey slums where the poor prayed gently for less of the next world and a little more of this, were built out of Abereiddi waste. When the slate trade in Abereiddi came to an end, the crushed stone trade of Porth-gain Village Industries Limited carried on and provided employment for locals and for many from St. David's. Some walked all the way daily, in their 'yorks', ribbed trousers with a piece of string tied round below the knee. Others, at least fifty at one time, walked to Milford to look for work on the trawlers. Porth-gain too came to a halt, in 1931.

The second natural cause was, obviously, unemployment, lack of work, lack of any prospect of work. There was perhaps the unspoken itch for something better in life and home. People left, reluctantly, and asked no questions when the troubles came.

They came again in 1938. In February of that year Abereiddi found itself afflicted with the typhoid epidemic that struck the parish of St. David's. Troubles come in battalions, as Shakespeare said, and on top of the epidemic the Atlantic gales came in, and the six cottages and one storehouse at the base of the tramline hill were swept away. The steady erosion of the slate beach, Bible-black when wet, carried on, which is why they built the sea wall.

The natives went, to find other homes.

CHAPTER FIVE

Trade and Communications

Its geographical position made it inevitable that from earliest times the St. David's headland was acquainted with traffic. Trade routes from immemorial times became the routes followed by the early Christian missionaries, and the Headland became a focal crossing point of trade and Christian routes, a synthesis immortalised in Gwenallt's rich choice of words – the merchandise of Christianity, '*marsiandiaeth Calfari*'. Not surprisingly, therefore, the first record that we have of trade through Porth Glais involves the Church. It begins with two monks. On Friday before the Feast of St. John ante Latinam in 1385 Hugh de Pickton was sworn in as supervisor of the fabric of St. David's Cathedral, the equivalent of the Chapter Officer who later became known as Master of the Fabric, the office now held by the Dean. For the fifty-two weeks of his year's office, his scribe, Hugh Felton, entered into 'six rolls of Communicata' all payments for labour and materials, and was paid £1. 10s for his labours. Copies of these records form part of the accounts of the Cathedral called *Liber Communis*; they were printed in an appendix to Jones and Freeman's *History and Antiquities of Saint David's*, and were later translated into English in Francis Green's 'Pembrokeshire in By-gone Days' in Volume 9 of *West Wales Historical Records*, the Magazine of the Historical Society of West Wales.

This first record of trade in Porth Glais and the City – what does it tell us? For the first three weeks there was much work done in the quarry, and much mending of tools. David Bole and David Yrist, Jak Coce, Jak Skinner and Philip Rosse worked for 3d per day with no payment for liquid refreshments. And William ap Phillip Vawrer spent nineteen days busily carrying with his truckle cart, for which he was paid 6d per day. In the fifth week one pyckard (a boatload of fifteen tons) of lime stones was landed in Porth Glais and William Kyley was paid 4s for carting them from 'Porthcleyes to the churchyard'. In the eighth week another load of lime stones were landed in 'solfach'. And in the tenth week came a climax of preparations: 15 poles for a scaffold and 15 'Hoselstanes' from

Ireland; lead and iron from Tenby; another load of lime stones; and 40 bushels of coal at 2d per bushel brought in to Porth Glais and carted to the churchyard. Expenses, which included flagons of ale, were paid only to people who had to travel. Stone was cut from a quarry 'near St. David's', and from Caerfai, and lifted by windlass. Not once throughout these records was there any direct reference made to the Caerbwdi stone which is so often linked with the Cathedral.

What was the work done? Payments were made for making and repairing doors and windows, and making hooks, hinges, keys and nails. The general assumption is that there had been vandalism in the Cathedral, and that windows in the aisles were being walled up because of threats from robbers. Work was done within the Church, the gates of the Treasury were repaired, and more than one reference indicated work on the doors of dwellings or chambers of the clergy. Bars were made for outside gates, gates were made for the ramparts, and the north wall of the Close was repaired. It all looked like a great exercise which involved repairs to damaged property and the building of defences against intrusion. Above all else, this was 1365, the time of Adam Houghton, a great organiser and builder, and it was the year of the founding of the College and Chapel of St. Mary, the great and magnificent backcloth to all his work.

Over sixty men were involved, and their names would have charmed Charles Lamb into an essay on whimsy. Did Llewellyn Siglo (seeing that 'siglo' in Welsh means 'to shake') suffer from 'tremblings' when he made his nails and repaired his tools? And Jak Lokyer (this is the way that English surnames sprouted into use) spent his time making hinges, locks and keys. Amongst the labourers who sometimes found themselves promoted to masons was Jevan Degan, a John Tegan, the first record of a very familiar name in the records of the parish. There are many instances of the name Goch ('redhead') or Gough, and of Coce and Coke which may also be variants of this name. In 1625 a William Richard Goch was fined 3/4d for obstructing the King's highway between St. David's and Haverfordwest. Philipe Robert Goch of St. David's bought one brown colt for 14/8d at Ffair Feigan in Eglwyswrw in 1599. And a Philip Goch was vicar of Llanrhian in 1661.

As the Cathedral was the prime provider of employment so also it was chief user of the port of Porth Glais. The land of the bishop's manor stretched along the river Alun down to the harbour, and it would be sensible to assume that the protecting or harbour wall was built by the Cathedral authorities to make the harbour safer and more efficiently available for their needs, and that they continued to make use of it for centuries to come. One entry of the tenth week suggests that timber from Ireland come in through Porth Glais. So must the Irish bog oak used by Treasurer Owen Pole (1472–1509) for the making of the nave ceiling. And through the little port came the nine tons of lime stone and the culm to burn it, and the eleven tons of lime that were carted at 9d per load for work on the fabric in 1743–1774 when Chancellor David Lloyd was Master of the Fabric, and the work in hand was the renovation of the Chapter House.

Next come the Elizabethan records, and a reputed Cathedral scandal. Thomas Bansby, an English merchant, complained to the Privy Council in 1541 on behalf of two Bretons who had been robbed and plundered by English pirates off the coast of St. David's, and their goods reputedly sold to, among others, Thomas Lloyd, chantor of the Cathedral. He was accused by William Barlow of being implicated in piracy. The story, true or not, was symptomatic. The peace and drive of Elizabeth the First's reign meant a vastly increased maritime activity, and it was this activity in the Bristol Channel that invited piracy. Tales of piracy have clung around the coast ever since. Stories of boats being coaxed on to rocks, and luring lights, and the bludgeoning of crews and looting of wrecked cargoes are as common of Newgale or Ceibwr as of Solva and Ty-gwyn and Llanunwas. Fenton tells of the wreck of the *Resolution* off Newgale in 1690, when the owner and master were 'almost totally robbed and deprived'. The parish register of Nolton tells of eight wreckers killed and several injured when gunpowder exploded in a wreck they were looting. When the *Nimrod* perished off St. David's Head in 1860 a letter in the *Haverfordwest and Milford Haven Telegraph* scathingly commented that church and chapels in St. David's had the capacity to seat two thousand worshippers and that the foremost in despoiling the *Nimrod* were 'those most distinguished in their profession of religion.' The same kind of story appeared when the *Szent Istvan* was wrecked, but the religious enthusiasts accused this time were the people of Solva. In the *Pembroke County Guardian* (cuttings in Volume 11 of Francis Green's scrapbook files in the Library) are two grimly gory ballads descriptive of what Howel Harris called 'the theft and cruelty' of looting. One celebrated the wreck and looting of the *Pennsylvania*, passenger liner, off Solva about 1799, and a gruesome stripping of rings off the fingers of women passengers who were later buried in Brawdy churchyard. The other was on the wreck of the *Bordeaux*, equally lurid. This time the pillagers of Newgale got there first.

The Elizabethans did their best to encourage and establish effective control over this coastal trade and to curb piracy. They ordered that the Welsh ports and all creeks be grouped under three

Head or legal ports, of which Milford was one. Porth Glais was then, and still is, registered under Milford. The Elizabethan State Papers of 1574 to 1579 listed the names of all these creeks and ports; once Milford and St. David's were bracketed in an order as if on equal terms. All of them – Nolton, Solva, Porth Glais, Porth-mawr, Trefin, Fishguard, Newport, St. Dogmaels – were to be

> under the governance of the Quenes Justices of the peace of the said countie except the townes of Pembroke and Tenbie . . . and Purclays, Trevyne, Solvach before named be under the governance of the Reverend father the Bisshopp of St. Davids and yet nevertheless no shipp vessell nor boate in any of the places above said may have authoritie to lad or dislad but only of the Quenes majesties officers.

Significantly, the bishop's proprietary right over Porth Glais was recognised, but he had no further control over the trade that passed through it.

Two boats were listed under St. David's. Thomas Williams and Thomas John ap Philipe were owners and masters of boats (one of them named *Margaret*), each of eight tons, each with a crew of four, each trading with Ireland and North Wales and each going 'up Severne afishinge'. The names of the men deputed by the commissioners 'for the kepinge and surveying of havens' were given. Thomas Perkyns from St. David's was one of those in charge from Solva to Fishguard.

The Elizabethan Thomas Williams who, according to the Welsh Port Books, owned a boat in Porth Glais, lived in Treleddin. It is one of Francis Jones's most intricate delvings into family history, 'Rickeston and Scotsborough' (published in *The Pembrokeshire Historian*, Volume 2), that proves the point. The year was 1633. Thomas ap Rice (or Price) farmed Ramsey, leased from the bishop, and ran a ferryboat between island and mainland. His ferryman saw a Breton ship enter the Sound, and the captain and two men land, steal a sheep, and sail away. In the following May the ship came again, and the ferryman saw that the crew were aided and abetted by a group of local men, one at least of whom was a vicar choral. The ship finally dropped anchor close to the island, other locals arrived, and the captain and thirty men ranged over the island and came back after midnight carrying four cheeses and one sheep. That was not all. A little after sunrise there was another raid, and eight cheeses, a lamb and some sheep were carried away. In the middle of this flurry, when the second lot of St. David's men arrived, another came with them – Thomas Williams of Treleddin, carrying a jar of milk which he wanted to swap for wine, and a couple of hens, a cock, and a capon, which he hoped to sell. There were four Thomas Williamses of Treleddin before the last, who was a different sort of man. He was magistrate, Trinity House representative for Solva, High Sheriff of the County of Pembroke, merchant and owner of two boats.

How old, one wonders, are the names of features along this coast? Who was Bet of 'Pwll Bet'? Or Elen of 'Trwyn Elen', not far from Tre-fin? There is Trwyn Shôn Owen (John Owen's ness or nose) on Ramsey, and Ogof Mary (possibly a wrecked boat) near Castell Heinif, and Ogof Mrs. Morgan near Porth Lisgi. Was Ogof Thomas Williams on Ramsey named after one of the Williamses of Treleddin?

Details of Porth Glais men and boats, given above, come from the *Welsh Port Books* for the years 1550 to 1603. Here also can be found entries of particular interest to St. David's, names of boats, names of owners and masters, and cargoes and ports of origin and destination. Boats brought into Porth Glais a mixture of some of the essentials of living and some of the luxuries, wine, hops and raisins, calico, pepper, salt, and timber from Ireland. What went out was predominantly grain, to the Severn ports, Barnstaple and Bristol, to the ports of North Wales, Barmouth and Caernarfon, for North Wales was a land not well suited for the growing of grain, and to Wexford. According to Barbara George (*Pembrokeshire Sea-trading before 1900*) corn was the most important export of the county after 1600.

From the beginning of the seventeenth to the beginning of the nineteenth century there is hardly a record of any maritime activity in Porth Glais, and only incidental references to men like Thomas Williams of Treleddin. In 1722 the Cathedral was again involved – Precentor John Davies (of the same family as Richard Davies the bishop) repaired the pier wall 'in order to bring the ancient town back again into some repute'. Fenton visited Porth Glais in 1811, as did Treble in 1818, and both saw boats but no great sign of trade. But in 1833 Samuel Lewis wrote in his *Topographical Dictionary of Wales* that

> of late years the quay has been extended, and the harbour considerably improved.
>
> To this small port belong 7 vessels, averaging about 25 tons burden, which are principally employed during winter in conveying grain (chiefly barley) and butter to Bristol and other ports on the Severn, and during the summer in bringing limestone, coal and culm from the shores of Milford Haven. In the year 1830, 3000 quarters of grain and 250 casks of butter were shipped from this place.

Five years after the publication of the *Topographical Dictionary* appeared the *Report of the Commissioners on Municipal Corporations in*

England and Wales (1835). It referred to Porth Glais, and paid tribute to one man, unnamed, 'who keeps the only respectable shop in the City, and at whose expense the pier is kept in repair.' Who was he?

The farm of Treginnis Ucha was destroyed by fire and the farmer, Henry Williams, moved into St. David's. His son was George Williams, merchant, who had a shop in Nun Street known in the family papers as 'The Old Shop'. In the Record Office in Haverfordwest is a bill-head on which he advertises himself as 'Linen and Woollen Draper, Silk Mercer, Hosier and Haberdasher. Tallow Chandler. Funerals Completely Furnished'. That bill, a signed receipted invoice of goods bought by Mrs. Martins of Trefelly, shows that he also sold ironmongery and bought butter and cheese. The goods entered are black gloves and ribbons, silk handkerchiefs, and materials in black and white, things that belonged to the occasion of a funeral in the old Welsh tradition, and the final settlement was an adjustment between the cost of materials sold and the price of butter and cheese bought from Trefelly, in effect a barter of goods. This, as far as can be proved, was the shop mentioned in the Boundary Commission Report, and George Williams was the man who kept the pier in good repair.

George Williams, in partnership, owned two boats. *Favourite Nancy*, a seventeen tonner built in Milford in 1817, he held in partnership (16/64 shares) with George Perkins, farmer (16/64), John Rees mariner (16/64), William Davies farmer (8/64) and John Williams farmer (8/64). *Kitty* (there seems to have been at least one other boat of that name sailing from Porth Glais in these years) he shared equally with George Perkins. The old Methodist historians of St. David's tell us that George Williams prospered immensely, and that he sent one of these boats, with his brother John on board, to Liverpool to collect building materials for the first of the Goat Street Tabernacles. There was every reason, obviously, why George Williams should attend to the pier in Porth Glais. He had a sister, Phebe, who was mother of John Phillips, the Parish Clerk, and three brothers, William Williams of Penlan, John Williams of Clegyr, and Thomas Williams, husband of Martha Williams, who, according to the Tithe Commutation Returns, owned a malt house and a coach house in High Street. According to Francis Green, Thomas Williams was described as a cabinet maker, but in 1828 he appeared as owner of the Commercial Hotel in High Street, the site on which Bonvilston now stands.

There is nothing in the records to prove that Thomas Williams was responsible for any greatness in the commercial life of St. David's in the nineteenth century. His brother, George, was as important as the Boundary Commission Report indicated he was:

he kept the harbour in repair, and he developed in the Nun Street shop a versatile and substantial trade as buyer and seller. Both, however, had sons who comprehensively developed the commercial potential of the place and the time.

Of George Williams's children, Ebenezer was a druggist in St. David's, George (better known as George Williams Llysyfran) became the second minister of Tabernacle, following William Morris. The third, born in 1819, was Samuel Williams. It was Samuel Williams who went to school on the family boat. He started in the Chapter Grammar School and then went to Prospect Place Academy in Bristol, a commercial school which flourished from 1800 to 1847, patronised by comfortable middle class Bristolians and providing education for men of business, with Latin, Greek, French, Italian, Music and Drawing thrown in to leaven the culture of commerce. It was run by an eccentric character by the name of George Pocock, a tent preacher or field Methodist who was a notable teacher and a precocious inventor of such things as 'a royal patent self-acting ferule', a beating machine for recalcitrant boys. Samuel Williams was a general merchant in St. David's from 1838 to 1856, and a ship broker in Cardiff in 1856–1857; and lived in Fagwr Gaiad (Rock House, now known as Y Fagwr) in the 1840s. His papers and letter books (in the National Library of Wales in Aberystwyth) cover a vast amount of correspondence, and a vast amount of local history between the lines: contacts with ports in every part of England and Wales (and with Methodist ministers everywhere), and orders for timber and other building materials, coffee, lobster pots, garden and farm seeds, and innumerable letters to captains and owners of boats, some local, often with requests for information on sailings. One letter, to Swansea, asked Captain Thomas Davies to check on a lad on the schooner *Andromeda*, at the request of an anxious mother in St. David's. His notebooks – a sentence or two on law and order, on the problem of drink, references to chapel rebuilding and to a considerable rebuilding of houses in the 1870s, notes on property deals and rents, and pages of notes on the electoral lists, and notes on wrecks that he could remember (he was sub-agent for Lloyds) – add enormously to our knowledge of the City in those years of its greatest growth. His notes on the 'railway project' are valuable; and most valuable of all his comments on the 1870 Education Act in answer to which he wrote a report which formed the basis of the organisation of elementary education in the City.

Samuel Williams's first cousin was William Williams, son of Thomas and Martha Williams of the Commercial. He became farmer, property owner, shipowner, hotelier, agent for agricultural stuffs, agent for Lloyds, member of the School Board, chairman of committees, and precentor of Tabernacle. The second half of the century belonged to him. In retrospect he appears to have been active in three major fields: in farming, the continuing basic industry; in maritime trade, which grew into particular significance in his time – continuing on a larger scale the old combination of farmer and merchant; and in tourism, which was then beginning to expand towards the proportions of today. In 1869 William Williams advertised that he was moving from the Commercial to more convenient premises in Grove House, and from then on he cultivated with great skill the holiday appetite of shooting gentry and nobility, of new tourists whose interest lay in the Cathedral and the antiquities of the place, and of the commercial gentlemen brought in by new waves of commercial enterprise. He farmed Ramsey, and operated four boats named after his daughters. He rented the lime kilns in Porth Glais, he was postmaster, he owned stables and ran three coach services to Haverfordwest. He brought coal and culm in to Porth Glais: one of his boats, *Le Courier*, was making for home with a load of culm from Little Haven in October 1879 when she missed her stays and drifted on to the rocks at the entrance to Porth Glais, a total wreck. He advertised enormous areas of shooting rights: there were plover and pheasant and snipe around the 'Grove'; and Ramsey was a favourite resting place for migrant birds.

In May, 1900, six months after William Williams's death, Ramsey was advertised 'To Let', and that began a long history of changing fortunes. Agriculture and tourism had to wait for the end of World Wars and depressions to see the revival that led to the prosperity of today. Other members of the Williams families continued to participate in trade. There were men of the sea amongst the Inkerman Williamses. Watts Williams became the most distinguished coxswain in the history of the Lifeboat. Adrian (Owen) Williams carried on, in local government and in the Old Cross, but his coal business, with George Nicholas as his right hand man, was based on Solva.

Solva's busiest years were those of the early nineteenth century. After the early 1840s it began to decline; the last Bristol boat, which had been in service for at least forty years, did not survive the beginning of the First World War. It is to the credit of the men of St. David's that they managed to maintain the local trade for another two decades after the First World War: there were others – Perkins, Greenish, Rees – besides the Williamses who owned boats and carried on trading. Bristol Presentments of 1827 to 1859 record that *Kitty* (Richards) and *The Brothers* (Davis) traded in and out of Porth Glais. They also record that the corn trade had moved to Solva and

Abercastell with their better anchorage and larger boats: William Morgan of Abercastell built and owned boats of one hundred tons and more, and the heavy corn exports to the Welsh Back in Bristol were carried in these. *Eliza* (J. James), *True Bess* (D. Williams), *Rechabite* (James) and *Alligator* (J. Reynolds) are also mentioned. The only pre-1850 newspaper, the *Carmarthen Journal*, printed its weekly shipping lists, but the only boats that came to Porth Glais, it vouched, were small boats carrying coal. Entries for St. David's are few and far between: *Jane* of Solva, cleared Pembroke, carrying coal; *Maria*, owned by Perkins of St. David's, on ballast, entered Pembroke Dock; and *Nancy*, cleared Pembroke for St. David's with a load of coal. The ten St. David's boats listed on the Milford Register (1828 to 1836) tell their own tale – they are small boats, because Porth Glais harbour was limited in size, had a difficult entrance, and lacked facilities. Invariably these boats were owned in partnership by farmer, mariner and master mariner. And trade was agricultural and local. This is also true of the boats whose names and captains are still alive in the public memory: *Agnes* (Captain Mitchell); *Annie* (Jenkins); *A.T.* (the Willie Morris family boat); *Azure* (Beer); *Bessie Clark* (Tucker); *Cornish Lass; Dasher; Democrat* (Walsh); *Dolphin* (Jewel); *Edith; Elizabeth; Favourite Nancy* (John Rees); *Kitty* (Henry Grinnis); *Mary* (George James); *Mary Jane Lewis* (Phillips); *Nimrod* (Oakley); *Portland* (Bruford); *Resolute* (George Beer); and *Water Lily* (Tom Mortimer and Bill Jenkins). These Porth Glais boats depended on sails, or, to be more precise, they carried sails. The winds were their friend, and their enemy. A few found themselves eventually fitted with engines – *Democrat* was one. But what happened to them all? The ketch *Dasher* was broken up in Porth Glais. The *Bessie Clark* became a hulk in a barrage balloon system in Falmouth in 1940. *Agnes* was abandoned in the West Indies in the 1950s. *Portland* sank in Porth Lisgi harbour in November 1928. *Mary Jane Lewis* and *Water Lily* became engaged in the Angle sand trade after 1945, working for a construction firm based on Haverfordwest. One of them (some say it was *Mary Jane Lewis*) was metamorphosed into a luxury cruiser.

Ultimately the coming of the railway and, in the 1920s, the development of road transport, spelt the end of coastal trade and the small boats. The threat had been there for some time, particularly for the small boat. *The Dewisland and Kemes Guardian* of 28 June 1869, carried an advertisement giving notice that the directors of the Aberaeron Steam Navigation Company had

> placed their fast-sailing screw steamer, Prince Cadwgan, upon the trade between Solva and Bristol. The steamer will be taking in goods at Bristol weekly for Solva, St. David's, Mathry, Castle Morris, Trevine and Llandeloy and places adjacent. For further particulars apply to Mr. John Williams, Merchant, etc., Solva.

Later the Aberaeron Company introduced *Norseman* and *Bristol* to the Solva route. In February of 1889 the United Welsh Slate Company Limited bought the quarries and the harbour at Porthgain, and in March following they bought the Trinity Quay in Solva; their steamers then replaced those of the Aberaeron Company. Then in July 1899 the branch line of the railway to Goodwick was opened. With the subsequent opening of the very important station yard in Mathry Road the old coastal trade virtually came to an end.

The only survivor as far as Porth Glais was concerned was the small boat coal trade. In 1891 W. M. Mortimer opened a coal business in Goat Street. At the beginning of the new century came the coal business of Willie Morris and his father in Porth Glais Yard and in New Street. And later William Morgan of the Farmers opened a coal business at the top of Deanery Hill, behind the old grain store. The small boats continued to supply them, and the Gasworks; the last to come in is said to have been the *Agnes*. But coal that came in by boat had to be unloaded: the captain of the boat hired one man, the coal yard another, and the time came when not even a high rate of unemployment would drive them to do this backbreaking work. The unloaded coal still had to be brought to the coal yard and again loaded and distributed. And weighed. Once operated as a limited company, the weighbridge outside Hafod was used by the farmers, who loaded their own coal, checked their loads, and handed in their load tickets monthly. The minutes of the Parish Council tell the brief story of this weighbridge. In January 1897 the Parish Council was told by Canon Lewis that at the next meeting he would be moving a resolution for the erection of a weighbridge 'for the parish'. In April 1944 the Clerk told the Council that he had forgotten to advertise that the weighbridge was for sale. The question was deferred. At an ordinary meeting in February 1945 the bricks of the building were offered to whoever would demolish it, for ten shillings.

Long before this coastal trade came to an end, the cottage pub, which some say was called the Mariner's Arms, and the last cottage in Porth Glais had come to ruin. It was 1967 when the Gasworks and its dwelling house were demolished. The place was derelict. But the fishermen, part-timers all, and their boats were still there, and it was pressure from them and from the growing tourist trade that eventually got something done. Cei Coch was rebuilt by voluntary labour. Now the harbour wall has been rebuilt by the same good spirit. It was generally intact in the early years of this century, in spite of cracks. But wind and weather got hold of it, and a photograph by W. Morris Mendus, reproduced in *Country Life* in

April 1939, showed a jagged and battered ruin of a wall. Now it is strong again, 115 feet long and 15 feet wide at its base, but not as high as it once was. And the boats are still there, fishing for lobster, and for the mackerel that still bite in the bay in April. The Penzance fishermen, old visitors, are said to be coming back. And the herrings, once a common catch in St. Bride's Bay. Old-time tales say that the vicars choral in their greed tried to impose tithes on the mackerel fishermen, and the mackerel went away in protest. Thornhill Timmins tells another tale, of the fishermen's chapel near the shore of the little haven of St. Bride's that fell into ruin when put to degenerate use as a salt-house.

Lettice Peters, heroine of *The Captain's Wife*, tells us that there was a time when the sea involved every family in St. David's. The story of Porth Glais is only one aspect of a great participation. Men have always owned boats here; it is said that some of the old farmers farmed on the basis of one horse and cart and two boats. John Lewis, Treasurer of the Cathedral (1539) willed 'both my botes with seyne' to his brother William. Thomas Martin of 'Goorydbach' (1694) gave a fourth share of his boat, kept at Porth Stinan, to his grandchild Thomas John. Thomas Williams of Cwm-wdig (1709) owned one third of a boat called *the Catherine sloope*. William Davies of Barry Island (1800), gave to 'John Harries, Philip Nash and John Evans my sloop called *The Royal Oak*, and my share of the sloop called *The Young Eagle* and one eighth of a sloop I lately purchased from Thomas Harries of Fishguard, merchant.' And Thomas Meyler of Tremynydd, gent, in his will of January 1807 gave 'to my brother William Meyler and my sister Lettice Thomas my share of the sloope called *The Hope of Milford*.' This Thomas Meyler sold Tremynydd, went to live in Solva, and bought a trading vessel which, according to some information in the Francis Green manuscripts, he sold about 1840.

There were hundreds of mariners, master mariners, and captains and so-called captains in the St. David's of the nineteenth and early twentieth century. John Roberts of Epworth spent his early childhood in Maendewi, was apprenticed to the sea as a boy, started with sail, went over to steam, and ended up, a true Cape Horner, with his first love, sail. Thomas Williams of Gwrhyd Bach was the last of the Cape Horners from the parish, another of the splendid few who were master mariners in both sail and steam. He was born in 1884, went to sea from Trellwyd (or Treliwyd) as a boy of fourteen (off to Barry and lost his little luggage on the way), and retired as a captain in 1929, and spent the rest of his life farming and as twelve times chairman of the Parish Council. The lists of names of these men of the sea can be found in all kinds of places, in the Rate Books, Parish

Council minutes, and the registers of the Cathedral, best of all in the marriage registers, where groom and fathers of bride and groom signed their name or made their mark. They can be found on gravestones in church and chapel, and in a strange little booklet called *Monumental Inscriptions copied from the Tombs and Monuments in and around the Cathedral Church of St. David's*, published in 1864 and in 1884 by the resourceful Martha Williams of Solva, which includes also the burials of Tretio.

The 'Liberator' episode has now been forgotten. It was a disaster, a financial wreck, but it revealed the close link with the sea of the people of St. David's. In 1892 the Liberator Building Society, part of the financial empire of Jabez Balfour, collapsed, and the population of St. David's, then fewer than two thousand, as a result faced a reputed loss of £38,000. Some two years later, when the disastrous backwash had reached and clawed at the life of this remote area, a reporter of the *Haverfordwest and Milford Haven Guardian* wrote a long article on what he had found. He had walked the streets, had knocked on cottage doors, and had asked questions, and found (it could hardly have been intentional) that most of the families he had questioned had links with the sea. Thomas Tegan, old sailor, living in a white-washed cottage in Goat Street, had lost £450. He had been at sea for forty-two years, nineteen of them in the service of Trinity House, and had helped in the building of the Bishop Lighthouse. Anne Richards of Catherine Street, whose sailor husband worked on a smack, was too poor for any loss. A woman of Lower Moor, wife of a common sailor, had lost all her savings. Captain Tudor had lost £300. He had sailed the seas for thirty-five years. And Andrew Morris of New Street had been caught by the temptation of an eight or ten per cent rate of interest. He too was a sailor.

Amongst all the records of St. David's that remain lost or undiscovered, none can be regretted more than the records of the old sea captains. St. David's could have done with an Anthony Trollope to prove the history of this cloisterless cathedral and the hidden corners of the Close and the histories of its vicars choral. A Caradog Evans could have spun his caustic art between the Farmers and some chapel of this chapel-haunted land, of furtive trips after morning worship to the little pub in Rhodiad, of bouncings in the hay of some dark farmyard, a red-hot mix of religion and life. What is wanted is a writer with the salt of the sea in his blood to track the old bearded masters of the Atlantic run, or running the Sound. Their names are on the gravestones, but that is all. They played their part in the great nineteenth century explosion of trade between Bristol and the Americas that made busy the sea lanes around St. David's Head.

Hard facts of rock, the south face of Ramsey, the Smalls, the Bitchy entrance to Ramsey Sound: if anyone were to ask the question why they built the Lifeboat Station in St. David's, these would provide the answer. There is a lifeboat station in Fishguard, and one in Angle. Between these is the lighthouse on Strumble Head, built in 1908; another on South Bishop; another on the Smalls; and on St. Anne's Head, which is now the Headquarters that St. David's once was. It is a dangerous coast, cluttered with islands, the Bishop and his Clerks, Ramsey's jagged teeth, Skomer, Skokolm and Grassholm, the Horse, Midland; vicious currents and hidden rocks: Jack Sound; and Ramsey Sound, the corridor, the most dangerous of all. This, said George Owen, is where rocks speak 'deadly doctrine' and where the 'westerlye and southwinds are found very sharp and tempestuouse.' It has always been a dangerous coast; it was worse in the Elizabethan heyday, worst of all in the boom years of nineteenth century progress along the great seaway west. St. David's then, as always, sat astride the sea routes. In the Appendix are two lists, the first of passing ships wrecked, the other local, lost boats of the coastal trade. Samuel Williams compiled the second list of 'vessels wrecked or disabled since 1835'. Here are the names of small coasters, trading with Solva and Porth Glais, and the small ports of Cardigan Bay and St. George's Channel and Severnside. Here are their cargoes listed: slates from Abereiddi; iron and other ores; food and general cargoes; grain; lime from the south of the county; timber, and pit wood for the Newgale Valley collieries; and coal and culm. Ivor Arnold entered their names in his diary. Many years earlier David Evans of Twr y Felin noted in one of his many autobiographical essays that he often saw between sixty and eighty of these little sailing ships going through the Sound on the turn of the tide.

Storms were their vicious enemies, and 1859 was bad for storms. *The Pembrokeshire Herald* tells of the devastation of October of that year, when four ships were sunk near St. David's, the *Royal Charter* lost, and eleven other ships off the coasts of Wales. The same storm destroyed the old church at Cwm yr Eglwys near Dinas, and the old pub in Newgale, standing across the road from where the 'Duke of Edinburgh' now stands. People felt consternation and anger at these disasters, and their emotions drove them to petition and to protest that something should be done to save life at sea.

The lighthouse came first. According to Douglas Hague's *Lighthouses, Their Architecture, History and Archaeology*, a Quaker called John Phillips, master of the St. George Dock, Liverpool, obtained a lease in 1775 to put a light on the Smalls, and it was Phillips who hired a musical instrument maker, Henry Whiteside, as designer. The two planned an open structure built on stanchions (originally intended to be of cast iron; rough oak posts were later chosen instead), topped by the keepers' quarters and the lantern with its fixed oil lamp. That first structure survived from 1776 to 1861. In Volume 16 of the Francis Green scrapbooks in the Library in Haverfordwest is a history of this, *The First Structure*, published by John Williams in Solva in 1851. The agents to the Establishment, according to this, were Thomas Williams of Treleddin, Henry Whiteside, John Oakley, William Henry Kemp of Solva, and Captain Clarke and Lieutenant Nott of the Royal Navy. The first communications boat was *Amity*, Captain Richard Williams of the Ship Hotel, Solva, then *Nancy* of Porth Glais (William James), *Pilgrim* (William Thomas) and *Eliza* (George Lewis). The journey across could sometimes be completed in twenty-four hours; in poor weather it took five or six days.

Meantime an Act of 1836 abolished all private lights. Trinity House took over, and it was a Trinity House engineer, James Walker, who designed the strongly built tower 142 feet high which still stands on the Smalls.

In answer to popular petition the first lifeboat, *Augusta*, was allocated to St. David's. In the same year, 1869, the Lifeboat House on Trinity Quay in Solva was built. After eighteen years the Solva lifeboat, *Charles and Margaret Egerton*, was sold, and in 1879 it was a joint Committee of the St. David's and Solva Branch of the Royal Lifeboat Institution that sat in the Grove Hotel in November to inquire into matters relating to the wreck of the brigantine *Messenger of Exeter* in Ramsey Sound on 5 October.

The *Augusta* of St. David's spent some time under tarpaulin on the green in front of what is now the Old Cross Hotel before the Secretary of the Lifeboat, a dignitary of the Cathedral, summarily banished it from the Square to Port Lisgi, where David Hicks, the first coxswain, lived. And there it stayed until the completion of the new Lifeboat Station at Porth Stinan, where there was deep water and a safe launch.

The legend of the St. David's Lifeboats – *Augusta, General Farrell, Swn-y-Môr, Joseph Soar* – has been told in *The Story of the Lifeboat*, published by Desmond Hampson and George W. Middleton in 1974, the Year of the Lifeboat. On the Honours Board in the Lifeboat Station are the names of the coxswains – David Hicks, Thomas Davies, William Narbett, John Stephens, Sidney Mortimer, Ivor Arnold, Eleazer James, W. Watts Williams, David Lewis, W. T. Morris; and the lives lost – John Stephens, Henry Rowlands, James Price, Ieuan Bateman. Two hundred lives have been saved: on occasions memorable in tragedy and success – the *Mystic Tie, Graffoe, Democrat* and *Gem, Moseley, World Concord,* and *Notre Dame de Fatima*; and all the wartime rescues. Long service and loyalty are the characteristics of lifeboat history, as well as of the City and the Ladies' Guild in supporting it. The Rowlands family of Pencnwc, the Griffiths family of Rhosson: these, fathers and sons, have contributed their century of service in which a love of the sea has joined with an awareness of the dangers of this coast.

In *Slater's Directory* of 1880 George Owen Williams was named as representative of Manby's Apparatus for Shipwrecks: G. W. Manby, the man who invented the rocket firing gun and who wrote *History and Antiquities of the Parish of St. David's*, lived at one time in Carnwchwrn. In February 1891 the crew of the Board of Trade Life Saving Apparatus were inspected and examined at their drill ground, the Clegyr Valley. Then the Coastguard authorities decided to remove the Rocket Brigade practice post from Clegyr to Dowrog Moor, because of claims of alleged trespass. In 1906 Thomas Tyser of Nun Street was in charge, and in 1923 the Coastguards took over from the Royal Navy. Since then there have been many changes. The tall houses of Royal Terrace were originally built as coastguard houses, and in the Council Chamber are three prints celebrating the visit in 1822 of Alfred, Duke of Edinburgh, who inspected them. The present-day Post Office in New Street was originally built to house the Apparatus, and the block of houses between Gospel Lane and Seion Baptist Chapel were all originally coastguard houses. Today at the north end of Nun Street is the flagpoled Coastguard Station, and alongside it two other houses built for coastguards, empty. The sea lanes have retreated from the coast; new electronic wonders have revolutionised modern communication, and a much reduced station now guards this vital coast from Porth-gain to Newgale.

Many years before the institution of lifeboat stations, Sir William Hillary had appealed that something should be done to reduce the appalling loss of life at sea. In 1824 the Royal National Institution for the Preservation of Life from Shipwreck was formed. The *History of the Shipwrecked Fishermen and Mariners* quotes the *Morning Post* of Friday, 22 February 1839, which announced that a public meeting held the previous day at the London Tavern in Bishopsgate Street proposed to form a fund for the relief of shipwrecked mariners and fishermen and their widows. A retired medical man, John Rye, of Bath, who had heard of a terrible disaster with great loss of life to a fleet of fishing boats in the Bristol Channel in 1838, was the man who planned it. Honorary agents were appointed, and in 1850, a year which saw the loss with all hands of a vessel off the coast of North Wales, the nineteenth on that coast for want of a lifeboat, the Society was incorporated under a special Act of Parliament, and nine boats were purchased. Following the Merchant Shipping Act of 1854 and a request by the Board of Trade that all lifeboats should be under the control of one society, a Special General Meeting was convened on 29 November 1854, at which it was decided to transfer all lifeboats, gear carriages, boathouses and the balance of lifeboat funds to the National Institution for the Preservation of Life from Shipwreck, which was then renamed the Royal Lifeboat Institution. It is on those lines that they have functioned ever since, the Lifeboat Institution to take charge of rescue work at sea, the Shipwrecked Mariners Society, for which two generations of the Nash family have been secretaries for over sixty years, to take charge of the rescued as soon as they are brought ashore.

How many were never saved alive no one will ever know. The names of some are in the Cathedral registers, others in Martha Williams's little book :

> 1825. Edward Humphreys, master mariner, of Aberystwyth, and his son, a mariner. With another son, and the remaining one of the crew, whose bodies were not found, perished by shipwreck on the rocks of this Parish, together with many others along this coast on the doleful morning of Friday, the 7th of October, 1825.
> 1828. John Jones, Captain of the *Susannah*, lost near Porthllysky, on his voyage from London to Bangor.
> 1829. John Williams, mariner, Aberaeron, lost his life in the sloop Three Sisters, on St. David's Head.

The rest – their names were writ in water.

In 1886 the sea was still busy and cluttered with wrecks. And the House of Lords was discussing the construction and improvement of large and small Harbours of Refuge in Great Britain and Ireland. At the same time a report appeared which for romantic colour and adventurous idealism takes the breath away. This was the report of 5 April :

> The labouring poor of Pembrokeshire want to be roused to a sense of the advantages which would accrue to them if, by the formation of Harbours of Refuge, and railways leading from them, trade were to be brought to them. Surely the landowners and well-to-do yeomen of the district ought to interest themselves in the matter. In *The Welshman*, a fortnight ago, there appeared a letter on this very subject. The writer points out the great improvement that might be affected in the small but well situated harbour of St. Davids and urges that if the channel known as Ramsey Sound which at its narrowest part is only half a mile wide and from three to six fathom deep for a considerable distance, were filled up as it might be without any great outlay, it would be a boon to the neighbourhood.

Nothing more was heard of it. Trade looked for larger boats and larger harbours, and for larger warehouses and other facilities. There is in the Porth Glais of today no remnant of a ruined warehouse nor anything else, for that matter, except the harbour wall, to remind us of the old maritime trade. The Tithe Map tells of a warehouse in Porth Lisgi, but that too has gone. The end of the coastal trade followed improvements in roads and the coming of the railway to Haverfordwest and to Fishguard.

Charles Hassall in 1794 had reported that there had been some improvement of roads 'in the previous thirty years'. A petition of 1790 envisaged a trust to take over the roads from Haverfordwest, towards St. David's, Fishguard and Cardigan. Various parishes, the original caretakers of roads, protested, and the trust became responsible for only one road, that from Haverfordwest to Fishguard. The St. David's area remained free of turnpike trusts: there must have been one in Roch Gate; and the nearest to the City was the Newgale Turnpike Gate, whose lessee was Samuel Griffiths of Poyntz Castle, High Constable at one time of Dewisland Hundred and Collector of Taxes for Brawdy. Absence of toll gates explains why there were no Rebecca Riots in the St. David's area.

Copies of the 1791 Acts which followed the petition can be seen in the Regional Library in Haverfordwest. One was for amending, widening and keeping in repair, the road from Fishguard to St. David's. Turnpikes were to be erected and tolls to be charged, but no gate was to be placed between Fishguard and St. David's till five miles of road had been repaired and £450 raised. No great progress was made, and in the Report on the Roads of the Turnpike Trusts of 1884, we find a comment by one witness – 'The road from Fishguard to St. David's, I think is given up.' The other Act, for widening, amending and repairing the roads from Haverfordwest to St. David's, contained one peculiar extension – 'to the City of St. David's, and from the said City to Caerfai.' The explanation came later in the Act, and both explanation and comment appeared in Manby's *History and Antiquities of the Parish* which had been published in 1801. 'Near this place,' said Manby, 'an attempt was made, some few years since, to form a road, for the convenience of procuring sea sand, as a manure; in which much money and labour have been wasted . . .'

Authority for the maintenance of roads remained with the parish. In the Quarter Sessions Rolls of 1826 is a draft presentment by James Propert to secure the maintenance of a road neglected by the parish – he sued the parish, complaining that from time immemorial there was an ancient king's highway leading from the City of St. David's to Haverfordwest, and that a portion of it commencing at a place called Nine Wells and ending at a place called Ffynon Degfed in the Parish of Whitchurch was 'ruinous, deep and broken, so that carts and carriages cannot pass as they were wont to do.' The road from St. David's at that time went, not through Solva, but through Whitchurch and Middle Mill, and 'Ffynon Degfed' was Ffynnon Ddegfel, named after the Saint who drank at the well and bathed his eyes there on his pilgrimage to St. David's.

When the modern road through Solva to St. David's came into being about 1840, advertisements began to appear and the stage coach came to the City. In 1869 the *Dewisland and Kemes Guardian* advertised the 'St. Davids Omnibus':

The St. Davids Omnibus leaves the Mariners Hotel, Haverfordwest, every Tuesday and Saturday afternoon at 3 o'clock p.m.

List of Fares	Inside	Outside
St. Davids to Haverfordwest	2/6	2/–
Solva to Haverfordwest	2/–	1/6
Penycwm to Haverfordwest	1/3	1/–
Victoria to Haverfordwest	1/–	1/–

N.B. passengers are allowed to take 28 lb of luggage free of charge.

On 10 September in the year 1875 the *Pembrokeshire Herald* carried an advertisement of a different kind:

David Lamb has established a contract with the Postmaster General for the conveyance to and from of mails between Haverfordwest and St. David's.

Leaving Mariners	6.30
Arrive at Grove Hotel	9.00
Leaving Grove Hotel	2.15
Arrive Haverfordwest	5.00

Permission to carry passengers. 7/6 return 5/– single.

The mail coach had long been established in England, but private stage coaches, speeding up with improvements in roads, had begun to steal revenue from the Post Office. The mail coach, however, remained steadier and safer. Mabel Thomas of Hafod, half a century after the *Herald* advertisement, recalls how as a child she came from Pointz Castle to school in Solva as a passenger in a mail cart, a long and narrow vehicle, passengers in the front, mail at the back. Charles Hassall had criticised the typical Pembrokeshire cart for being too long and narrow; width of cart and axle, he thought, were determined by the narrowness of the roads. Narrow carts suffered at the toll gates – they were assumed to be more damaging to road surfaces: narrow wheels paid 6d, carts with wider wheels paid 4d.

From the 1860s to the first decade of the twentieth century these horse-drawn buses galloped their rough rides to Haverfordwest and back, and in competition with one another. Some went to Letterston to meet trains on the new Fishguard line. They changed their times but very little in the nature of their ride. They were criticised, increasingly, and not without reason, by the tourists, who in any case had to walk the long hills of Solva and Newgale. They were scathingly criticised for their treatment of horses. Fast driving was fashionable, and as far back as 1813 Thomas Burgess, bishop, had helped to form a society to prosecute wild drivers. In the records of Mathry Sessions, June 1899, were two classic examples – William Davies of Caerdegan, charged with furiously driving a horse and trap through Letterston; and Lewis Griffiths of Priskilly Terrace, charged with furiously driving a horse along, and presumably down, Goat Street.

William Williams of the Grove at one time ran a triple service, the Omnibus, the Brake, and the Van. John Sime's Eclipse left the Cross House Hotel at 7 a.m. every Tuesday and Saturday (Menai was then a guest house called Cross Hotel) and left the Swan Hotel in Haverfordwest on the arrival of the 3.51 p.m. train. There was the City Hotel Omnibus, the Getawayo; and in 1895 W. H. Jones of Prospect advertised that a passenger conveyance would run from St. David's to Letterston on Monday and Thursday commencing 6 May. It was a busy time for Isaac Evans the saddler and the blacksmiths, for the stable men of the Grove, and the stables alongside Manor House, and Jackson's stables and those of the City Hotel. Remnants of stables, in the City, on the farms, can still be seen. But where, with all the horses that there were in the parish, did all the harnesses go?

The carriers were also busy. Besides James Lamb, hotelier of the Mariners in Haverfordwest, there was George Beynon, who took over her business from Mary Price of Solva. Pritchard, proprietor and driver of the mail cart from Haverfordwest, announced in the *Dewisland and Kemes Guardian* of January 1875 that he carried the mails 'on Thursday last for the last time.' There were others: Stephen Williams (1865); John Stephens (1866); William John (1872); Fred Butler (1901); and later still, Moriarty, father and son, of Journey's End in Nun Street, whose horse, they said, stopped automatically at every pub on the way. And there was James John, Y Wern, near Tretio, who ran his conveyance for passengers and parcels through Hendre Cross and the Old Middle Mill road to Rhydygele and on to Roch Bridge and Haverfordwest. He advertised his service in 1895 – every Saturday, leaving Boncath Cross at 6.30 a.m., Hendre 7.30 a.m., Roch Bridge 7.30 a.m., and returning from Haverfordwest after the arrival of the newspaper train. And there was, also in this century, Tom Furlong's service from Fishguard.

There may well have been many more, unsung. Their importance in their time cannot be over-estimated. They were the communicators, carriers of people, goods and news. Their successors were the single-handed bus drivers of forty or fewer years ago, when the motor bus began to open up the rural areas and the bus-driver-conductor collected newspapers and prescriptions and odd messages as part of his daily work. When the buses came, when roads improved, the romance of covered wagon and galloping horses was soon to join with the romance of master mariner, peak-capped in his little boat, and disappear into a less hurried past.

It was the family of the Phillipses of the Swan in Upper Solva that began a motor bus service in 1915–1916 between St. David's and Haverfordwest. Two years later the Great Western Railway began a service of, it is said, three trips daily. The later Western Welsh depot was in New Street, at first an old zinc-roofed hut between the City Hotel and the Mount, then a new building that now houses the St. David's Assemblies. Each in its time was a landmark, ultimately, counting drivers, conductors, mechanics and cleaners, employing upwards of forty people, a significant element in the economy of a small place permanently lacking in variety of job opportunities.

The last episode in this story of trade and transport is that of the railway that never came. It is a tale of seeming effort fighting against delay, of lack of money and changes of plans and, in the end, lack of support. The project failed after sixty years of talk and conflict. The railway first came to Haverfordwest in 1854, to Neyland in 1856, to Milford in 1863, and to Pembroke in 1864. Towards the end of the century it approached Fishguard, but the original line was inadequate and badly built and it was not until 1906 that a reliable link was established. Originally any plan to bring the railway to St. David's depended on the success of this Fishguard line.

A report reprinted in *Y Cymro* (*The Welshman*) in the County Library in Haverfordwest states that in 1870 a public meeting was held in Mathry, under the chairmanship of Canon Reed, whose purpose was to promote the formation of a railway from St. David's to Heathfield (near Mathry Road) to join the projected railway from Haverfordwest to Fishguard. In his opening address Canon Reed emphasised the potential advantages, to agricultural, mineral and passenger traffic; he mentioned the coalfields of Nolton, Southwood and Roch Castle, the slate quarries of Abereiddi and Porth-gain, and the lime trade. Frank Green gave his legal advice and stressed the enormous advantage of a line that would meet no geographical difficulties, called for no bridges to be built, and a prospect that had at that early stage drawn the support of seven strong sponsors. Two years later, in November 1872, a letter in the *Dewisland and Kemes Guardian* represented an obvious attempt to allay doubts and to maintain hopes: it was signed by George Harries of Rickeston, Ebenezer Morris of Tremynydd, William Davies, and W. V. James of Haverfordwest, and Frank Green of Carmarthen. Another letter in 1873 confirmed that plans had been lodged with the Board of Trade, agreements with landowners, with the exception of a few, executed, and the Government inspector was ready to come down. In June 1875 the promotors of the Clarbeston and Fishguard Railway indicated that they were determined to withdraw their Bill from Parliament.

The local papers of 1877 announced a change of plan: St. David's was a booming resort, plans were in hand to build an hotel and aquarium at Whitesands Bay and to expand the Bay as a resort. For seven successive issues there were articles and leaders in support of a new railway that was now to be called the Clarbeston Road and Whitesands Railway. The *County Guardian* of December 1878 reported that Sir Hugh Owen had presided at a meeting in Fishguard to consider a proposal that the railway be extended from Rosebush to Goodwick, travelling through Puncheston, Little Newcastle, Jordanston and Manorowen. The length of this line was to be fourteen miles and the estimated cost £89,000. William Davies (Member of Parliament) of Haverfordwest promised £250 when the line reached Letterston, another £250 when it reached Fishguard, and a further £500 if it were extended to St. David's.

In November 1879 prospects were said to be bright, but the proposed route had been changed – Boulton Hill to St. David's via Foul Bridge, Belmont, Broad Haven, Nolton Cross, Llandeloy, Hendre, St. David's. In July of 1880 a leader in the press said that 'The promotors were prepared to commence work as soon as they find that the public will take reasonable practical interest in the project, and therefore the sooner a certain number of promises are made the sooner will operations be commenced.' In August 1880 contracts for shares in the railway were ready for signature. In 1898 an extraordinary meeting of the Parish Council considered a communication from the solicitors of the projected plan asking the Council's consent to pass it over Council land. Dowrog was mentioned, and there were objections. Meetings were held in St. David's, Llanrhian, Mathry and Letterston, and the *Guardian* of August 1899 categorically stated that

> It has now been definitely decided to proceed immediately with the St. David's Railway, the Fishguard Water and Gas Works and the St. David's Water and Gas Works. 'You may rely on this if only landowners will give their support, and not see, immediately to make a fortune out of what is now useless land . . . there is a good time coming for the St. David's end of Pembrokeshire.'

It never came. *The Pembroke County Guardian* of 25 April 1930 headlined the news 'Death of the light railway proposal'. Farmers who saw some possible benefit for agriculture were still collecting towards the funds late in the 1920s. The last hope they clung to was that a branch line might come to Croesgoch.

There survives a plan for the complete Heathfield project, sectioned in miles, showing stations at Mathry and Croesgoch, with a planned siding from Croesgoch to Porth-gain, a halt at Treglemais, a station at Caerfarchell, and the terminal inside St. David's, a station between Nun Street and New Street (opposite the City Hotel), with a passenger exit to Nun Street and the goods exit to New Street. The 'good time coming' never came. Neither were there any developments from a meeting held in 1898 at Carnhedryn School to consider the advisability of establishing a creamery in the neighbourhood. Much more recently there was another scheme to establish a fruit and vegetable cannery in the district. The St. David's Assemblies, with a largely female payroll, has made a substantial contribution to the wellbeing and prosperity of the place; this apart, the evidence of history suggests that St. David's is not industrially inclined.

There are still horses on the moorland below Cruglas, and a few riding ponies in the City. It is difficult to imagine the City when horses were in their prime on its streets. Farmer preachers and Methodist evangelicals rode them, as the pilgrims had done centuries earlier. When they went there was no one to succeed Isaac Evans the saddler, and no need for anyone. The stables have disappeared, although there are still at least two sets of mounting steps in City and Close. Chapels had their stables and yards. There was one at the top of Deanery Hill, where William Lewis lived and where William Morgan kept his coal yard. There the farmers from Cylch Gwaelod parked their pony and trap, on their way to evening chapel.

Donkeys also went. They were once prominent in the City's population. 'Milly fach', daughter of Mrs Bevan in P. E. F. Thomas's *Purely Local*, knew them all: 'Fanny the old thing that goes like lightning', and Fanny the Second from Goodwood in Nun Street. Sidney Gronow remembers six donkeys on the 'patchin', the green in Caerfarchell. There were donkeys in Abereiddi, and nine in Lower Mill for carrying corn in the days of William Owen. And there was a convoy of six carrying coal from Nolton Collieries to Solva.

Old shops went out of business. Tŵr y Felin stopped grinding corn, as did all the other mills, except Lower Mill. Tossell in New Street, the oldest established bakery, closed. So did Willie Moss's bakery. In 1894 J. W. Evans of City Clothing Stores was advertising men's suits for 16/11, boys' suits for 2/½, and men's suits made to measure for 20/–. He had six tailors in his workrooms. M. Downs, milliner of High Street, made bonnets and hats of leghorn straw. In that same year Miss Catherine Phillips, dressmaker of Cardegan Terrace, appeared before Mathry magistrates, charged at the instance of Mr Augustus Lewis, H.M. Inspector of Factories and Workshops, for on January 17 not having affixed to her workroom a copy of the prescribed abstract of the Factories Act. She was fined 5/– with costs. The weavers have gone. So have the jewellers – Henry Morse, John Eynon, Gwilym Evans. Their sidelines, the miscellanies that Henry Owen sold, are now to be found in the craft shops, geared to summer tourists. On the pilgrim way from Gwalia down to the Tower is a bookshop that would have gladdened the heart of Francis Kilvert, and might have stopped Daniel Defoe from coming and going as fast as he did. Perhaps he would have relished the news that at one time it was a beer store. Next door up were the stables; next door down the Tower Inn itself.

Things change. But at the centre the permanencies remain. Agriculture remains the basic industry. The Cathedral remains, and this story of trade and communications still turns around these two. It is the means of transport that have progressed.

CHAPTER SIX

The Coming of Nonconformity

In 1536 William Barlow, prior of the Austin monastery in Haverfordwest, favourite of Anne Boleyn, protege of Thomas Cromwell, Catholic turned Protestant, became bishop of St. David's. Its first Protestant bishop, he destroyed relics and abolished pilgrimages, regarded the legends of St. David's as spurious and the Patron Saint as a saint by trickery, and the place as a monument of corrupt medieval superstition and Roman allegiance. St. David's was never the same after him.

In 1548 Robert Ferrar, his successor, Protestant caught in the backlash of Catholicism, was martyred at the stake in Carmarthen.

Richard Davies was bishop from 1561 to 1581. His translation of the New Testament meant that people could have the Bible and their services in their own language. That provision of the Welsh Bible was, however, intended (by Queen Elizabeth the First, who ordered it) to enable Welsh people to obtain a better understanding of English, to fit them into the Elizabethan establishment of national discipline and order.

In 1621 William Laud, Catholic ritualist, hater of Puritanism, became bishop. His *Book of Sports*, to be read after Sunday morning service, demanded that those who came to worship in the morning should spend the rest of the day in fun and games. When William Wroth and Walter Craddock refused and walked out of their churches and were joined by those who refused to 'conform' to the Act of Uniformity in 1662, nonconformity as a religious movement was born. Laud, nevertheless, appointed Rhys (Vicar) Pritchard as Chancellor of St. David's, and encouraged the appointment of Welsh clergy and of Welsh-speaking bishops.

In 1678 a Bristol Welshman, William Thomas, became bishop, and it was he who encouraged Stephen Hughes, Welsh Protestant vicar of Meidrym (on the old pilgrim road from Holywell to St. David's) to publish Vicar Pritchard's *Cannwyll y Cymry*, the thousands of simple little Welsh verses intended to show the uneducated masses the duty of a Christian – 'to guide my blind and ignorant countrymen to serve God.'

In 1705 an old and venerable man, George Bull, a great scholar and a man full of compassion, ordained Griffith Jones, a father figure of a priest, whose Circulating Schools continued the process of preparing and educating the country people in readiness for a religious revival that was to lead them away from the Church.

Some time between 1732 and 1743 Nicholas Claggett ordained Howel Harris as deacon and refused to ordain him as priest, an event which may or may not have precipitated the Methodist Revival.

Some of those acts involving bishops of St. David's were acts springing from a hard state-imposed religion; they were politically motivated. Others produced unexpected results and effects quite opposite to what their authors had intended. Religion, as has happened in all history, got itself involved with state security and with politics.

In 1947 the Honourable Society of Cymmrodorion published *Disaffection and Dissent in Pembrokeshire* by Francis Jones, the result of his researches in the Public Record Office into this entanglement of religion and politics, of 'how political disaffection and religious dissent were closely involved in bygone days.' Here are some examples, chosen because of their involvement with the parish itself or with the fringes of the parish, and because in the end they led to the establishment of Nonconformity in St. David's. In the autumn of 1642 Haverfordwest magistrates committed a number of people taken 'at an unlawful meeting, pretence of religious worship and evil principles in great disobedience of His majesties government.' Some of these were Quakers, and they apparently were the earliest of the dissenting movements to live in the City. David Salmon in 'The Quakers of Pembrokeshire' (Volume 9 of *West Wales Historical Records*) mentions that Quaker meetings took place in the City at the end of the seventeenth century but that regular meetings were discontinued in 1732. In the Francis Green manuscripts in the Library in Haverfordwest is a transcript of the 1731 will of John Green, Quaker, of St. David's, shoemaker, who 'left the residue to my housekeeper and executrix, Elizabeth James, she being one of the people called Quakers.'

In 1663 Phillip Thomas of St. David's caused offence by being too loudly anti-royalist, and in the same year the Rev. Peregrine Phillips of Dredgman Hill in Haverfordwest refused to attend church and was charged with holding unlawful assemblies. It was from these that Congregationalism began in Haverfordwest and spread outwards until it came to Rhodiad and to Ebenezer. It moved first to Trefgarn Owen, where a chapel was built with the help of a churchman landlord, Thomas Jones of Brawdy.

Lastly, *Disaffection and Dissent* reminds us twice of the old and never-to-be-forgotten significance of the St. David's peninsula, the 'western approaches' significance which from the time of the Romans has always had to be watched. In 1696 fear of contraband around the coves and creeks and Ramsey, fear of danger from Ireland, compelled that the coastline be closely watched. The contraband was Catholics. At the time of the French invasion of Fishguard there was another fear, vividly described in D. K. Broster's novel, *Ships in the Bay*. This time it was fear that the invading force of General Tate was being helped by local dissidents. Suspicion fell on the Protestants. Treglemais, home of John Reynolds, Baptist minister, was searched, and two well known Nonconformists, Thomas John of Sumerton in Little Newcastle, farmer and Baptist minister, and Samuel Griffith of Pointz Castle, were arrested and put on trial in Haverfordwest in September of 1797. The fact that both were discharged and that there was very little evidence against either is beside the point: what was obvious was the suspicion, the fear of the unlicenced meeting, the fear of a country and government that suspected underground religious movements. They were old fears, although ever since the middle of the eighteenth century there was no longer any difficulty in getting licences for religious meetings. In June 1739 the house of George Morris in Trefin was licenced, in January 1740 the house of Evan David in Treglemais. James Griffiths of Rhodiad sent in a petition in November 1815 for the registration of Ebenezer in a field called Parcycycwyll adjoining the City of St. David's; and in December 1824 the dwelling house of John Roach called Lleithyr was registered.

Our immediate concern, however, is not the growth of dissent but its beginnings in the face of the old belief that City and Cathedral formed such a bastion of established religion that no dissenter dared venture across the boundary. On three sides of the Cathedral is the sea, once the easiest way to enter the parish. On the landward side are the churches of neighbouring parishes, Llanrhian, Llanhowel, Tregroes, St. Elvis or Llaneilw. This was the bastion, and Baptists and Independents had to break this line. That is why the chapels that were built are like arrowheads thrusting at the gaps between. In any case, the building of the chapel was the act of consolidation. The groundwork had already been laid, in *seiadau* and in preaching sessions in the farms. The farmer was a leader in nonconformity, and he was often the preacher; the converts met in his farm; the pulpit erected in his kitchen. They met in Llaethty and in Pwllcaerog long before they began to meet in the City.

Revival from Within – The Methodists

Independent and Baptist drew their inspiration from across the border, from English Puritanism; from Llanvaches in Gwent and

Olchon in the land of John Penry. From Ilston, Rhydwilym and Haverfordwest they spread still westwards. Methodism was later, and different, and Welsh and native, a revival from within to revive and cleanse the Church, a revival which led to a break that was never intended. Because it was Welsh and native, it became involved eventually through religion with all aspects of Welsh life.

The Bible in Welsh had become available. It took some effort to get hold of it, and a greater effort to learn to read it. And it was in this wider sense of what was needed for Wales that the Methodist Revival became involved with language and education as well as religion, and ultimately with politics and nationalism in one comprehensive movement. The creation of a new denomination, as R. T. Jenkins said, was the least of its achievements. Traditionally, education had been the responsibility of the Church but with time it became neglected, and even by the middle of the seventeenth century a Welsh clergyman had attacked the material and spiritual decay of the Established Church in Wales.

> Often does sorrow strike my heart in observing and reflecting upon the great deficiency and utter neglect which prevails among us Welsh clergymen in taking pains to teach our flocks conscientiously, through our not giving ourselves with full purpose of heart to reading, to exhortation, to doctrine. We are ourselves unskilful in the word of righteousness, and therefore incompetent to direct others . . .

Gerald the Welshman had said that the Welsh people hankered for religion. They also wanted education. They were getting neither. The fact that the little religious verses of Vicar Pritchard and, later, the hymns of Williams Pantycelyn became so enormously popular proved that they fell on minds and hearts starved of spiritual enlightenment, of poetry, of music, of an emotional satisfaction that was more important to the Welsh than to the English.

The great leader of Revival, Howel Harris himself, visited St. David's on several occasions between 1739 and 1752, and spoke of the things that were around in his day in Wales. He talked of drunkenness, of common whoredom, swearing and ignorance. He disliked denominational rivalries. He defended the forms and articles of his church, but he despised the vile example given in the behaviour of the less worthy priests and he criticised the behaviour and corruption of the leaders. The country was poor and overpopulated, there were paupers and beggars, there was ignorance and superstition, and the trembling fear that comes from ignorance. People yearned for something they could not find and could not put into words. William Williams, his great co-worker, said in 1773 that Wales was enveloped in the thickest darkness. Thomas Rees,

Trepuet, and David Evans said much the same thing of St. David's: the land lay in wickedness, and in listless sleep, wrapped in a mist of ignorance and darkness. The Church was asleep. Crowds gathered in houses where there was music, dancing, gaming, in thoughtless ignorance of their peril. Even if this darkness of sin was exaggerated we can not overlook the fact that the Church was neglectful in two respects – lack of preaching, lack of teaching. Griffith Jones was the pioneer in teaching the common people in Welsh, whilst it was Howel Harris who began the preaching. He was the man 'of immediate strong impulse, felt in the soul' – ''Tis the presence of the Spirit that is my all to preach.' The Church refused to ordain him except on its own terms that he promised 'not to go about.' His answer was that 'he would not be confined.' It is, however, in some ways ironic and, indeed, a warning to us that we must not overemphasise the 'darkness' of the times even as far as the clergy were concerned. Some of them were able and active men seeking the salvation of souls, for the leader himself was converted after hearing the Rev. Pryce Davies, Vicar of Talgarth, preaching on Palm Sunday, 1735.

It is always worth remembering that the leaders of the Revival were all members of the Established Church and ordained at least as curates in the Diocese of St. David's. Howel Harris was ordained by Bishop Nicholas Claggett who, however, refused to ordain him as priest a few years later because he would not keep himself to the confines of his parish. The second outstanding leader of the Movement, Daniel Rowlands, son of a clergyman, was ordained curate and thrown out after thirty years in Llangeitho; then there was William Williams, three years curate in Llanwrtyd, refused ordination as a priest because he preached outside his parish. Thomas Charles, the great organiser, was educated at Oxford, and was in effect thrown out after some years as curate in Bala. Howel Davies, the 'Apostle of Pembrokeshire', was ordained priest in 1740, came to Llys-y-Fran, and was the only one who managed to stay in, despite his determination to be a free traveller. They were all very young, and their father-figure was Griffith Jones, who remained throughout a devout churchman, advising them against the dangers of 'enthusiasm', trying to keep them within and always reluctant to condemn them outright for what they did. The early 'societies', Howel Harris's fellowship of believers, were equally careful that their meetings should not clash with those of the Church. Years afterwards, the now separated Methodists of St. David's were fond of walking down to the Cathedral, after evening service, crossing the nave from south to north, and looking around as if at a long-lost home. The Peters family in *The Captain's Wife* always attended

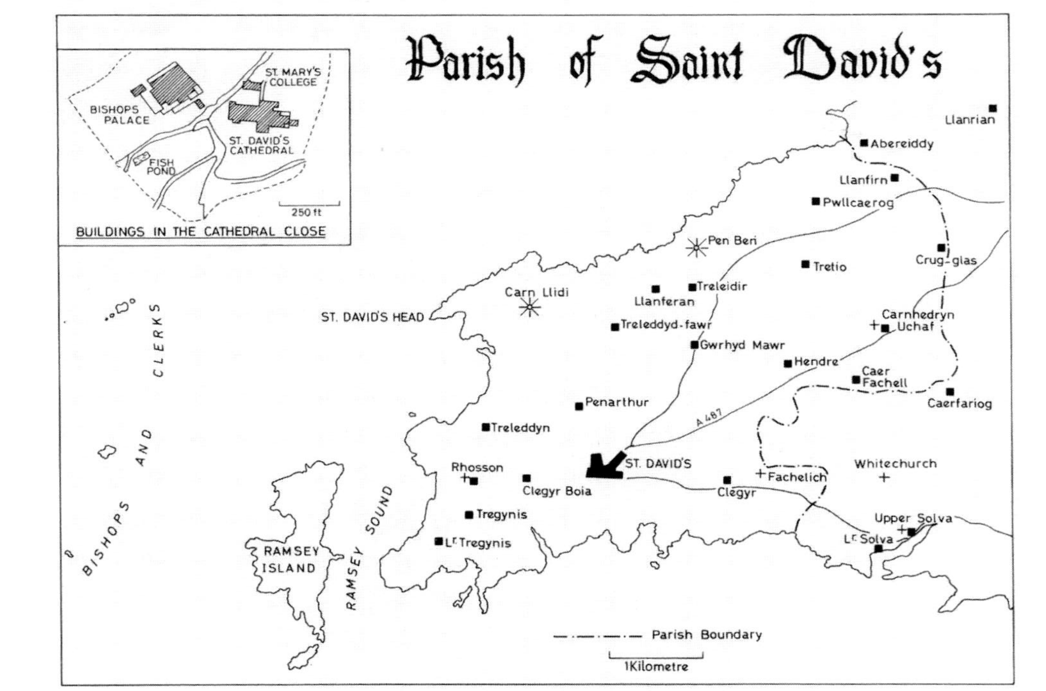

Parish of Saint David's
BISHOPS PALACE
ST. MARY'S COLLEGE
ST. DAVID'S CATHEDRAL
FISH POND
250 ft
BUILDINGS IN THE CATHEDRAL CLOSE
Llanrian
Abereiddy
Llanfirn
Pwllcaerog
Pen Beri
Tretio
Crug-glas
Treleidir
Llanferan
Carn Llidi
ST. DAVID'S HEAD
Treleddyd-fawr
Carnhedryn Uchaf
Gwrhyd Mawr
Hendre
Caer Fachell
Caerfariog
Penarthur
A 487
Treleddyn
ST. DAVID'S
Whitechurch
Rhosson
Clegyr Boia
Fachelich
Clegyr
Tregynis
Upper Solva
Lr. Solva
Lr. Tregynis
RAMSEY ISLAND
RAMSEY SOUND
BISHOPS AND CLERKS
Parish Boundary
1Kilometre

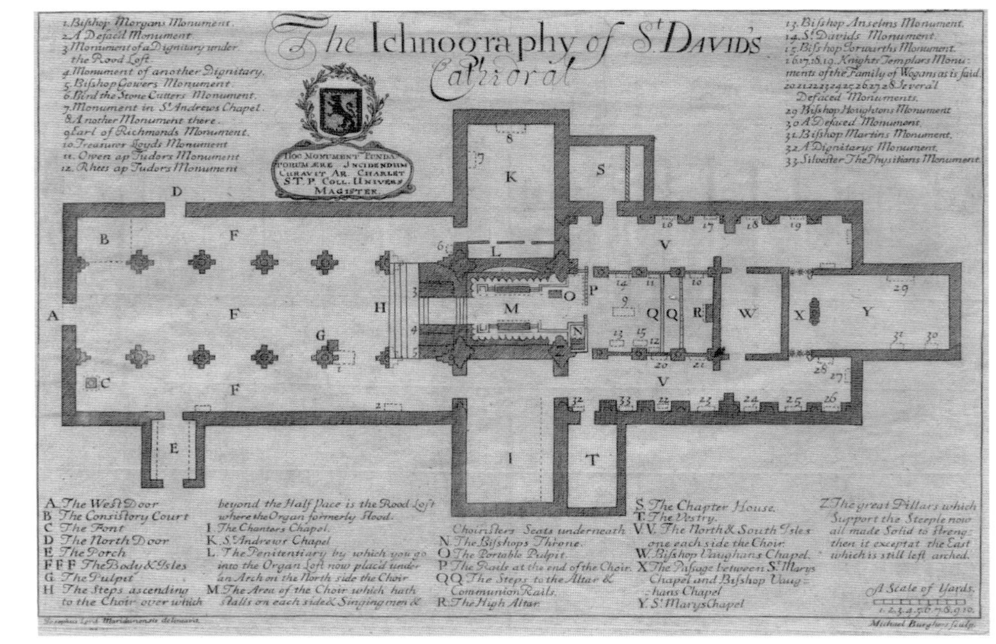

The Ichnography of St. David's Cathedral by Joseph Lord, from Archdeacon Yardley's *Menevia Sacra*, 1720

Regional Library, Haverfordwest

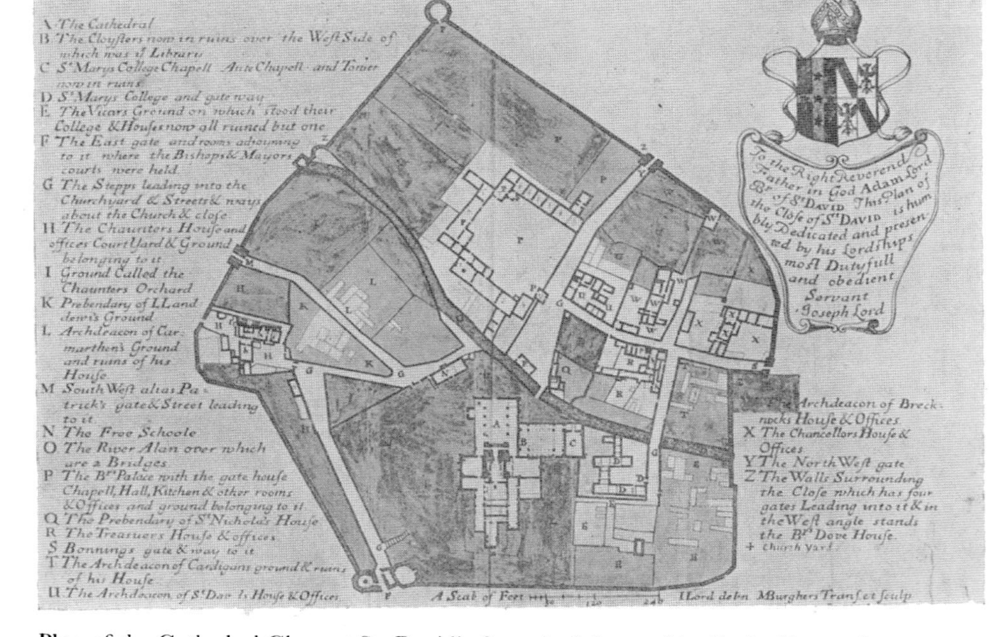

Plan of the Cathedral Close at St. David's from Archdeacon Yardley's *Menevia Sacra*, 1720
Regional Library, Haverfordwest

Manor of the City and Suburbs of Saint David's in the County of Pembroke } The Court Leet of our Sovereign Lord the King and Court Baron of the Right Reverend Father in God John Banks by Divine Permission Lord Bishop of Saint David's Lord of the said Manor holden and kept at the Dwelling House of Thomas Williams situate in the said Manor on Tuesday the twenty first day of October 1828

Before

Wm Harris

Depy Steward

List of the Jury

app Thomas Hughes	sw	app George Stephens	sw
app Thomas Rees	sw	app George Roberts	sw
app John Owen	sw	app Henry Lewis	sw
app Henry Perkins	sw	app Thomas Morgan	sw
app Josiah Griffiths	sw	app Thomas Arnold	sw
app John Roberts	sw	app Thomas Oakley	sw
app John Phillips	sw		

Who having sworn and charged upon their oath present that several residents of this Manor owing suit and service thereto have made default in appearing this day (for their names refer to the suit roll) and we amerce each defaulter as follows

	s d
Freeholders ———	2 . 6
Leaseholders ———	1 - 6
Cottagers ———	- - 6

We also present

Revd John [illegible] Freeholder 2.6
Capt Thomas Hughes Leaseholder 1.6
James Davies Leaseholder 1.6
David Richard Do 1.6
Josiah Griffith Do .6
Wm Roach Do 1.6
Thos Hughes Do
George Hughes Do 1.6

Court Leet Minutes dated Tuesday, 21 October, 1828

Above: Coetan Arthur – the druidical monument near St. David's Head. The line drawing is dated 30 April, 1867, and signed Jas. Thos. Irvine. *Below:* The slab used as a gate post at Pen Arthur Farmyard (*left*), fixed with its wrong end upwards and the slab in the base of a fence wall near Pen Arthur Farm (*right*). These drawings are also dated April 1867 and may also be the work of James Thomas Irvine

Regional Library, Haverfordwest

Old Cottage near St. David's. This line drawing shows distinct similarities with two other sketches, one in *Archaeologia Cambrensis*, 1902, and the other in the *Report of the Royal Commission on Ancient Monuments in Wales and Monmouthshire*, 1925. Both name the building as Porth Mawr, the old farmhouse above Whitesands Bay

Regional Library, Haverfordwest

Treletwr 'Church'

W. M. Mendus

St. David's Square and Cross at the turn of the century
D. G. Hampson

Porth Glais at the turn of the century
D. G. Hampson

Aerial View of the Cathedral Close

Crown Copyright M.O.D.

matins in the Cathedral on Christmas Day, since no service was held on that day in the nonconformist chapels. 'This was *their* Cathedral.' Even more revealing is the story of old women of the City, not so many years ago, walking down to the Cathedral in their clogs, taking them off at the South Door, and walking in their stockinged feet *o barch*, in reverential awe.

How did the Revival affect the 'little City' dominated and controlled for centuries by episcopal power? Howel Harris came to the parish of St. David's for the first time in July 1739 – 'towards St. Davids, and Caerfarchell, Bridaeth or Brawdy (Bready), and in the evening Wolff's Castle'. The next day he was seven miles from Hendre Gwyn, ten miles from Llanddowror, and could have had time only to look at St. David's, let alone preach there. He came again in September of the same year, to Newgale, Porthiddi and Fishguard. In 1740 he came to Trecadwgan, and 'rode hard to Penarthur, Captain Davies's.' And then on to Hendre Eynon and Tre-fin. Later he was to make acquaintance with Longhouse which with Hendre Eynon became the centre of all his subsequent visits. In Longhouse, it is said, in the time of the Thomases, there was always a double-bedded room ready aired for passing preachers – the old Welsh custom of 'the preacher's room'. In 1741 he came again to Longhouse, 'tired and bruised', and went to the Cathedral, 'came out and discoursed to near 6 (o'clock) to about 3 or 4000, in Welsh and English.' The terrors of hell and damnation came in Howel Harris's first sermon. In 1748 he was again at the Cathedral, worried at seeing 'the old Cathedral and the ruins of colleges and palaces.' In March 1752 he came to St. David's for the last time. This is the only time there is a reference to preaching on the Cross Square – he discoursed, he said, 'in the great open street.' There may be some significance in the dates of his visits. Nicholas Claggett, who had ordained him deacon and refused to ordain him priest, had threatened to take him 'up by a warrant' if he (Harris) came into St. David's. By 1741, the date of Harris's first recorded visit to the Cathedral, Claggett was no longer bishop: in 1748 and 1752 Harris seems to have been free from ecclesiastical intervention.

Of the many other exhorters who helped the Revival on its way, one of the most violent was Wil Edwards of Rhydygele, a carpenter who compared his sermonising to a cannon loaded to the muzzle. What happened when a firebrand of that nature fell on a mass of ignorant, superstitious people, living in poor homes, thoughtless of anything but existing, grabbing what little fun they could find to make existence tolerable? This is how Henry Evans tells of Wil Edward in the 'History of Caerfarchell' –

Ac y mae ar gof gan yr ysgrifenydd glywed un o hen drigolion y pentref dan sylw yn adrodd more hapus ac heddychol oedd yr hen bobl yn byw yr amser hyn. Elem i eglwys B- are foreuau y Suliau ac yn y prunhawn aem i chwarau pêl neu bitwel (football) ond daeth Wil Edward a rhyw scamps melltigedig fel ef ei hun ac ni orffwysant nes rhoddi yr hen arfer da i lawr a 'tawn i'n marw dda'th llun byth ar y wlad ar ol hynny.

[The old inhabitants of the village used to tell how happy and peaceful life was in those days. They went to church on Sunday morning and in the afternoon played football, but Wil Edward came from Rhydygele accompanied by some damned scamps like himself and they never rested until they squashed the good old custom, and, strike me dead, the country hasn't been the same ever since.]

The Methodist Revival smashed that little world where misery and thoughtlessness lived cheek by jowl. What else it smashed (and some argue that it knocked all kinds of ancient joys, some innocent, out of Welsh life) is debatable, but the old Sunday went with its coming. And with the old Sunday went the football match in the afternoon in the churchyard, City against Parish, with the clergy as referees – the sop, perhaps, to sleeping consciences in fear they should awake. Dewi Ddyfrwr was back in the City waging war on drink. Canon Richardson of the Cathedral thundered on temperance in the *sêt fawr* of the old Ebenezer. The Independent Order of Good Templars and the Temperance Drum and Fife Band were formed. In one of Samuel Williams's letter books is a delicately scripted page in coloured inks :

To the Honourable the Commons of Great Britain and Ireland in Parliament assembled . . . The humble petition of the inhabitants of the City of St. David's . . .

showing

That your Petitioners are deeply impressed with the fact that the common sale of Intoxicating Liquours is the chief cause of the Drunkenness Immorality Lunacy Crime and Pauperism of the Nation . . .

Whether or not that petition was sent we do not know. We do know that the result of the national appeal of which ostensibly it was a part was the Local Option Bill for Wales and the Sunday Closing Act of 1881.

Nonconformity began as a religion of the home. 'By reading or discoursing,' said Erasmus Saunders, 'to instruct one another in their houses.' First the cottage, then the farm, then the small chapels built by the farmers, Capel Bach, Tre-fin, built by Lloyd of

Longhouse; Blaenllyn and Newton by the Thomases of Trehale; and Berea fostered by the Roaches of Llanfirn. Then came the domination of chapel and sermon and the coming of the larger chapels. The Revival left altogether three Methodist chapels in St. David's, and it may be interesting to look at them briefly in turn. Although the early Methodists seem to have held their meetings around the steps of the Cross or at Y Llew Du (the Black Lion) where Lloyds Bank now stands, early indoor meetings were also held at the home of Sion (John) Griffith or at the house of Richard Bowen. As it grew in numbers the society moved to the loft of a building near to The Old Shop in Nun Street, a few hundred yards from the Square. Nevertheless, the oldest chapel in the parish was built by the Methodists in Caerfarchell, on the parish boundary, in 1763. Landowners protested, and many others for various reasons feared the invasion of a new way of life which was certainly not popular with all. The story goes that one formidable old female, protesting against the convoy of carts bringing materials to the site, took it upon herself to lie across the narrow lane leading to the site, waving a piece of red flannel at all and sundry. Williams of Carnachenlwyd (father of William Williams of Llandigige) tried to arbitrate. Thirteen days after foundation the meeting place was finished. It stood for sixty four years. We know what it looked like. On a blank page of the family Bible of Elizabeth, mother of Henry Evans, was drawn a plan of the layout of the original chapel; Elizabeth Evans was one of the *plant yr eglwys* catechised by Thomas Charles of Bala, *Yr Hyfforddwr*, when he visited Caerfarchell; and Henry Evans was uncle to H. W. Evans. A reproduction of that plan appeared in the ninth volume, 1924, of the *Journal of the Historical Society of the Presbyterian Church in Wales* in a little paragraph, submitted as an addition to the history of the chapel printed in the *South Wales News* in 1923 by H. W. Evans of Solva. Caerfarchell's seniority has given it a measure of conservatism, backed by a record of faithfulness and independence. Its greatest strength was its Sunday School, founded in 1800, and probably the first in the district, and visited by the founder of the Sunday Schools, Thomas Charles. The Revd Ebenezer Richard, father of Henry Richard of Tregaron, Member of Parliament, Apostle of Peace, kept school there from 1797 to 1800. Henry Evans, an ordinary farmer, taught illiterate locals to read in the Sunday School. Its first minister was John Griffiths, father-in-law to a later minister, A. H. Rogers. John Griffiths was an early visitor to the new elementary school in St. David's established after the Act of 1870.

Caerfarchell has another claim to fame. The original chapel was notoriously bad acoustically, the present building is outstandingly good. The legend is that this is so because when the foundations were laid a horse's skull was buried under each corner by William Lewis, faithful chapelgoer and seaman. Here is one example out of many spread throughout the country of an old custom originating perhaps in a foundation sacrifice, or to protect a house from evil; or as an accepted direct means of improving acoustics, under dance floors in Ireland, or under the choir stalls of churches. George Ewart Evans quotes many more in *The Pattern under the Plough*.

When we look for the origins of the second Methodist Chapel in St. David's, set up originally in 1785, we have to return to the area of the village Cross. The first Tabernacle was built in New Street near the junction with Gospel Lane. A new chapel was built in Goat Street in 1817, and the present chapel on the same site was opened for worship in 1877. On 1 May 1977, the chapel held its centenary services, on the same day and date as the Revd J. Rees Owen, nephew of Thomas Rees of Trepuet, preached the first sermon one hundred years before. The old warehouse in Nun Street belonged to William Davies of Barry Island, and it was he who donated the land and built at his own expense the chapel in Gospel Lane. Here the old pioneers met, Thomas Griffiths, Thomas Williams of Ty Gwyn, Reuben Morgan, who lived at the junction of Nun Street and Cross Square, Molly Williams, who was called Molly Moths, mother of John Williams the shoemaker, and Sally Lewis, aunt of Ebenezer Richard of Tregaron and Thomas Richard of Fishguard, the preacher who was said to be 'very powerful in his velvet cap.'

George Williams the merchant, who became a Methodist while his father remained a staunch churchman, was influential in building the second chapel. In 1825 John Elias came to preach: the old chapel was overfull, and the crowd outside stretched from 'Warble Lane' to Cross Square. In 1838 William Morris, the 'melting preacher', came to St. David's, and he is generally recognised as its first ordained minister, a man recognised as a great preacher, and at length, as his collected sermons (edited by his successor, George Williams of Llys-y-Fran) amply prove. William Morris travelled far and wide on his little grey mare, and preached at the opening services on the occasion of opening Trefecca College in 1842. George Williams of Llys-y-Fran had been in Bala since 1840 and became the first student of the College. In later years two others with close St. David's connections, Edwin Williams and J. Young Evans, became prominent members of its staff.

According to Thomas Williams of Gwrhyd Bach, historian of Rhodiad, the first Independents or Congregationalists came into the parish as the Old Celtic Saints had come, by sea. The persecution of English Puritans that followed the defeat of the Monmouth Rebellion at Sedgemoor in 1685, and the Bloody Assize of Judge Jeffreys, led to the escape of a family named Perkins to Milford, then to Porth Glais, and ultimately to the common land of Dowrog, before they finally settled in Pwllcaerog. John Perkins (1697–1763) was born in Pwllcaerog and was buried in the Cathedral Yard. He had married a Meyler (another strong Nonconformist family), and it was their son, William Perkins, who joined the church 'with an open mind and an insatiable thirst for truth.' The name of Perkins, however, was known in St. David's long before the days of the Monmouth Rebellion and the refugees knew this. The spur to action came from Haverfordwest. James Richards, a Cardiganshire man ordained minister of Trefgarn Owen, a branch of the initial 'Green Meeting' in Haverfordwest, came once a month to preach in Carnachen-lwyd Farm. There William Perkins heard him and invited him to preach at Pwllcaerog. Other neighbouring farms became centres of dissent, Trefochlyd, Caerhys and Llaethty, and not far distant was Carnachenwen, well-known in Methodist history.

To find a site for a Nonconformist chapel was another matter. And the first Congregational chapel in the parish was built on land given by William Meyler of Tremynydd. This old and historic chapel in Rhodiad, near the old settlement of Gwrhyd Bach in the Alun valley, still stands, and carries its message above the doorway, which translated reads:

> This building was erected 11 June 1781, and opened as a place of worship 19 January 1785, and called 'The King's Way'. Renovated and re-opened 17 and 18 June 1884.

It stands as a shrine and memorial to men who cherished freedom and an independent way of life.

In 1795 James Richards went to America, lost his worldly wealth because his bank went bankrupt, and died soon after and was buried in Elizabethtown. In that same year William Harries, a lay preacher carpenter of Trefgarn, was ordained minister and soon afterwards began to preach in Solva, where a chapel was built in 1798. In 1814 James Griffiths became joint minister of Rhodiad with William Harries, and it was he (having married Sarah Phillips of Llanferran) who gave the land on which the first Ebenezer in St. David's was built in 1815. Eighteen years later another Congregational chapel was built in Berea. The link between Rhodiad and Ebenezer is James Griffiths, who was born in Clungwyn, near St. Clears. When he left the Graig Chapel in Machynlleth to come to St. David's he started a ministry which was to last for forty years; the memorial to him and to his wife in the Cathedral Yard speaks of 'exemplary diligence and piety', and in *The Nonconformist Principle and the*

Congregational Idea, a pamphlet published in 1949 to celebrate the story of the South Wales Congregational Union, James Griffiths and James Meyler of Rhosycaerau are bracketed together as men who fought to the benefit of Congregational churches within both the Welsh and the English parts of the county. The original English inspiration had safely merged with the Welsh. From the same family came David Griffiths of Trellwyd, who built the Old Town Hall in St. David's, and Eiluned Lewis, the writer of *The Captain's Wife*. There is a legend that this James Griffiths kept in touch with Machynlleth during his forty years in St. David's, travelling on horseback, a journey of eighty miles, twice a month. Like his fictional counterpart, the father of Lettice in the novel, he was also a farmer.

Farmer, preacher; preacher, farmer (said the novel); often they filled both parts and the word of God was sown no less vigorously than the crops of oats and barley in the sea-girt fields. These men looked on the two aspects of their work as one in kind; they practised the metaphor of the Bible; the corn of the field, the gift of God, was something to be reaped with infinite care, and they saw the simple barn-like chapels they built with their own money as the granaries of God.

The Baptist spirit of Olchon came to Pembrokeshire in 1668 when the church at Rhydwilym was incorporated. Out of Rhydwilym grew Llangloffan and Felinganol. And from Felinganol grew the two chapels within the parish, Tretio (or Treteio) and Seion. The early Baptists were people of great determination and method, and they walked immense distances from widely scattered areas to their mother churches. And when any one area had grown sufficiently in numbers, then the mother church released some to form or incorporate a daughter church. In 1706 Rhydwilym released a cell of the faithful to enable Llangloffan to be established with a membership of two hundred and six. In 1794 Llangloffan released seventy to establish Felinganol. Solva branched from Felinganol in 1816. Then came Tretio, and in 1866 Felinganol released ninety-nine to establish Seion in St. David's. Tretio was built earlier, in 1849, by Henry Bevan. When he realised that his wife, Phebe, could no longer walk to Felinganol, he donated some of his land and built on it at his own expense the chapel that was bequeathed to the Baptist cause in 1851, long after the days when John Clun, farmworker, and William Reynolds, joint ministers of Felinganol, had conducted services in the kitchen of Henry Bevan's Tretio farmhouse. The chapel now stands closed, on the fringe of a village of many ruined cottages, a memorial to a very different age that has gone.

It is said that there were some Baptists within the parish before the middle of the eighteenth century, but the first proof of their presence in the City came in 1816, when John Reynolds and Peter Perkin bought for £25 a thatched cottage in High Street owned by a mariner called William Richards. In that thatched cottage (owned, according to the 1838 Tithe Schedule, by the Trustees of Felinganol) they began to hold services on Sunday afternoons. Seion in the City was built in 1843 and in 1864 Daniel Davies became its first minister. The first baptisms by immersion in St. David's took place in 1843, when David Jones of Felinganol baptised Thomas Preece, Ebenezer Thomas, Joseph David and Jemima David in the river Alun by Penitents Bridge.

Bethel, the Wesleyan Methodist foundation in Goat Street, is the youngest of the Methodist chapels. In the same street is Epworth House, named after the market town in Lincoln where John Wesley was born. John Wesley obviously had difficulty in Wales, and apart from the Societies he founded along the roads to Ireland in North and South Wales, and his firm family links with the anglicised Borderland in Brecon and Radnor, he was face to face in the rest of Wales with the language problem which worried him considerably. 'Oh, what a curse is this Babel of tongues', he said. Nevertheless, he came to St. David's and this in itself is proof of the existence of a strong English element in the population of the parish. The first chapel, built in the time of Lot Hughes, was completed and dedicated in 1818. George Harries of Cruglas was one of the original trustees. The chapel's most interesting document is its Register of Births, which dates from June 1843. In the list of circuit ministers is the name of Dr Thomas Jones, D. D., of Wellfield (who married Elizabeth, daughter of William Rees of Cwmwdig), one of the most distinguished in the history of Wesleyanism. And amongst the entries are the names of many old families of St. David's: Prosser of Porth Glais; George and Mary Owen of New Shop; the Morrises of the Mariner's Arms; Lile of Ty Gwyn and the Llewellyns of Ty Gwyn; Oakley; Frederick Lewis of Mitre House and Honddu Villa; Mathias of Farmers Arms; Pritchard of Epworth House; Thomas and Anne Roberts of the Farmers; Owens of Harglodd and Gwrhyd Bach; and the first trustees, George Harries; Henry Harries of Treginnis; James Hughes; Henry Roberts of Mynydd Du; William Williams of Penlan; James Sinnet of 'Hafhesp'; and Henry Stephens. Bethel now belongs to the English circuit of Haverford-west and Milford Haven, and is very far removed from the fierce controversies of the 1800s, and the wranglings of Calvinist and Armenian.

The early chapels dominated the visible evidence of the Great Revival. It was the sermons preached within them that dominated the unseen contribution of the Revival, and it was the sermons that changed the lives of ordinary folk. We have examples of students preparing for Holy Orders in the Church and after hearing a Methodist sermon joining the Methodist chapel even when their parents remained staunchly church. George Williams the merchant was on the point of going to India as a young personal secretary, but he heard a Methodist sermon and changed his mind. He went instead to Newcastle Emlyn, where for two years he was in charge of a school before coming back to St. David's to take charge of his mother's shop. The Revival produced an amazing interest in and a desire to hear sermons – the Sunday circuit of the Methodists went like this: Service in St. David's at 8 o'clock in the morning; to Caerfarchell as soon as possible for a service at 11 a.m.; Trefin between 2 p.m. and 3 p.m.; and Carnachenwen in the evening. It is even said that large numbers of the congregation, given a good preacher who could easily excite the emotions, would follow him on his route all day long.

The sermon was the centrepiece of all Sunday chapelgoing. We must not forget that the chapels in the weekdays developed into the pivot around which turned most of the community life. Margaret Richards spent every evening except Wednesday and Saturday in chapel and vestry, and from the mid-nineteenth century the local press was dominated by reports of church and chapel events. There was Bethel's watch-night service; the Girls' Friendly Society meetings; Sunday School teas and entertainments. Fachelich Sunday School held its Good Friday tea for upwards of fifty years attended by over two hundred children and adults; the League of Youth had their teas; Nursing Association meetings were organised by the chapels; there was the annual festival of the Calvinistic Methodists of Tre-fin, Treffynon, Caerfarchell, Solva and Tabernacle; Tewyn Baptist Sunday School had its tea and entertainment; there were organ recitals by W. H. Harris; and the Seion Baptist Church annual outing to Cardigan in the G.W.R. car; and Puleston Jones, the blind preacher, and M. P. Morgan preached at the anniversary services in Tabernacle. They were halcyon days in chapel and church. The Revival had affected all.

Families were often denominationally divided; father and sons went one way, mother and daughters another. If from the Square to Treginnis was mainly Methodist, from the Square to Lleithyr was mainly Congregational; and Tretio was Baptist. These boundaries were, however, happily crossed when it came to Sunday School. There was no question of denomination when children went to Sunday School to John David in Treleddid Fawr, or to Rhosycribed, to William Davies. These children had to learn and recite their verses, and the child who forgot had to meditate, feet on the *sciw*, head in the dark womb of the chimney, out of sight. This learning of verses, the 'memory deposit', was the direct result of Sunday School work, and it proved more influential, more lasting, than all the seiadau and preachings of the Revival. Thomas Charles revived the Circulating Schools in 1785 and established the Sunday Schools about 1800. One of their greatest achievements, which shocked Dean Allen's sister on her visit to St. David's, was that they attracted and taught both young and old. In his essay on 'Evangelisation of Wales', Henry Richard said that 'by this means the people almost universally, not only learn to read with an understanding mind, but acquire very considerable stores of sound Scriptural and theological knowledge, which, among other things, prepare and qualify them to be intelligent and appreciative hearers of their ministers' public teaching.' Part of Sunday School was the practice of *holi*, catechising, basically that of Church catechism but much more comprehensive: it was not only the rote learning of question and answer from *Rhodd Mam* but the intelligent grilling by ministerial catechists of a whole Sunday School, a public questioning over a whole field; and the occasion of a vast gathering of peoples that made *Holi Pwnc* of Whitsunday and Monday a great annual event.

The Revival had, indeed, achieved its first objective, which was the reformation and regeneration of the church. The outward and visible signs of that great movement, the field chapels and the Sunday School centres, are now closed: Rhosson and Fachelich have reverted to the farmers who had leased the land on which they were built. The normal Sunday audience has evaporated. And the other great consequence of the Revival, the fact that church and chapel were the seats of religious and social and communal and entertainment activities, has also disappeared. *Cwrdd pishin* and that tradition of St. David's, the singing and reciting of topical verses, have gone. One old custom survives: the 6 a.m. Christmas morning service, the *plygain*, in Tabernacle. To all of this there is no simple and comprehensive explanation. Churches have given up educational work – the early nonconformists believed that it was the duty of Sunday School and home, not the secular school, to give religious education. There have been shifts of population, a relaxation of family discipline, the disappearance of the paternalism of *mishtir*, the loss of charisma of preaching, and the neglect of such a thing as 'memory deposit': these and two World Wars have each and all helped the disappearance of the centrality of church and chapel in the community.

The greatest liability in terms of today is the largeness of the second and third generation chapels that were built, which were even in their own time too large for the normal Sunday congregation. It was Henry Harries, one of the most eminent of the ministers of Seion, who said that the greatest mistake of nonconformity was to surround its worshippers with walls.

That time of building walls was the City's busiest age. The granaries; the Old Town Hall; the Memorial and the City Hall; the 1902 County School; chapels and their branches and the field churches; the old cottages and farmhouses rebuilt, re-roofed with Abereiddi slates, and grouted; and the great Sir Gilbert Scott restoration of the Cathedral, tower, presbytery, aisles and nave, the south porch, the Chapter House roof – all at a cost of £17,000: the substance of St. David's as we know it today belongs to these decades. Behind all this activity was a new spirit of faith and enterprise, and behind that was the spirit brought into church and chapel and the whole community by the Revival.

There is no great point today, even in the most charitable of Christian ecumenical moods, in trying to assess the relative positions of contemporary church and chapel. Perhaps – to paraphrase The *Captain's Wife* in its interpretation of the mood of its time – the nonconformists knew in their bones that their faith was the same faith that had built a great Norman cathedral on the site of a far older shrine, and on the bones of a Saint whom their revivalism came to recognise as worthy of their respect; that its great tower had the air of grey simplicity of their faith; and they knew, although they now went to the nonconformist chapels of the City, that the rain-washed gravestones of their ancestors from both church and chapel still lean in the shadow of the 'blue-grey eminence' in the Valley.

Nonconformist Growth

Caerfarchell (M)	1763	1827			
Rhodiad (C)	1781				1949
Tabernacle (M)	1785	1817	1877		
Ebenezer (C)		1815	1838	1871	
Bethel (W)		1818	1837		
Berea (C)		1833	1878		
Tretio (B)		1839	1851		1902
Seion (B)		1843	1866	1897	
Rhydygele (M)		1821			
Treleddid Fawr (M)		1838			
Rhosson (M)		1866			
Treleddid Fawr (C)		1871			
Fachelich (M)		1885			

1873 Restoration of the Parish Church of Whitchurch (Tregroes).
1877 Restoration of the Cathedral completed.
1879 Corner stone of the new Church of St. James the Great in Carnhedryn laid by Dean Allen.

CHAPTER SEVEN

The Parish and its Administration Past and Present

Nowadays the Dean, the Archdeacon, the Canon in residence, and the lay vicar choral Organist live in the Cathedral Close. In 1851, according to the Census returns, it had 53 residents. That is the degree to which the Church administratively has shrunk. Economic pressure has compelled a shedding of numbers. And the voice of legislative government, of Parliament, under the combined pressures of Liberalism and nonconformity, has removed the Church from all involvement in the general administration of the parish. It has been stripped to its first task of spiritual care.

The entanglements of the Church with the old feudal tenure of land came to an end in 1920, with Disestablishment. The severance of the Church from the civil administration of the parish had already come in 1894. The dividing line was clearly marked out. All registers and papers containing entries relating to affairs of the church or its ecclesiastical charities were to go to the Church authorities. These are now in the National Library of Wales in Aberystwyth, although copies of Consistory Court records and the Registers of Births, Marriages and Deaths are kept in the Cathedral Library. 'All public books, writings and papers' otherwise should be in charge of the Parish Council and finally in charge of the County Council. In effect, some are to be found in the Parish Chest, traditionally the repository of all parish records, now in the Community Council Chamber, some in the National Library, some (or copies of some) in the Record Office or the Regional Library in Haverfordwest.

History tells of an ancient rivalry between lord of the manor and parish priest, and that the priest, backed by the power of the Church and the terrible power of religion, ultimately became more significant than the lord and his manorial courts. The priest and his parishioners meeting in the vestry of the church became the medieval vestry with its officers, and that was the traditional administrative body of the parish. How this worked out in St. David's is not clear. Here originally was a church that was a tribal church owning land given to it by the tribal chief, a church that was much older than the Norman manor. Monastery became church and Cathedral and Parish Church, the bishop's vicar presumably became parish priest, and the bishop himself was lord of the manor and autocratic ruler over many manors. The ancient Celtic four-fold division of tithes became a division of three: in the English way, the priest had his share which maintained the chancel; the parish vestry maintained the nave; and the parish vestry took care of the poor. At one time it was also responsible for the roads, and in particular the bridges, because they were essential crossing places for pilgrims.

The bishop as ecclesiastic had his consistory court, and as lord of the manor he had his courts leet and his courts baron. There is evidence that many of the manorial courts around St. David's lapsed centuries ago, but the Court Leet and Court Baron of the Manor of St. David's, and similarly of the Manor of Dewsland, summoned by the Steward, who was an officer of the bishop, carried on meeting as late as the mid-twenties of this century. Some of the minutes of these Courts, and what work they performed and what officers were elected by them, can be seen in the National Library.

Apart from the Local Government Act of 1972, when the Parish Council of St. David's became the St. David's Community Council (reminiscent of and coinciding with the old Cwmwd of Pebidiog), the legislative landmark in the history of local government was the Local Government Act of 1894 which established the Parish Council. Following the circular of the Local Government Board of November 1894 a Parish Meeting was called by the Overseers, Theophilus Jones of Carnwchwrn, Henry Williams of Trelerw, and John Thomas of Treleddid Fawr, to meet at the Old Town Hall on 4 December to accept nominations and vote for Parish Councillors. The first meeting of the new Council was held at the Old Town Hall on 31 December 1894. There were fifteen members:

William Peregrine Propert (Dr)
Thomas Bleddyn Rees, Tremynydd
Luther Bowen Rees, Mynydd Du
John Perkins, Llanfirn
James Williams, carpenter, Beehive
William Preece, Trefaeddog
William Howard Jones, Prospect Hotel
William Wilfred Williams (Dr)
David Propert Williams, Penberi
Gilbert Beavan Martin, Belle Vue
William Davies Beynon, Harglodd
John Owen, Gwrhyd Bach
George Gibby Perkins
Thomas Preece, Rhodiad
John Phillips (Revd)

The first elected chairman was David Propert Williams and the first clerk George Gibby Perkins: these and their councillors now faced what seemed to be the most ancient of tasks, the administration of the parish. It had always been a difficult task, but now there were two differences. The authority of the Church had been severed. And the heaviest of all medieval burdens on the vestry, the care of the poor, had been taken away by an earlier Act of 1834, and deposited elsewhere. The old and traditional autonomy of the parish had been broken. That first meeting of the Parish Council passed two resolutions: that the new Council should next meet on Tuesday, 29 January 1895, at the Board Schoolroom and not at the Old Town Hall; and that the keys of the Parish Chest should be taken to the Board Schoolroom forthwith. It also asked that a committee consisting of W. P. Propert, W. W. Williams and J. Owen be commissioned to make an inventory of the contents of the Chest. That inventory was duly entered into the minutes and it tallies with the present contents of the Chest except in one regrettable detail – a bound volume of Parish disbursements from 1754 to 1780, the oldest item, is now missing.

With that exception, the oldest document in the Parish Chest is an apprentice indenture of 1757, between Thomas Jenkin, son of a mason, and George Hugh of 'Trelerwr', tailor, signed and sealed by Thomas Jenkin, sealed with the mark of George Hugh (the apprentice could write, his prospective employer and teacher could not), and witnessed by William and Mary Laugharne. This indenture, formal, precise, contained everything that appeared in another (of 1880), signed by Levi Evans of Solva (later of the *Fishguard Echo*) and Henry Whiteside Williams (of the *Dewisland and Kemes Guardian*), and has the same guarantees regarding teaching, housing and feeding, and the customary list of moral and ethical obligations on the part of the apprentice, such things as avoidance of gambling, marriage and erotic entanglements, matters which had much less to do with high moral standards than with guaranteeing that the employer's time, money and property should not be wasted.

The majority of the other Parish Chest papers concern the greatest of all medieval problems, the care of the poor. This was traditionally the duty of the church, a duty made heavier when the monasteries, great distributors of alms, were closed. The population grew and ultimately there were not only people who could not work but others for whom there was no work, and those, the vagabonds, who would not work. The vestry, the body of church worshippers, and later a select body of those worshippers with their own elected officers: they became responsible for the poor and the ailing, the tramp, the widow and the bastard. Their numbers grew, and there came a time when alms and church money were totally inadequate to meet the problem. An Act of 1388 had penalised vagabonds, and all who could not be maintained by a parish were to be sent back to their birthplace. An Act of 1572 established the office of overseer, and another of 1597/8 clarified his duties and ordered that he should be appointed by the Justices of the Peace. The Elizabeth the First Act of 1601 ordered the nomination of churchwardens and a certain number of substantial householders as overseers of the poor and ordered the provision of funds from taxation on occupiers of houses and lands. An Act of 1662 established the law of settlement and withdrawal – a person belonged to a parish if he fulfilled certain requirements and a stranger could not settle in a parish unless he fulfilled those conditions. That remained the system until 1832 when the vastly increased burden of the problem compelled a commission of enquiry. The result was the abolition of the control of the parish and the amalgamation of parishes into Unions governed by Guardians elected on property qualifications, all of which ultimately to be controlled by the Poor Law Commissioners.

The system that was abolished in 1834 had depended on these churchwardens and overseers, on the money and time of men of property (there was no payment in salary, expenses were refunded, all else was voluntary), on the Parish Constable, and on the confirmatory signatures of all documents and accounts by the Justices of the Peace. It was based on the vestry and on voluntary effort; in it the parish was the prime unit, confirming Theodore of Tarsus's definition of the parish as the territorial basis of community service. The great mass of documents in the Parish Chest are accounts of these parochial efforts to help the poor and to meet growing social problems and changes. Many are documents which defend the parish against maladministration and against having to carry the burden of those poor whom it was not its duty to maintain.

In the Parish Chest is a batch of documents which are Bonds of Indemnification, dating from 1766, and orders of Affiliation and Removal from 1794 to 1825. The Indemnity Bond began with the ominous words, 'Know All Men', and was an attempt to counteract the economic problems of bastardy which deluged the whole country after 1750. Poor social conditions and bad housing brought promiscuity, and panic, and parishes were faced with the problem of maintaining vast numbers of single women and bastard children. Fathers, or putative fathers, or others were bound to repay the overseers for 'all manner of Rates, taxes, impositions, whatsoever, that shall happen by maintaining or educating or bringing up' the poor victims of social circumstance in their charge.

The same parochial economic urgency, and the same painful state of affairs in which men and women and children moved or were moved around the countryside looking for some ease and safety and were then found out by the overseers and carted like farm stock from parish to parish, formed the background to another bundle of documents, the removal orders dating from 1775. One particular document, dated 18 February 1848, illuminates the process and gives some of the background history of nineteenth-century St. David's:

> To the Overseers of the Poor of the Parish of Llanelly in the County of Brecon and to the Overseers of the Poor of the Parish of St. David's in the County of Pembroke and to each and every one of them.
>
> Whereas Complaint hath been made unto us, whose names are hereunto set and seals affixed, being Two of Her Majesty's Justices of the Peace acting in and for the said County of Brecon (one whereof being of the Quorum) by the Churchwardens and Overseers of the Poor of the said Parish of Llanelly that M. L. (the widow of J. L. deceased) and her three children by the said late husband have come to inhabit, and are now inhabiting in the said parish of Llanelly not having gained a legal Settlement there, nor having produced any Certificate acknowledging them to be settled elsewhere, and that they are now actually chargeable to the same Parish and now receiving Relief therefrom, We, the said Justices, upon due Proof thereof as well by Examination of Witnesses, to wit, of the said M. L. and of one E. L. upon Oath, as otherwise, and upon due consideration of the Premises, do adjudge the same to be true, and that the Place of the last legal Settlement of the said M. L. and her said three children is in the said Parish of St. David's . . .

The Order went on to state that within twenty-one days the Churchwardens and Overseers of Llanelly would inform the Churchwardens and Overseers of St. David's, and then in due time 'some proper person or persons' would remove and convey the said M. L. and her three children from and out of the Parish of Llanelly to the Parish of St. David's and hand them over.

What of the Examination? This order is dated 1848. The 1834 Act meanwhile had taken administration out of the hands of the parish and transferred power to the Board of Guardians of the Union. The Overseers carried on with their work in the parishes, and the Board at Crickhowell had conducted their Examination of M. L. She was twenty-nine years of age, the lawful widow of J. L., formerly of the parish of Aberystruth in the County of Monmouth miner deceased, to whom she had been married by banns about ten years before in the parish church of Llanelly. Three of the children of the marriage were alive and with her; none had gained a Settlement. Since the marriage and up to the time of her husband's death about two and a half years earlier in the parish of Aberystruth the husband had never rented a tenement of the yearly value of £10 nor served in any parochial office nor ever did any other act in his own right whereby to gain settlement. He was a native of Pembrokeshire but she had no information as to his place of settlement. The wife had removed from Aberystruth to Llanelly the day her husband was buried at Brynmawr. Her brother-in-law had then written to the authorities in the Parish of St. David's telling them of the death of her husband and asking for relief. She received relief at the rate of three shillings per week through her brother-in-law which she believed was sent to him by her father-in-law who lived in the parish of St. David's. This continued for eleven months and was then discontinued. It was the consequent poverty and inability to provide for herself and her children that had made her chargeable to the parish of Llanelly.

That was not enough. The mother-in-law of M. L. had also to be examined. She, now upwards of seventy-six years of age, lived in Aberystruth, was the wife of M. L. who lived in the parish of St. David's and to whom she had been married about fifty years before in the parish of St. David's and by whom she had had seven children. One of them was the husband of the examinant, the widow M. L. This son had been legally settled in the parish of St. David's by living and service and residence in such service with Mr Williams of Hendre Eynon Farm as a farm servant for three years. That was the last place he lived in before leaving the neighbourhood and coming down to the Blaenau Iron Works in Monmouthshire, where he met his death.

That was the statement, taken and sworn in the town of Crickhowell, date 18 February, 1848, which confirmed that the widow and three children should claim legal settlement in the parish of St. David's. That also was the statement, after its anxieties and questionings and travellings and expenses, which relieved the parish of Llanelly of the weekly expense of three shillings of maintenance money.

No firm statistical conclusions should be drawn from the total of Removal and Examination forms that have managed to remain in the Parish Chest. Most belong to the years 1830 to 1850, years of great poverty and distress when the population of the parish was at its highest point. But it is difficult to avoid the conclusion that St. David's was at times used as a social sanctuary – we remember that the Saint himself, according to Rhygyfarch, had made the place a sanctuary and 'that it should apply to every ravisher and homicide and sinner'; we remember also stories of refugees claiming sanctuary in Dowrog in days when dissent was oppressed – and that people escaping from the pressures of the Poor Law found refuge on its masses of common and waste ground. Of forty-five Removal Orders copied immaculately into the Removal and Affiliation Book by John Perkins, clerk, nine were orders to 'convey' back to St. David's people from other parishes. The remaining thirty-six were orders for the removal of people out of the parish who had no business to be there.

Examinations and removals were lengthy procedures. They involved long journeys; distress in body and mind to those questioned; parish was pitted against parish; people moved from place to place not because they wanted to, but because of economic pressures: examinations and removals inevitably meant suffering, hardship, expense. Here was a young husband who had worked on a farm in his native parish, was forced to leave for the ironworks, met his death, by accident, and through no fault of his own precipitated his family into a mess of legal complications and a chain of past-raking for the sake of a few shillings weekly. Its worst vice, this system that pitted parish against parish, was that in spite of the best intentions it created misery and unemployment. After 1834 and the amalgamation of parishes into Unions, the Overseers of St. David's collected their rates and sent them to Haverfordwest. It was a mechanical and impersonal process, and Edward Perkins of Pwllcaerog was not the only one to regret the passing of an older, clumsier but more compassionate method of dealing with the most persisting of all social problems. In 1845 the total of in-door and out-door adults and children within the parish who were given relief was over three hundred. A national comparison shows the enormous growth of the problem: the poor rates of 1785 for the whole country were rather more than two million; by 1817/19 they had crossed the ten million mark.

The Account Books show this pain and suffering measured out in doles of shillings and pence, and spoonfuls of wine for the convalescent, boots for the young, vinegar for a bad leg, coffin and burial expenses for the dead. Henry Phillips, Overseer, claimed his charity expenses and payments for the Easter Quarter of 1803: 4/- for removing M. T.; 2/- for a warrant to take G. M. to Fishguard; to David Phillips as per order ½ bushel barley, 7/-; to 'christning Mary R's child 2/6; to Sarah L. for nursing D., 3/-; to Mary P. being unwell, 1/-; and a staggering £1.11.6 to three horses and two men for two days removing M. W. to Llanstadwell Parish.

In the Parish Chest is a very heavy leather bound tome whose first page reads: An Account of the Sums laid out for the support and relief of the Poor, from the 25th day of April to the 25 July 1820. Thomas Owen, Overseer. The officers of the parish are named:

Overseers – Thomas Owen, John Perkin, Richard Lewis, Thomas Jenkins, Henry Robert, Thomas Martin, William Lewis, Thomas Nash, Abel Lloyd, William Beynon, Watkin Lewis.
Constables – John Martin, John Lewis, Thomas Oakley.
Justices of the Peace – William Richardson, William Williams, William Harries, Thomas Mortimer, George Harries, John Mortimer, Thomas Owen, George Perkin.

Twenty-three people were listed as having been assisted from the Parish, one from Caerfarchell, one from Solva, one from Kingherriot, one from Whitchurch, one from Fishguard, one from Waterston, two from Haverfordwest, two from Clegyr, one from Torbant, one from Talbenny. Weekly allowances ranged from 1/- to 4/-.

Journey to Mathry	2/-
Journey to Tremarchog to visit W. G.	3/-
Vestry Room	1/-
Medicines for a Plymouth woman	9/6
Appointing Overseers	2/2
Journey to Dockyard concerning M. D. and wife	8/-
Guarding & conveying T. T. to Haverfordwest	£1.14.6
To coffin for a corpse found under Porthclais	17/-
To bill for John Morgans surgeon	£12.10.0
To fox kilt by Saml James	1/-
To order of affiliation on Peggy R.	5/-
help to buy a blanket	3/-
towards a rug that went off with a vagrant	6/-
Two pairs clogs	5/6
Her husband off	3/6
Clothes for Joab	16/10
Shoes for Joab	8/-
Keeping Joab for a week	1/6
To bill of William W. repairing the Highway	8/6
To a boat to go on board the *Lazaret* re D. B.	2/6
Expense at Ramsey for collecting the Rate	10/-

Journeys to Mathry are mentioned time and again in the Overseers' Accounts. They paid rent for a house in Mathry, and the constant references to payments of rent to George Arnold suggest that in St. David's as well as in Mathry there was a house used for lodging, a doss-house for the homeless poor and the vagrant. There is one reference, and one only, in the Accounts to 'Parish House'.

Some of these payments seem irrelevant and odd. The most obvious, perhaps, is the shilling paid for killing a fox. Since about 1532 churchwardens had had the duty to remove certain kinds of vermin, clarified in 1566 as 'noyfull Fowles and Vermyn'.

The maintenance of roads was of major importance, a duty advocated at one time by the Church as strongly as was care for the poor. Later the burden of maintenance fell on owners and occupiers of land. The history of this considerable burden is marked by three great Acts, the first of which was the Statute of Winchester of 1285, which confirmed the medieval view that road maintenance was a duty of the manorial lord. He promptly passed on the burden to his tenants, and put the Constable in charge. The Highways Act of 1555 became the basis of developments for the next three hundred years.

The parish took over, with the landowners and occupiers of land putting in four days per year of work on their local roads, with the surveyors taking over from the constables. Even as late as 1852 the surveyors of the highways of St. David's acted on these duties, for the simple reason that there were no Turnpike Trusts affecting St. David's, which consequently remained free of toll gates. This situation was due to the fact that there was no 'through traffic' affecting St. David's as a town. 'Through traffic' across Pembrokeshire to Ireland was via Milford Haven or Fishguard and it was along such roads that profits were to accrue. In the Parish Chest is an Order for Contributions (District Highway Board, acting under the South Wales Highway Act of Queen Victoria) asking William Roach, William Martin, Wilkin Beynon and William Williams, Surveyors of the Highways in the Parish of St. David's, to pay to Mr Thomas Gibbon, District Surveyor of the Mathry District Highway Board, the sum of £107 towards the maintenance and repair of the highway. (Here and in many other ways Mathry seemed to have a greater importance than St. David's as an administrative centre: Mathry marts and fairs were larger and more important; and the Magistrates Court of much more recent times was in Mathry, not in St. David's.) The last and third Act, the General Highway Act of 1835 allowed the Parish Vestry to continue in charge, until 1894, when the powers of the parish in this as in other fields were swept away.

These systems had their problems. The four days of statutory labour became tiresome: men repaired their local roads and neglected those that were of less importance to them. Roads deteriorated. The great surging mass of medieval pilgrimages had long gone, but the new tourist pilgrimages from England reported (as did Jones and Freeman in 1856) that all the roads around St. David's were atrociously bad. Then came the suggestion that worsening roads and a growing total of paupers should be regarded in conjunction and that paupers should repair the roads at 1/- per day. There was hardly any improvement. The Boundary Commission had stoutly condemned St. David's roads; the local papers of 1891 and again in 1899 carried letters bluntly stating that 'the roads at St. David's were a perfect disgrace to any respectable community'.

The more interesting of two Roadbooks in the Parish Chest is 'The Weekly Account of the Money Expended on the Highways of the Parish', starting with the week 10–17 June 1850. Six men were paid 1/- each per day for working on the Caerfai road. Fifty loads of rubbish were carted from 'the hill' in the week ending 21 October. Many references in Parish Council meetings to the dangers that nearby quarries presented to Board School pupils suggest that 'the hill' was Quickwell. In the last week of January 1851 rubbish was carted from Porth Glais. And in May of the same year work was being done on New Street.

In the Record Office in Haverfordwest is the Highway Rate Book of 1846, arranged according to the 'Cylchs'.[1] The rate then was 3d in the £, and among those assessed were Henry Williams of 'Porthclais'; William James, Porth Glais; Dorothy Roberts of Penarthur; Thomas Rees, Emlych; William Davies, Rhosson; David Hicks, Rhosson; Henry Phillips, Pencnwc; William Walters, Trevithan; Thomas Lewis, Pencarnan; Mr Morse of Ramsey Island and St. Justinan; John Mortimer of Treginnis Farm; John Perkins, Porth Lisgi Isaf; George Perkins, of the same address; William Griffiths, Miners Arms; Martha Williams, Malt House and Coach House; John Roberts of Lower (the bishop's) Mill; and many others whose names are now blurred out of recognition. The Highway Rate Book of 1864 gives the rate as 6d in the £. The Rate Book of 1870 (in the Record Office) gives an assessment for the Relief of the Poor at the rate of 1/-, a massive inflation. Later this tax, along with others for other purposes, was compounded into a County Rate, and the cost of road maintenance became divorced from that of maintaining the poor.

Most intriguing of all strange references in the Poor Law accounts concerns the 'Vestry Room' and the rent paid for it. This is a little history on its own. Traditionally the Vestry (or a committee of the Vestry) met in the only place where at one time it could meet, the vestry of the church, and all its documents were kept in the Parish Chest, which traditionally was kept alongside the north wall of the presbytery or, fitted with padlock and keys, in the priest's house or in the home of one of the churchwardens. The records of its meetings were written out by priest or churchwarden or Parish Clerk. Where was the St. David's Parish Chest kept before the new Parish Council of 1894 ordered it to be removed to the Board Schoolroom? And where did the Vestry or the Parish Meeting assemble?

Our first clue can be found in the Receipt and Payment Book of the Overseers, where receipts and payments were summarised quarter by quarter from 25 June 1837 to 25 March 1848, and signed in each case by James Saies, Auditor of the Accounts of Haverfordwest Poor Law Union, produced at the Quarter Sessions, and

[1] The Welsh plural 'Cylchs' has been used in English in Pembrokeshire. It can be found in Jones and Freeman's monumental *History and Antiquities of St. David's*. That volume also uses 'townships' as a translation. This (like all other translations – circle, district, ward, region) is unsatisfactory in conveying the peculiar connotation of a territorial allocation of tithes which may, after all, be peculiar to this parish. Henry Evan's *Twr y Felin Guide*, written in English, uses the Welsh plural *Cylchau*.

counter-signed by two Justices of the Peace. Here also were entered the expenses of the Parish Constable: costs of postage (7d for Cardigan, 2d for Haverfordwest); payment to a messenger boy for taking out notices, and to the boatmen for taking the Rate Collector over to Ramsey; 10/6 for Mr J. Marychurch for two pairs of handcuffs; payments to Potter of Haverfordwest or to William Perkins for printing. The last three lines of expenses for the quarter ending 29 September 1839 were crossed out and an explanatory note written alongside:

> The answer from the Poor Law Committee respecting this item is not to hand. J. S.

What had been crossed out was:

> To David Bennett for the Year's Rent of a Vestry Room for the Parishioners, they not being allowed to meet in the Cathedral.

David Bennett was paid regularly up to and including 24 June 1840. Previous accounts had made no reference to Vestry rents. After 24 June 1840 rent was paid regularly to Martha Williams (receipts can be seen in the Parish Chest) of the Commercial Hotel 'for the use of a Room in Her House as a Vestry Room'. Martha Williams, incidentally, was Martha Williams, born in Emlych, the wife of Thomas Williams, the cabinet maker, who became occupant of the Commercial Hotel in 1828. Why had the Vestry departed from traditional practice? Why was it refused permission to meet in the Cathedral? The answer must lie in the growth of dissent. As more and more of the parishioners became Nonconformist, the break became inevitable.

The next link in this history of the parish meeting comes from a chain of events that led to the building of the Old Town Hall and eventually to the building of the Memorial Hall in 1922 and of the City Hall in 1924. Tucked in between the last page and the cover of the Museum Scrap Book in the Parish Chest is a copy memorandum written in pencil which states that David Griffiths, Trellwyd (the Treliwyd of the locals) promised to grant the Trustees (yet to be appointed) a lease for the term of ninety-nine years from 29 September 1866 on a plot of ground with the buildings 'now in course of erection thereon situated in New Street, St. David's, for the purpose of a Concert and Lecture Room', on condition that an annual rent of ten shillings clear of all deductions be handed to him on 29 September in every year 'and that all rates and taxes be paid by the Trustees and that such building or buildings be kept in a good state of repair'. This was dated the 27th day of July, 1866, and signed by David Griffiths.

This building, partly constructed in 1866, was planned to be a concert and lecture room, but in 1869 it was still unfinished. In the meantime David Griffiths had died, and his widow offered to advance sufficient funds to complete the project. Rent and rates were to be the responsibility of the Trustees, and parishioners were invited to become shareholders at £1 a time, and John Owen, George Owen Williams, George Owen, Dr Hicks, Watts Williams and Phillip Bowen were elected to form a building committee and to complete terms and agreements with Mrs Griffiths. This explains an advertisement which appeared at the time in the *Dewisland and Kemes Guardian* asking for tenders to furnish the place as Concert and Lecture Room.

To 1883 belongs a memorandum of an agreement made on the first day of March by virtue of an Act passed in the thirteenth and fourteenth years of Queen Victoria in order to prevent the holding of Vestry or other Meetings in Churches – 'between George Owen of St. David's in the County of Pembroke draper George Owen Williams of St. David's gentleman John Rees Owen of Pembroke Minister of the Gospel and Catherine Williams of Solva being the executors of John Owen late of St. David's and Henry Hicks of Heriot House in the Parish of Hendon Doctor of Medicine proprietors of a certain building situate in New Street in the City of St. David's known as Town Hall (the lessors) and William Perkins Lewis Davies Henry Walters and Henry Williams of St. David's the Overseers of the Poor and their successors (lessees) and with the sanction of a majority of the Vestry . . . the Lessors agree to let and the Lessees to take the buildings called the Town Hall for the purposes of the Act – for holding of any Vestry or other meetings, for the transaction of any business of or relating to the said Parish . . .'

The Vestry, sent into the wilderness by the Chapter, and having sojourned in the Commercial Hotel, now had the right to meet officially in the Old Town Hall. At its very first meeting the Parish Council decided immediately to hold its next meeting at the Board School and to get the Parish Chest moved (from the Town Hall?) to the School. The new Parish Meeting also met in the Old Town Hall for the first time, but it too moved into the Board School in 1895. In 1901 the minutes reveal that the Council discussed a motion from the Parish Meeting that the Town Hall, then for sale, be bought to be used as a Parish Hall. From 1917 onwards there were plans to build a new Town Hall, but it was 1925 before for the first time a Parish Meeting was held in a new Town (or City) Hall. The Parish Council continued to meet in the Board School meantime, then migrated to the old Reading Room in New Street and to the Library in the new City Hall before it came to roost in its present quarters. The Memorial Hall was opened in August 1922, in memory of the fourteen men from St. David's who had lost their lives in the First World War. It was also the home of a museum, the dream project of Henry Griffith Owen. In 1952 economic and other difficulties emerged and the Museum reached an unfortunate and untimely end in March of 1954. It was then that the first floor was converted into a Council Chamber.

At the opening ceremony of the Memorial Hall, performed by Sir Evan D. Jones, M.P., the man who presided over the ceremony was Alderman J. Howard Griffiths, and in his address he referred to the history of the Old Town Hall. His father had built it. It was its inadequacy, its barnlike appearance and awkward accommodation that had made Captain Samuel Roach think (as he passed it on his daily walks) that the City deserved something better, which was why he gave his donation of £1,000 towards the building of a new City (rather than Town) Hall. On the other hand, the Old Town Hall had played its part and served its time, not least as first home of the new St. David's County School. Concerts and plays and lectures were held there – and many of the older citizens of today still remember its concerts and dances with pride and joy. It became British Legion headquarters, evening classes were held there, it became a cinema for some time, before reaching its present and well re-constructed state as the Catholic Church of St. Michael.

1894 and After

In the Minute Book of the New Parish Meeting, post – 1894, stuck on the inside cover, is a document listing the privileges and duties of parish meetings, under six headings –

(a) To discuss Parish affairs
(b) To adopt the Adoptive Acts
(c) To consent to expenditure on Parish Councils
(d) To authorise expenditure of Parish Councils involving a loan
(e) To complain about defaults of R. D. C.
(f) It has the power to enter into Contracts to accept gifts.

In a heavy hand (signed H. L. D.) a seventh has been added –

A Parish Meeting is not a Local Authority.

We do not know precisely why this seventh note was added by Herbert L. Davies of Hendre Eynon. The Parish Meeting was no longer a local authority, although it continued to meet. Much had gone by the board – the control of the Church over the affairs of the parish, the very powerful administrative authority of the Justices of the Peace, and, much earlier, the full representation when all parishioners gathered together and made their decisions. Old functions had been lost, new ones gained. The parish had lost its liberty and autonomy and had been stripped of functions and demands which, strictly, it had never been capable of satisfying. New men had new power, superseding squire and Justice of the Peace, overseer and churchman. The new Parish Council for the first time included representatives of all the people, including the nonconformists. It was a difficult transition, and Parish Councils throughout the country were not particularly popular, for the men who had owned the monopoly and the experience for centuries were not likely to smile at the change. This new and untried body was to be maligned and frustrated for years to come, because it too never had the resources to carry out all its expected duties. It had, however, to test its muscle. The St. David's Parish Council immediately challenged the Church to a long duel over Dr Jones's Charity, and over the distribution of charities generally, including that of Thomas Beynon. It wanted them out of the hands of the Church, to be distributed elsewhere than in the Church, and on a non-sectarian basis. It was wary for a long time of wrongful enclosure of commons, especially Waunfawr. It strove hard to get triennial elections, ostensibly to save money. Once in its earlier years (and once in the very recent past) there were moves to get a redistribution of seats on the Council based on a new division of the parish into wards. It worked hard to get allotment fields and the Trenergy Recreation field out of the hands of the Church, deeds and all. It showed enormous concern for the public water supply; the wells of High Street and Lower Moor and Waun Gwla were under discussion for years, and they were endlessly cleaned and deepened. Strong protests were made against the washing of carriages from the public supply, as happened at Quickwell. It was very concerned with land on the Burrows – which was why it strove desperately to get the Parish Map out of the hands of the Church. Finally it got the Map and bought the Map Chest from the Cathedral to hold it. It concerned itself with bad drainage systems, with open drains, and with the horrible habit of dumping garbage indiscriminately on back streets. It accepted the parish hearse as a free gift from the Church, a Grecian gift which cost much money and more discussion later. Surprisingly, it had spells of fierce opposition to the projected light railway, and turned down plans that it should cross Dowrog Moor. It showed equally fierce opposition to the 1902/3 Education Acts, and to any possible wastage of money on education. According to these Acts, all authority over education would pass to local committees of the County Council, the distinction between Board and Voluntary Schools would disappear, and all schools would be financed from the rates. Some protested against an inevitable rise in rates; the Nonconformists protested because they saw liberties and their educational independence being threatened. The Council did not want any of this, nor new lighting for the City, nor new houses, nor a new weighbridge on Lower Moor. It criticised moves and proposals that could have been regarded as very much for the public good. Behind its refusals were old quibbles, wrangles over religion, matters of rights and freedoms for which they had fought. Neither old emotions nor old bitterness were easily forgotten.

Membership of the Council was always regarded as a matter of serious responsibility. The Reverend John Phillips once submitted an apology for non-attendance; it took much consideration and much hesitation before the Council decided that it could be accepted. This attitude got scant mercy from the local press. In September 1895 a letter, signed by 'Elector', appeared in the weekly paper:

> Sir, The St. David's Parish Council is dragging on an ignoble existence, and the electors are leading a life of disappointment. A long time ago, we elected as Parish Councillors, as we vainly thought, men of ability, of pluck, of energy, of promise, but during the whole of their official career they have done absolutely nothing. It is true there have been many meetings which were at first frequented by the public but the public have ceased to be entertained by empty twaddle.

What was this civic critic complaining about? The erosion of commonable rights; methods of allocating Dr Jones's Charity; allotments; the Council's attempts to get allotment land at prices below their reasonable value; the need for a public weighbridge; and lighting for the town; nuisances; the need for a public library and museum; the desperate need for an improvement in the appearance of the town and for the provision of cliff walks.

In January 1899 the papers reported at length on the St. David's Gas and Water Scheme. A company, said the report, comprising William Bentham Martin, Charles Edward Benney and Arthur Henry Brown was formed 'for supplying with water and gas the City of St. David's and adjacent places'. A pumping station was to be erected at Nine Wells. On 10 June 1899, the St. David's Gas and Water Bill received the Royal Assent, and six months later the papers carried two items of news. 'About 15 navvies have commenced operations on the road near Upper Clegyr Farm on the water project.' 'Gasworks – artisans and labourers required to commence at Porthclais are expected shortly.'

Two years earlier at a committee meeting, Dodd Griffiths and W. D. Williams had been asked to inquire regarding the probable cost of providing St. David's with lighting by electricity. The Parish Council of 1934, forty years later, was still negotiating with Captain Beer to get the streets adequately lighted by electricity. They were still negotiating in 1945. Captain Beer, in fact, was the man who on his own initiative provided the City with electricity from 1926 to 1952, when the South Wales Electricity Board took over. It was in 1952–53 also that the Wales Gas Board promised to put right the poor quality of gas supply: a new booster was installed in Porth Glais, an operation which damaged the harbour wall in the process, damage that took another twenty years before being put right.

The most noticeable changes that the City has seen are little more than fifty years old. In the aggregate they are what has affected most places in recent years, the change that was aimed at lifting places, villages as well as towns and cities, seemingly by the bootstraps out of past heritages of poverty, bad building, lack of amenities, to bring them into line with what is desirable in the sophistication of our present and affluent society. No more than three or four decades ago High Street and the Pebbles and Goat Street had their open gutters, bridged at intervals by slabs of stone. The neat and attractive appearance of the City of today – typified best, perhaps, in the pleasantness of the City Green and Memorial Garden – is very recent. The Parish Meeting had put pressure on the Council for years: even in 1934 the Green was in a deplorable state, a dogs' playground. The wall of sea-washed Caerbwdi stone, the ecclesiastical massiveness of the four entrances, these were put up in the early 1950s, and much of the work was done by a County Office clerk of works, Bryn Rees, and by one of the most respected of St. David's characters, Morris Mendus.

The first Parish Meeting following the Local Government Board circular of November 1894 was called by the Overseers, and its first job was to arrange the election of Parish Councillors. That was its outstanding job for many years to come: to elect Parish Councillors annually by nomination and show of hands, after due heckling, and always subject to the danger that any five parishioners had the right to call a poll. Nothing much else disturbed the far from serene atmosphere of these meetings. It was a relief when elections became triennial affairs in 1952. At times the voice of the parish as expressed in these meetings was practically unheard. The 1912 meeting – it met once a year except in emergency – touched rock bottom. The Clerk was the only being present: and he made a note that there was no business done. Occasionally there were spurts of activity – the 1918 meeting adopted the Libraries Act; in 1926 moneys were voted towards doing something with the City Green (the Parish Meeting had the right to call for an extra levy of rates); this was three years after they had discussed the light railway project, when the Engineer told them that the proposed station was to be between New Street and Nun Street. And in 1941, seemingly for the first time, Captain Thomas Williams of Gwrhyd Bach began the admirable practice of presenting the Parish Meeting with a full report of the year's work in Council.

From the early 1930s onwards all were faced with a major task – the provision of new housing. One thousand and three people had shared a total of 414 houses in 1801. In 1831 a population of 2,338 shared 503 houses. Today's population of about 1800 has much more room and a much larger choice – the building of Heol Dewi in the 1950s was a major contribution – and the chronic overcrowding of earlier years has been removed.

Again in the years after 1938 the Parish Meeting roused itself to demand a clean-up of the City. It demanded that all citizens should begin to take pride in their environment. It was equally concerned about health conditions; the typhoid epidemic had shaken public apathy. Five years earlier, in May 1933, Miss E. M. Davies had been appointed District Nurse. She retired in 1970, after thirty-seven years of public service. The history of today's compact clinic unit of Dr Middleton and Nurse Salmon and Nurse Iona Davies is very different from the beginnings. In November 1905 a meeting was held at the Old Town Hall to ask the several religious bodies to discuss an offer of £20 made anonymously towards getting a nurse for St. David's. *A pro tem.* secretary was appointed, the inevitable Frederick Lewis, who was to remain secretary until his death in 1920. On 28 November a provisional committee was appointed. The Management Committee, it was decided, was to comprise any contributor of one guinea, the doctors and the chemist, and two members from each congregation. The cost was estimated at £70 to £80 annually. The object – to provide a trained nurse to care for the sick, especially the poor, in their own homes; and to raise the standard of nursing by all means available. Emphasis was placed on getting a Welsh nurse, and a later stipulation insisted that she should be a cyclist.

The first appointed was Nurse Crowther (of the Queen Victoria Institute), provided she passed her examination in midwifery. Her first report indicated that she had recorded 1182 visits between 1 May 1906 and 31 January 1907. In September of that year she resigned to become Assistant Superintendent of Hampshire Nursing Association. In 1912 Nurse Dixon started inspecting the children of the three schools for a twelve month trial period. The Education Committee gave £5 in recompense. She was also asked to give lectures to the British Red Cross Society, on condition that the

Society paid £2. In March 1914 she resigned: there was too much work, too little money, and no relief. Then came Nurse Griffiths, Nurse Lloyd and Nurse E. M. Davies's immediate predecessor, Nurse Daniel. A much more recent development in 'civic care' can be seen in Nun Street. Doctor, nurses and Gwen Martin created the local detachment of the British Red Cross in December 1949. In 1957 its own quarters in Nun Street were opened by the Princess Royal with a presentation of colours in the Cathedral.

The Local Government Act of 1972 marked the restoration of one of the most ancient of Celtic historic names. The three counties of Pembroke, Cardigan and Carmarthen became merged into a new county of Dyfed, approximating to the ancient kingdom of that name. The Parish Council of St. David's, after a piebald and controversial history of eighty years, became the St. David's Community Council, looking after what is the equivalent of the old *cwmwd* of Pebidiog, one of the two 'cwmwds' of the ancient cantref of Dewisland in that kingdom of Dyfed. Over the last century or so, however, this most conservative of parishes had lost some of its old offices and customs, and it may not be inappropriate here to refer to some of them.

It was the duty of the Parish Constable to keep 'watch and ward' over the parish, to keep a sharp lookout for strangers, to keep violence in check, to help collect the County Rate, and, after deduction of his own expenses and relief of the poor, to take the remainder to the Chief Constable. He acted for and with the Overseers and like them had to submit to the supervision of the Justices of the Peace. It was this Parish Constable, possibly one of the oldest of parish officers, who from 1554 to 9 June 1857 controlled the City of St. David's under the supervision of the High Constable, who later became the Superintending Constable of the Hundred of Dewisland. In October 1840 Thomas Davies was High Constable. From December 1844 to June 1857 George Jones was Superintending Constable, and then joined the newly formed Pembrokeshire Police as Superintendent in charge of the Fishguard Division. Five years after the formation of the Pembrokeshire Police, in response to a complaint by John Owen of St. David's, draper, three labourers, Joseph Harnold of Hull, Joseph Shaw of Wolverhampton and Dennis Coghlan of Cork, were arrested for stealing 46 yards of shirting. All three were convicted on the evidence of H. J. Perkins, who five years earlier had retired from the office of Parish Constable.

In 1879 Samuel Williams wrote in protest to the Superintendent of Police in Haverfordwest. The City, he said, had in the last decade seen much greater expansion, and in population and trade and building, and in the number of visitors, was growing rapidly, and because of this deserved and demanded a greater amount of police supervision, not only for the comfort but also for the welfare of its inhabitants. There were noisy gangs and disturbances in the City, and growing complaints, and all because of a great increase of strangers accompanying the reconstruction of the Cathedral.

The Overseers as officers of the parish verstry date back to 1572. The Parish Records show that they worked in groups of four, corresponding to the 'Cylchs': in 1865 James Mathias, Thomas Hicks, William Roach and Thomas Rees; in 1895 James Rowlands of Cross Square for Cylch y Dre, Miss L. B. James (the only female name seen on the list) from Treleddin for Cylch Gwaelod y Wlad, Henry Evans of Caerfarchell for Cylch Bychan, and Thomas Richards of Cruglas for Cylch Mawr; in 1900 S. J. Watts Williams, W. Phillips of Cwmwdig, Samuel James of Llandridian, and David Roberts of Treginnis; in 1910 Henry Roberts, Brynawel, Richard Davies of Penberi, Thomas Lewis of Rhosson, and W. L. James of Caerfarchell. At the Annual Meeting of April 1926 a precept of £30 was made to the Overseers, and the following were appointed for the parish and their respective 'Cylchs' – John Didwith of Goat Street, William Walters of 'Clegyr Boia', Gwilym Evans of Trelerw, and Richard Davies of Penberi. That was the last batch of appointments to this ancient office, and, as far as can be proved, the last official appearance of the Cylchs. When they disappeared as part and parcel of the system of local government, St. David's lost an institution that Jones and Freeman had called 'immemorial'.

In 1835 the Boundary Commission Report demolished the legality of an office cherished by the people: it declared that there could be no official 'mayor' because there was no charter. They forgot that in the earliest extant version of the Laws of Hywel Dda are references to two officers whose duty it was to guard the king's waste land. One was called *kymellaur* (the enforcer). The other was called a *mayr*. And it is hardly likely that Walter Jones, the blacksmith of Nun Street, remembered about Hywel Dda when he became the last 'elected mayor' of St. David's. Samuel Lewis's *Topographical Dictionary* said that the 'mayor' held his office in the south-east wing of Tower Gate, and was appointed annually by the Steward of the bishop. His duty was to collect dues and rents of the Manor of the City and Suburb. Francis Jones gives further details of the history of this office in the 1967 volume of *Journal of the Historical Society of the Church in Wales*, and gives one example of the 'mayor' in action. On 26 October 1844 John T. James published a notice that the Court Baron of the Bishop was to be held at the Commercial Hotel on 5 November. Mrs Elizabeth Williams was charged with non-payment of £1, five years chief rent due to the bishop on lands called 'Davies land'. And her son, Samuel Williams, was on the same day to be distrained for 1/8d being two years chief rent due on land and premises called 'Allen's Land', all within the manor. Meanwhile the 'mayor' seized a corn screen, a Winchester measure and a striker of their property, which he impounded in the Mitre Inn.

In the National Library in Aberystwyth are parchment documents, records of the Minutes of the Manorial Courts of St. David's. Old and different manorial courts had been merged in the Court Leet of the King and Court Baron of the Bishop of the Manor of Dewisland and the Court Leet of the King and Court Baron of the Bishop of the City and Suburbs. And they met, the Court of the Manor of 1826, for instance, and the Court of the City and Suburbs of 1828, in the same place, the dwelling house of Thomas Williams, and before the same Deputy Steward. Both kept an eye on hedges and commons, fined people for letting animals stray, saw to it that pathways were kept open. In one instance, the Court of the Manor acted on a ruling that was in existence as far back as the *Black Book*. John Mortimer of Treginnis had come into possession of Treleddid Fawr and had not reported it. He was fined 5/-, which was the amount charged on tenants of the *Black Book* for alienation, that is, for transfer of land.

The Court Leet of the King and the Court Baron of the bishop, lord of the manor, appeared to be dealing with the same problem, land, transfers of land, common land, and the rights attached to these things. Originally the court baron was an assembly of the free tenants of a manor under the lord; and the court leet was the assembly of the men of a township. Into these mergings had come another court. The press notice calling for a meeting of these courts ran, 'The Courts Leet and View of Frankpledge of our Sovereign Lady the Queen, and Courts Baron of the Ecclesiastical Commissioners for England' (this was the time of Queen Victoria, and the Commissioners had taken over episcopal lands since 1835). The frankpledge was an ancient Anglo-Saxon court, a meeting of men from the ten households of a 'tithing'. They had to meet in the presence of an officer such as the sheriff and answer questions on the unity, the honesty and social health of their members. Did they know of people 'such as continually haunt taverns, and no man knoweth whence they came; or of such as sleep by day and watch by night, eat well and drink well, and possess nothing?'

The Court of the City and the Suburbs elected officers. The Court Leet of our Sovereign King and Court Baron of the Right Reverend Father in God John Banks by Divine Right Lord Bishop of St. David's lord of the said manor holden and kept at the Dwelling House of Thomas Williams situate in the said manor on Tuesday the twenty-first day of December 1828 made three such appointments – of John Harding Harries as Lord Mayor of the City of St. David's; of John Griffiths as Pond Keeper; and Thomas Oakley as Constable. It is easy to assume, knowing the elasticities of spelling of old documents, that keeper of the pond meant keeper of the pound. There were two pounds known to have been in operation in St. David's: the fold or 'ffald' below and north of Tower Gate, which went out of commission in the early nineteenth century; and the other south of Back Lane, clearly marked on the *Twr y Felin Guide Map*, and adjacent to the old Tennis Courts. Some elements of the six foot high wall of this pound were demolished as recently as the 1950s, when the lay-out of the Penygarn Council estate and of Hafan, the Old People's Home, were being prepared. It would be natural to assume that John Griffiths's office was to attend to these. On the other hand, one is reminded of Thomas Tamlyn's Enclosure Award, where there were specific references to ponds in the parish reserved for the use of grazers on the common. If they were important enough for specific mention they would have been important enough to demand maintenance and supervision.

The disappearance of another of the ancient offices of parish and church came on 30 March 1895, when John Phillips, Parish Clerk and Deputy Registrar, died. Nobody seems to know exactly what, in England or in Wales, this ancient office entailed. The Parish Clerk read the hymns in church, he took care of the vicar and the building, he was verger, he completed the registers. John Phillips spent most of his life in and around the Cathedral, he was Cathedral Guide, with Canon Richardson he knew more of the history of Cathedral and parish and their customs than anyone else. He was made assistant parish clerk to his grandfather in 1825 (Henry Phillips held the office for fifty years), and succeeded him in 1827. He held the office, therefore, for sixty-eight years, and with his death it disappeared. It is said that he spent his boyhood with Henry Williams in the Old Shop in Nun Street – his mother was the sister of George Williams the merchant – and later learnt the craft of joinery with Thomas Williams, the cabinet maker of the Commercial. His obituary in the *Dewisland and Kemes Guardian* said that his knowledge of local lore was immense, and that he knew great masses of Vicar Pritchard's *Canwyll y Cymry* off by heart.

According to Jones and Freeman, the Close in very early days contained some encroaching private houses. Vigorous efforts were made to remove these and this was achieved by the time the Close was defined and protected by the encircling Wall in the thirteenth century. Clerical independence was then gained and the Close became a *civitas*, a parish within the parish. The Boundary Commission recommended in September 1976, and informed the Community Council, that the Parish of the Cathedral Close, with an electorate of nine and traditionally with its own electoral roll, should lose its independence and be merged with the Parish of St. David's. As far back as 1883 the Haverfordwest Union had taken over St. David's and the Cathedral Close in matters of health and police. The maintenance of roads and lighting had also been transferred. When that recommendation of the Boundary Commission comes into effect, the Cathedral Church will have lost another 'relic'. And the process of secularisation, already evident in the fact that the Bishop's Palace and all the surrounding lands and buildings are now in the care of and maintained by the Department of the Environment, will have taken one further step forward.

CHAPTER EIGHT

Church and Chapel in Education

The monastic church of St. David's established its supremacy, we are told in Bevan's *Diocesan History*, partly through the saintliness of its founder, partly through the connexion between the bishop and civil power, and partly as a centre of education. Of these three, it is of St. David's as a centre of education that we know the least, and what we do know is throughout bedevilled by vagueness and a disturbing confusion of labels and dates. We are told that St. David was taught at a place called Vetus Rebus, which, according to modern scholarship, was not in St. David's. After this he went to Paulinus the scribe, who lived on a certain 'island' which has not been identified. Of the monastery of Ty Gwyn we know very little. The *Lives* of the Saints tell us that saints and scholars came to the monastery of Cell Muine to receive instruction of the fathers, but the man who centuries later wrote the first *Life* of the Saint was a member of another and more famous centre of learning, Llanbadarn Fawr. This man, Rhygyfarch, and his brothers and bishop father, Sulien, were all connected with Llanbadarn, and they all helped to transfer to St. David's enough of the greatness of Llanbadarn to make St. David's noted as a place of learning and a scriptorium for the writing of manuscripts. It is not now thought that Rhygyfarch's *Life* was written in Llanbadarn, and it is equally difficult to accept the view that the Welsh *Annals* were written in St. David's. King Alfred, looking for learned men, sent for some monks of St. David's and one of them, Asser, became his historian and confidential adviser. But there is little else to prove that St. David's was a place of academic distinction. Learning, one reads somewhere, ended in St. David's with the death of Sulien.

One of the most learned of his successor bishops, Thomas Burgess, called this early period (to the coming of the Normans) the period of austerity and venerable poverty. The next, from the Normans to the Reformation, he called the period of establishment and endowment, and it was in this period that the College of St. Mary, the most ancient of its kind in the country, was founded by

John Duke of Lancaster (John of Gaunt), with his wife Blanche, and Bishop Adam Houghton. The year was 1365. The intention was inscribed in a memorable charter. It was the duty of men that the divine service be devoutly and laudably increased in a wonderful manner. But in the church of St. David's, from ancient time metropolitan and solemn, there were only a few priests that sang well, and it was heavy expense to bring priests from England. The purpose, therefore, was to found, build, make and ordain a chapel or chantry of one master and seven priests in the form of a college, who would perform the divine services in their Chapel 'according to ye Salisbury Missale', and assist on Sundays and double festivals at High Mass and Vespers in the Cathedral among the Vicars there. They were given strict rules that they were not to go into 'St. Davids town', and never alone, they were not to frequent ale-houses and taverns, they should be daily clad in proper vestments, and they were to hold the canons of St. David's in due reverence within the church and without.

That College survived the dissolution of the monasteries, but in 1549 it was surrendered to Edward VI. Stephen Green was its last master. It had been a noble venture, noble architecturally, as the combination of the old and new in the renovated St. Mary's Hall (formerly the chapel of the College) is ample proof; noble also in its idealism, planned so that 'the Bridegroom of the Church should not be disgraced by the poverty of the servants and Ministers of the Bride'. We are told that it was built out of the personal wealth of the founders, and not by patronage of the church. And it was well equipped. 'After the foundation we ordered fair house and quarters sufficiently comfortable for the dwelling of the servants and the master and priests and of their ministers . . . we have begun to build an attached and useful cloister between the said cathedral church and the aforesaid chapel.' It is the stumpy relics of those cloister pillars that can now be seen between the Cathedral north door and the majestic steps leading to the door of the renovated hall.

In addition to this collegiate body there were the vicars choral, established by Bernard, a remarkably illiterate and ill-behaved body, and the choristers. Two years before the promulgation of his charter Adam Houghton had tried to improve the lot of these choristers. He had seen 'in bitterness of heart' that they were few in number, ill clad, attended the choral services irregularly and lukewarmly, and were very badly provided for in their temporal wants. It became his intention that these four choristers (increased to six in 1501 by Bishop John Morgan) should be housed, fed and educated free, and that the bishop's vicar should be given the duty of teaching them. This presumably was the foundation of the choir school, and it is logical to assume that their music master would also be master of what will later be called the grammar school. Adam Houghton insisted that the fellows of his College should reach a satisfactory standard in literature, music and church custom, and the master of that grammar school, the Cathedral School, of later years was similarly expected to give his pupils a good 'Classical and Mathematical Education'.

In 1549 St. Mary's College ceased to exist. In 1557 the Liber Communis recorded the building of a school at a cost of £10.15s. In 1560 Griffith ap Howell, communarius for the year beginning 1 August (the feast of St. Peter ad Vincula) recorded that payment was made to Sir Harrie Jenkinson 'for keeping the grammar school for one year'. His is the first name on the list of masters of the Cathedral Grammar School. The next logical step came in March 1565 when Richard Davies was bishop. A chapter order compelled the young vicars choral and the choir boys (the queristers) to attend this school daily at six in the morning and 'obediently to lerne and contenue with the scole mr all those accustomed times obeyng there saied scole mr'. Strict rules were laid down; a first or second disobedience were given their punishment; a third disobedience meant utter expulsion 'from stall and vicarage for ever'.

Traditionally a cathedral school was housed in the cloisters on the north and west. In *Menevia Sacra*, written by Edward Yardley, Archdeacon of Cardigan, and dedicated (1720) to Bishop Adam Ottley, there is a map of the Cathedral Close drawn by Joseph Lord of Carmarthen. On this map are drawn Adam Houghton's cloisters ('now in ruins'), St. Mary's College and Chapel, the Vicars' Ground on which stood their own College and houses 'now all ruined but one', and a Free School. In the west cloister, said Yardley, was formerly a Free School, or 'ye library for ye use of ye College, during which time, that which is now ye school, in ye churchyard, was a storehouse, or workhouse for ye use of ye Church'. This west cloister built by Adam Houghton (his architect was John Fawley or Foley, whose family name is commemorated in Foley House in Haverfordwest) had therefore at one time been the home of a Free School. And quite clearly that school had at a later time been transferred to a building in the Cathedral Yard. On the outside of the Yard Wall as it runs down from the Deanery Gate towards the ford one can see openings, doors or windows. That presumably was the workshop or storehouse, and it was above this workshop that a room was built to take the transferred school. It was in use as a schoolroom until 1791. In that year the architect John Nash converted the schoolroom into a Chapter House with a large dining room attached, and the school was removed (as Jones and Freeman tell us) to an ancient chapter house and treasury above St. Thomas's Chapel on the north side of the Cathedral. The etching in the Cathedral Library of 'St. David's Grammar School' is certainly of this treasury-chapter house. Nash's chapter house in the Yard was taken down in 1829 (it disfigured the landscape and ruined the view from both west door and south door of the Cathedral), but the foundation marks, grassed over, are still clearly to be seen. The ancient treasury and chapter house are today the ground floor and adapted gallery of the Cathedral Library. The question is, How long did the Cathedral Grammar School stay there?

The list of Masters of the Cathedral Grammar School provided by Francis Green in Volume 6 of *West Wales Historical Records* (1916) implies an unbroken continuity from 1560 (the time of Harrie Jenkinson) till 1885, when William George Spurrell was appointed. Spurrell, said Green's note, was by 1895 rector of Cosheston, and after his earlier (and undated) resignation the Cathedral Grammar School was discontinued. On the evidence of that list we should assume that Spurrell's school was a direct descendant of the school of Jenkinson; and of Henry Goffe, whose mastership, according to the records at the time of Adam Ottley's visitation, earned him £10 yearly; and the school that Dr George Harries had in mind when he wrote to the Chapter in August 1824 to tell them that he had been educated in the first place at the Free School in St. David's. Was it the school that Richard Fenton attended before transferring to Haverfordwest Grammar School? Was it the school that Nicholas Carlisle called a public Grammar School or a Free School? Later on that admixture of labels will cause confusion and argument. What again can we make of the statement in Samuel Lewis's *Topographical Dictionary* that 'the Grammar School attached to the Cathedral affords instruction to 6 choristers', and that another 'free school has been established by the Upper Chapter'? There are at present, said Samuel Lewis, upwards of 80 boys and 50 girls in this school.

The easiest way to solve whatever confusion there is may well be to work backwards from the time of Spurrell, from 1885, the time of his appointment. His predecessor was William Matthews, Master from 1879 to 1885. During the second half of the nineteenth century the *Dewisland and Kemes Guardian* displayed advertisements of this 'Cathedral School, St. David's', whose Visitor was Dean and Chapter, and whose Headmaster was the Revd W. Matthews, B.A., Jesus College, Oxford, formerly Assistant Master, King Edward School, Norwich. Here is Francis Green's list of nineteenth-century masters, with Matthews included:

1810–1829	William Richardson	1874–1878	Isaac Hughes Jones
1829–1840	Jonah Owen	1878–1879	Hugh Jones

1840–1854	Nathaniel Davies	1879–1885	William Matthews
1854–1867	Thomas Richardson	1885–	W. G. Spurrell
1867–1874	A. J. M. Green		

In the first place, it had not been a continuing history. The Parish Magazine of 1879 (one of three bound volumes in the Cathedral Library) announced (in August) that City and neighbourhood 'will hail with satisfaction the revival of the old Cathedral School . . . under the care of the Revd W. Matthews, Vicar Choral, as Head Master'.

Again, this Matthews school was different. It advertised for pupils, it charged fees, it looked like a little Eton, classically dominated, as its end of term programmes of plays and concerts show. They took place in the Old Town Hall and were well reported in the local paper. It prepared boys for the University, for the Preliminary Examinations, and for Commercial Pursuits. Its pupils were given the opportunity of living 'under licenced lodging houses'. There were other schools like it not far off. Solva had a grammar school conducted by the Revd D. E. Edwards, Master of Arts, University Medallist, First Prizeman in the University of Glasgow. Fishguard had another, with Revd Henry Miles of Llanstinan Rectory as Headmaster, Frederick Miles as Classics Master and D. Stuart Miles as English Master.

What had happened in St. David's? In May 1893, in Haverfordwest, an enquiry was held before a Charity Commissioner and amongst the matters investigated by it was Dr Jones's Charity of St. David's. Statements were made and recorded in the evidence that concerned the Cathedral Grammar School. It was said that there was no record of documents of the school; that there was imperfect evidence that the school was for the general use of parishioners; that the Grammar School of Mr Richardson and Mr Green had died a natural death; and that 'the Dean and Chapter now make contribution towards the education of Cathedral Choristers, who now attend the National School'. Despite this evidence, natural death or not, there had been some kind of continuation, and four appointments of Masters, since the time of A. J. M. Green. More surprising is that four years after the appointment of W. G. Spurrell (that is, in 1889) the *Dewisland and Kemes Guardian* carried a notice that the school would be opening in January. That notice (it gave details of fees) appeared in the paper from January to 2 November; there was no alteration in the wording after the passing of January. The thing was obviously dead. After 2 November, there was nothing but silence.

The Taunton Report on Endowed Schools of 1868 went as far as to say that there had been no mention of the school in any previous enquiry, in spite of its venerable antiquity as a school for chorister boys. The considerable endowments of the two bishops, Houghton and Morgan, were in 1868 in the hands of the Ecclesiastical Commission, which gave a chilling response to a request for assistance. In 1869 there were ten day boys and eleven boarders, the Master was Alfred John Morgan Green (M.A. Cantab.), and instruction was given in Classics, Mathematics, Divinity and English, together with 'Welsh, if not objected to' and 'Navigation, if required'. The Report also stated that the school was formerly held in an ancient building to the north of the Cathedral but was in 1867 held in a room rented in premises adjoining the house where the Master and his predecessors 'appear to have lived, at the opposite end of St. David's from the Cathedral'.

A third source of information is a printed report that appeared in 1853 on a comprehensively vindictive quarrel between Nathaniel Davies, Prebendary and Minor Canon of the Cathedral and Master of the Chapter School between 1840 and 1854, and Llewelyn Lewellin, Dean of the Cathedral. In actual fact, it was a matter of two reports, the first headed 'Notes on the Cathedral Church of St. Davids', printed in Haverfordwest by William Perkins, the other 'A Reply to the Rev. N. Davies's Notes on the Cathedral Church', printed by J. Potter, Haverfordwest.

Nathaniel Davies's 'Notes on the Cathedral Church' protested that the Chapter School was being deprived of funds that were legitimately its own either deliberately by the Dean and Chapter or through ignorance. The Dean in his reply emphasised the distinction between choristers and school, implying that whatever endowments or properties were held in the name of the choristers did not thereby belong to the school. More immediately relevant is a statement in Nathaniel Davies's reply to the Dean's defence. 'When I came here,' he said, 'I found the school in a most neglected state; there had been no Master to teach the boys for a considerable time, I believe nearly twelve months. There was no residence for the Master, and when I sought for a house large enough to receive my private school, I could not get one . . .' That brings us to a newspaper cutting now in the Francis Green scrapbooks in the Regional Library – a 'History of the Cathedral Grammar School' submitted in 1898 by W. Peregrine Propert to one of the local papers. He started with Adam Houghton's establishment of the cathedral choristers, and the new school built in 1557, and the order combining choristers and vicars choral in 1564. This, he said, was and had continued to be the Cathedral School. But some fifty years previously (that is, about 1848) a Master had been elected who, presumably under economic pressure, had brought with him pupils from leading families of Pembrokeshire and adjoining counties, and the school became a 'classics' school. The Master in 1848 was Nathaniel Davies, and in the Census returns we find a list of twenty-eight pupils, called 'classical scholars', attached to a school in High Street run with the assistance of James Wilson, B.A., Cambridge, a clergyman without cure of souls. These pupils came from Lampeter and Milford, West Indies, Jefferston and Carmarthen, Barbados, Taunton, Brighton, Llandilo and Bridgewater. The Dean, in his reply to Nathaniel Davies, referred to them – 'What say you to the fact that he has under his charge twenty-five or thirty boys, on an average, at sums of £40 a year each (some, I believe, at £60), the sons of the aristocracy of the three counties – the Owens, the Brigstockes, the Leaches, the Higgons, the Massies, the Lloyd Prices, etc.' He called it 'a sort of pocket Eton'.

In Volume 22 of the Francis Green Manuscripts is another reference to Nathaniel Davies, and to Grove House (now Grove Hotel) in High Street. It is a copy of a grant from the Revd Thomas Richardson, formerly of Fishguard, clerk, to Thomas Llewellyn, and a contract which included a list of properties. It referred directly to a coachhouse and schoolroom erected and converted on parts of the Grove House territory, and it refers to Nathaniel Davies. This was the house that Nathaniel Davies eventually secured to house his private school. The Taunton Report confirms that this Nathaniel Davies school continuing under A. J. M. Green was in Grove House in 1868. And the Charity Commission Enquiry confirms that this school, 'the Grammar School of Mr. Richardson and Mr. Green' died a natural death. From 1874, the end of A. J. M. Green's mastership, there were another four masters covering a period of nearly fifteen years, there was a revival with William Matthews, and a demise around 1889/90 in the time of Spurrell. This was the 'Cathedral School' of the advertisements.

Both Samuel Lewis and W. Peregrine Propert refer to 'another' school. In the last century, said Propert, there had developed a Free School in St. David's whose origin and purpose were entirely distinct from the Cathedral Grammar School and whose nature was that of a public charitable institution. According to Propert, this was the Benevolent School, supported by the Dean and Chapter. And this, we must assume, was the Free School of 130 pupils mentioned by Samuel Lewis in his *Topographical Dictionary*. And it was some confusion in local minds over the separate identities of Cathedral Grammar School (at one time called a Free School) and the Free or Benevolent School that had prompted

Propert to write his article. The Benevolent School, as will appear later, was mentioned in *Brad y Llyfrau Gleision*, the Blue Book Reports, and in the local reorganisation plans following the 1870 Education Act.

Private schools run by clergy or by relatives of clergy were not infrequent in the St. David's of the nineteenth century, but any positive or documentary evidence about them is scanty. *The County Guardian* of August 1893 reported the death of Henry B. Williams of Croeswdig, who, it said, had received his education from Mr Phillimore Appleby and Dr Propert. People say that there was a school in Manor House, where the Properts lived. Others say there was a school, a choral school, in Penygarn, which is now Warpool Court. A. J. M. Green, Master of the Cathedral School, lived in Penygarn. Clergymen, before or after retirement, certainly took in private pupils. A note in Samuel Williams's letter books states that Thomas Richardson was paid £2.6.4 for J****'s tuition. Thomas Richardson was Master from 1854 to 1867. There were private schools for girls. The Misses L. and C. James kept a school for girls in the Archdeaconry, and the *Dewisland and Kemes Guardian* of November 1879 advertised that the Misses M'Laren and John of Hamilton House were prepared to receive a limited number of young ladies to educate in English, Music, and other accomplishments. The best known of all headmistresses was Miss Appleby. There is some evidence that she had a private school for boys and girls in Royal Terrace, but her name is more frequently linked with Fossil House, by Ebenezer Chapel. Samuel Williams, reviewing the electoral roll, noted in 1870 that Miss Jane Appleby ran a private school in Nun Street. Very little documentary evidence has been found concerning the school at Y Bont, near Penitents Bridge; Essex Davies's Tithe Map on 1840 showed not even a house there. Nevertheless, many senior citizens declare without hesitation that their parents or grandparents were educated at Ysgol y Bont, and that an Appleby taught them. It is clear that there were two sisters of that name (and more than one male Appleby) who were teachers. The Miss Appleby that we know best is the tall, strict, commanding, the stern-eyed Miss Carlyle of *The Captain's Wife*, modelled on one of the two sisters. The two elder children of the novel's Peters family attended the school near the Cathedral, but 'Matty had recently joined the troop of boys and girls who ran every day to Miss Carlyle's school at the foot of the hill'.

The 'school near the Cathedral' was the Treasury School. Many of the old people of St. David's remember this school and one of its Masters, Revd J. R. Jones. Old family albums carry photographs, boys in their prim bow ties, of Treasury School groups. Captain

Peter Perkins and his son, the schoolmaster, were taught in this school; its schoolroom was demolished in 1976.

An article in Welsh in the *Pembroke County Guardian* of 12 February 1898 reminisced over two schools in St. David's. One was Ysgol y Canon. The other was Ysgol Twmi Dafi. What and where were these? The answers can be found in various reports of the time, in the Lingen Report, and in Samuel Williams's Report which formed the basis for the reorganisation after 1870. The first was the *Reports of Commissioners (Lord Brougham's Commission) to Enquire concerning Charities, Wales*, 1819–1837. This dealt with four St. David's Charities – Madame Bevan's Charity, which was a continuation of Griffith Jones's Charity Schools; Dr Jones's Charity; Adams's Charity, which had nothing to do with education; and Beynon's Charity.

Madame Bridget Bevan inherited the residue of the estate of Griffith Jones, and her will (1779) stipulated that this should pay, apply and be disposed for the use of the Welsh Circulating Schools as long as the same continued. The Commission referred to schools in Brawdy (1831 and 1832) and in Llanrhian, for twelve months, in 1836. Catechism and committing to memory were embodied in the curriculum; there was strict attention to attendance; when pupils had reached a satisfactory standard in Welsh they were transferred to the English class; scholars and masters had to attend divine service on the Lord's Day. Two reports on Llanrhian, by Morgan Morgan, Visitor for South Wales, were included in the Report.

Dr Jones's Charity (1698) originally made provision for the payment of £1 annually to each of four apprentices without indenture. In May 1893 a further report on this Charity was made after a full enquiry, chaired by a Charity Commissioner, which was reported in the *Dewisland and Kemes Guardian* in June of that year.

Adams's Charity derived from a deed, about 1700, under which Mathias Adams gave a rent-charge of £1 to the poor of St. David's, a rent-charge which issued from the 100 acre estate of Treleddid Fawr and was paid annually on 12 March.

Another Charity, Owen's Charity, dates from 1885. Thomas Owen gave £200 to the trustees of the National School, the interest to be used towards its maintenance.

Much more relevant was the Beynon Charity which finally explained Ysgol Twmi Dafi. Thomas Beynon of St. David's by his will dated 14 May, 1810, bequeathed to his widow, Mary Beynon, certain property, she paying several legacies, and amongst them £50 at interest at 'trevaine', £10 of which should be towards repairs to a meeting house, and the interest on the other £40 to the schooling of four poor boys, such as might be thought worthy by the persons appointed. The testator desired William Williams, John Roach and

David Hicks to appoint such children as they might think worthy. Lord Brougham's Report explained:

> Mr. David Williams, Pemberry, who is the eldest son of Mr. William Williams above mentioned, has in his hands the sum of £36 belonging to the charity. On the testator's death, the Rev. Francis Rees, who was requested by the testator to advise his widow, refused to pay over the £40 legacy to the trustees until he received a release, which cost about £4. The interest, amounting to 36s, was paid to a schoolmaster appointed by Mr. D. Williams. At the time of our enquiry, the schoolmaster, John Jenkins, was very ill, and the school was taught by Thomas Davies; he teaches six children in respect of the charity, one girl and five boys, children of poor people, nominated by Mr. Williams. They are taught reading, writing, and arithmetic, gratuitously; but the parents find books and stationery. The master teaches about 12 pay scholars, from whom he receives about 2s per quarter.

Ysgol Twmi Dafi, then, was the Beynon Charity School, and Twmi Dafi was Thomas Davies. Since 1962 a Thomas Beynon Prize has appeared annually in the prize list of Ysgol Dewi Sant. The original charity, unwanted in its original form and purpose in an age of state education, was rescued from anonymity in the Treasurer's Department in Haverfordwest and is now used as a prize to all pupils of the parish who proceed to a college of education.

From 1833 to 1845 Parliament voted moneys for education, to be devoted entirely at first to aiding local effort in the building of schools. A condition of award was that schools should be open to government inspection. One of the first to be appointed of these inspectors was a Pembrokeshire man, Revd John Allen. His father was David Bird Allen, vicar of Burton, his brother one of the most notable of deans, James Allen. It is said that the ancestral Pembrokeshire stock began with a Thomas Allen who came from Ireland and is said to have been shipwrecked in St. Brides Bay. John Allen was Archdeacon of Salop when appointed inspector by a Committee of Council on Education in 1839. A very strong character, he served for seven years on a roving commission, inspected all kinds of schools, found the conduct of the clergy scandalous, and had the good gift of getting his reports implemented. In 1845 he visited Pembrokeshire officially and examined the aided Church Schools and the surviving charity schools. These reports, to be found in the *Committee of Council Education Minutes*, Volume 1 (London, 1846), included one on St. David's:

> St. Davids. Intelligence and knowledge of the Scriptures satisfactory. School appears much indebted to the pains of the clergyman. £20 paid to its support by the Chapter. Master pleasing and intelligent. Room

ill-ventilated; hope of a new one. No necessary outbuildings. Desks arranged on Lancaster's plan.

On the day of inspection there were 34 boys and 27 girls present. Having analysed the groupings and the work in which they were involved, he commented generally on this district 'where most of the benefices are poorly endowed, residences are often wanting, and many of the clergy live away from their cures; consequently the advantages derived from the pastor's visits and the unbought labours of members of his family appear to be in many parts unknown'. He ended with the pungent 'As the attention of the clergyman is, so is the school.'

Where, then, was this Chapter-supported school within the City? The answer must lie in the Tithe Map, or in the *Blue Book* or Lingen Reports of 1847, or in Samuel Williams's report 'on the state of education in St. David's' in 1870/71. The Tithe Map and its schedule refer to two schools. One was 'House and Schoolroom', number 148, precisely south of the southern part of Tower Gate. Here, it is said, was a school run by an old warrior who may or may not have had a wooden leg, and who had a daughter whose job it was to replenish the tankard at his elbow, the level of which controlled his teaching ability and his temper. The other was 'Schoolroom, cottage and garden', Number 98, owned by Ebenezer Williams, occupied by Samuel Thomas, and standing where 'Menai' now stands.

The *Blue Books* were reports of a Royal Commission of Inquiry into the state of Education in Wales which was set up in 1846 and reported in 1847. The report on Carmarthenshire and Pembrokeshire (the Lingen Report) said that Dewisland was miserably provided with schools and that the conditions of schools and education generally were deplorably bad. It was its severe judgements on moral conditions that aroused intense antagonism and the anger of men like Ieuan Gwynedd, Samuel Roberts (S.R.), and Henry Richard, whose *Letters and Essays on Wales* refuted many of the severer accusations. Two factors had made the Report aggravating: Wales was growing strong in nonconformity, the investigators were Anglican; they were also English and failed to communicate, and, worst of all, regarded inability to speak English as indicative of a low standard of education, and a low standard of education as commensurate with a low standard of morality. It is only fair to add that the Reports were even more scathing on what they thought was one of the main causes of educational and moral backwardness, the weakness of the church. They reported bluntly that in some parishes the very machinery of ecclesiastical administration had ceased to function.

Four schools in St. David's are mentioned:

Benevolent School, established 1812. Held in a very low room over some cottages. Tolerably good condition, but windows in very bad repair. The master appeared a superior man for a country schoolmaster. The school was supported by the Dean and Chapter.

Bethania Day School, or Beynon's Charity. The master was a labourer who had broken his thigh some eighteen years previously. The school was held in the Methodist Chapel.

Ebenezer Day School, established 1842. Management by a committee whose qualification for membership was the payment of 1s per annum. No regular registers. Children more than usually shy and sheepish. But they sang very nicely, and nine of them read with ease from St. Mark. Arithmetic was occasionally taught. No blackboard.

Tabernacle School, established 1845. The new master an intelligent man. Schoolroom commodious and well furnished. Classroom in a wing of the chapel, raised at a cost of £150 advanced by friends of the undertaking. It was found that the dread of losing a privilege in one case, and a desire to get their money's worth in the other, made the parents diligent in sending their children to school. No register.

Both Ebenezer and Tabernacle were directly supported by religious congregations, although there did not seem to be denominational instruction or discrimination. Of the 73 on the books of Tabernacle, 4 were Wesleyan, 2 were Baptists, 2 Independents, 7 Church of England, 7 belonged nowhere, and 50 were Calvinistic Methodists. Ebenezer Williams vouched for the pupils of this school because Revd William Morris was away in Cardiganshire. James Griffiths (Treliwyd) vouched for the pupils of Ebenezer School. Of the 55 in attendance, 5, he said, were Baptists, 4 Wesleyans, one was Calvinistic Methodist, 5 Established Church, 28 Independents, and 6 were not connected with any denomination.

Our third source of information is Samuel Williams's report, which was printed in full in the *Dewisland and Kemes Guardian* on 21 January 1871. Having discussed the general and discouraging background, he came to the major consideration – that there were only three of six schools in the City that came within the requirements of the Education Department. These were Miss Appleby's, Miss Edmond's, and the Benevolent ('as it is called'). The reorganisation and rebuilding that would comply with the 1870 Act would have to involve these.

Miss Appleby held her school in two rooms, both small, and she had fifty pupils, which in terms of government stipulations on area/pupil ratio was fourteen pupils too many. Lingen had reported that she was losing pupils to other schools.

Miss Edmond's School had 72 pupils, and was in fact the Tabernacle School on which Lingen had reported favourably. In the log book of the state-aided Board School is an entry for 27 June, 1873 – 'Miss Edmonds, who has for many years carried on the school in connection with the Calvinistic Methodist chapel, has been engaged as Assistant Mistress.' An entry for 4 July reported that 40 pupils had been admitted, 39 of whom were Miss Edmonds' scholars.

The third of Samuel Williams's stipulated schools was the Benevolent, which had 78 pupils. The Blue Books had mentioned a Benevolent School, founded in 1812. Samuel Lewis had referred to the 'other' free school established by the Upper Chapter. Peregrine Propert, trying to keep apart the history of the Cathedral Grammar School, had referred to the 'other' Free School, and that Free School, he said categorically, was the Benevolent School or (according to the reminiscing Welsh article) Ysgol y Canon. And three years earlier (1895) one of the many letters to the local press on the teaching of Welsh and Scripture in the day schools, had mentioned Ysgol y Canon, 'as the Church School is called'. But Samuel Williams's report mentioned an older school. 'I am quite sure,' he said, 'that there is not a native present, who, being upwards of fifty years old, would deny that the school, now called old Mr Appleby's, and which was held from 40 to 60 years ago, was one of the best, if not the very best, that was ever held in the parish, to meet the necessities of the lower and middle classes, though it was a thorough church school, and the children were compelled to attend at the Cathedral every Sunday morning, and also at other times, to learn the church catechism, etc., but as it was supported partly by voluntary subscriptions and other gifts of a like nature, it gradually succumbed, and after suffering for many years from "decline" it died at last, much to the sorrow of many who had received nearly all the education they possessed under its wing.'

Was this the old Ysgol y Canon? In 1815 a William Appleby (was he the 'old Mr Appleby'?) had sent a letter to Archdeacon Davies which was a defence of his conduct of the 'Benevolent School'. The headmaster of the St. David's Board School which appeared after the implementation of the 1870 Act was Thomas J. Polinghorne. The headmaster of the National or Church School was – William Appleby.

These were the schools that together had formed an ill-assorted backcloth to the Act of 1870 and a reorganised primary school system and the 1889 Act which brought in state secondary education. The Taunton Report attributed the decline of the Cathedral School, rather unconvincingly, to the coming of the railways 'which made it possible for the gentry who had previously sent their sons to the Cathedral School to send them to English Public Schools'. The Charity Commission had reported a natural death. Economics must have been one cause. So without doubt was the overhanging debate on religion and disestablishment.

Samuel Williams's report had been based on statistics supplied by the Education Department which were based on returns from schools. When he compared his estimates of the total child population of the parish with figures of attendance at existing schools he saw that half of them never received any education at all. That was the problem. *Kelly's Directory* of 1884 said that the Board School in Quickwell was built in 1871 for 245 children. The National or Church School was built in 1873 for 150 places. The total was almost exactly what Samuel Williams had estimated.

The establishment of two sectarian schools in an area where the ratio of Nonconformist to Anglican was 5 to 3 did not bring any end to the rivalry between church and chapel. Religious instruction in school, compulsory attendance at church, the language question, the important question of how the new schools should be paid for (churchmen supported the rate or Government-aided system; Nonconformists favoured the voluntary system as protection for both language and religious freedom) – arguments over these continued, especially in such tense matters as the election of the school board. In 1876 came compulsory attendance for all children up to the age of 14; in 1891 the establishment of free education for all (the local rate, the 1d per week charged to all parents for each child, was replaced by a parliamentary grant); in 1902 the Education Act abolished School Boards and made the County Council working through its education committee the sole authority for all education other than that of university – the Board School went out, the Council School came in; and in 1907 the Welsh Department of the Board of Education came into being, with O. M. Edwards as its first inspector. Ten years earlier Henry Evans of Caerfarchell had commented in the local press that Scripture to Welsh children should be taught in Welsh. The appointment of non-Welsh speaking headmasters was criticised. It was the time of the 'Welsh Not'. There are still some St. David's people who remember the psychological tyranny imposed by that little domino piece of wood inscribed with the letters W.N., in primary schools where all the pupils were taught in English. The teaching of Welsh rested entirely on the Sunday Schools.

Inevitably the School Boards, before disappearing into history, had achieved a balance, between church and chapel, between English and Welsh, between town and country and trade and farming. The triennial elections of 1898 saw the following elected:

William Davies Beynon, farmer, Penlan; Lewis Davies, farmer, Hendre Eynon; Thomas Jenkin Davies, farmer, Treiago; William Davies, farmer, Rhosycribed; Isaac Evans, saddler, High Street; John Watts Evans, draper and clothier, City Stores; John Eynon, jeweller, Nun Street; Edgar Martin Griffiths, farmer, Trevelly; John Howard Griffiths, gentleman, Lleithyr; Macdonald Henry Jay, gentleman, Pebbles House; Mary Jane Jenkins, wife of Rev. William Jenkins, New Cross; John Richard Jones, auctioneer and valuer, Prospect Hotel; William Lawrence, contractor, Goat Street; David Lewis, clerk in holy orders, The Vicarage; Henry Lewis, physician and surgeon, Bodlondeb; Gilbert Bevan Martin, farmer, City Hotel; Claudine Isabel Winifred Morgan, independent lady, Brynygarn; Thomas Owen, retired farmer, Dyfrog House; John Phillips, clerk in Holy Orders, Cathedral Villa; Henry Rees, farmer, Treleddid Fawr; William Henry Thomas, C.M. minister, Caerfarchell; Adrian Owen Williams, merchant, Cross Square; David Propert Williams, farmer, Penberi; Samuel J. Watts Williams, sub-postmaster, Old Cross; Thomas Robert Williams, farmer, Grove Hotel; William Williams, merchant, Grove Hotel.

The original log books of the two new primary schools are now lodged in the Record Office in Haverfordwest. In them the first head masters, Appleby in the National, Polkinghorne in the Board, entered their first comments: bad weather, bad work, constantly bad attendance; a glimpse of talent in the occasional pupil; regret that a good scholar should have to leave school to work in a colliery because his family wanted the money; disappointment, books and furniture late in arriving; and among the legitimate comments, little notes on habits, customs, changes, the world outside school breaking in. They were years of extreme difficulty. The average attendance in England (1899) was 81.55%, in Wales it was 75.86, in Pembrokeshire a miserable 71.90. Every event in church and chapel was justification for a holiday. There were four fairs annually. A wreck in the bay, anything to do with the lifeboat, demanded its day off. The log book put it tersely – 'everybody going wrecking'. Child employment, for gardening, haymaking, potato picking and setting, made heavy demands, and the country children suffered worst. There was poverty, and children had to work. A child stood barefoot in the pools and gathered leeches, and sold them to Dr Lewis (or was it Dr Foley?) for a few pence a dozen. Those pence bought the children's boots. It is possible that absenteeism because of religious events was not quite so disrespectful of school and law as might appear: these were days of Nonconformity triumphant and the building and opening of chapels; and the opening of Tabernacle or great preaching meetings in Caerfarchell meant manifestations of great emotional experiences which parents did not want their children to miss.

More surprising were celebrations of the 'Old New Year'. *Hen Galan* celebrations traditionally belonged to other areas, the Gwaun Valley and Llandysul, areas bypassed by the severities of the Methodist Revival. But, Methodism or no Methodism, there were some people in the City who celebrated *Hen Galan*, and the school log books are proof of it.

Education was never entirely the prerogative of schools. Chapels were heavily engaged in educating young and old, and organised lectures by the great preachers and literary men of the time – Mynyddog, Thomas Levi, Gomer Lewis – were prominent on the calendar of the City. There was at one time a Literary Institute, meeting in the Old Town Hall. In 1891 the Science and Arts Institute was active with penny readings and lectures on such subjects as electricity and biology. 'A well taught school,' said an Inspector (H.M.) on the St. David's Evening Continuation Schools, 'though the attendance is much below what might be expected.' The Reading Room in New Street was opened in May, 1882, through the exertions of Canon Lewis. The aims were educational, but the people for whom it was planned, the poorer townsman, the working man, were not using it as they should.

Little evidence can be found of educational work in the two most prominent elements of St. David's life, agriculture and the sea, and no evidence that any Evening Classes were held to deal with the new methods of farming that were constantly reported in the press. In 1891 the University College of Wales, Aberystwyth, established an Agricultural Department – the first in the country to demonstrate the importance of '*crefft gyntaf dynol ryw*'. In consequence dairy schools were set up in various parts of the country following the granting of special powers to the County Councils towards that end. One such school, where demonstrations on the craft of butter-making were given, was in St. David's. The papers reported that there were twelve pupils in the first session, and ten of them gained certificates.

The Master Mariners were busier. From 1850 to 1900 the local paper reported successes in examinations in navigation, mostly in Solva. Captain Thomas Prosser of Upper Solva (and at one time of Nine Wells) was tutor. William Jones, C.M., late Master of the Board School, advertised the opening of the St. David's Nautical School in January, 1880. Another teacher of navigation and mathematics was James Rowlands, who lived in Gothic Villa and worked as carpenter and builder. In the evenings he turned his workshop into a school. William Morgan, one time of Mathry and later of Abercastell, appeared in the Milford Haven Customs Register as owner of ships sailing from Abercastell, the little port that exported vast quantities of corn in the eighteenth and early nineteenth centuries. He ran apprentice schemes for seamen. As the Cartlett Papers in the Library in Haverfordwest demonstrate, William Morgan was a busy man: there were twelve navigation apprentices on his books in 1778.

In retrospect, the history of formal education in St. David's seems to have been a history of impoverishment and absence. 'The general aspect,' said John Allen, 'appeared to me to be very melancholy.' The School Boards that followed the Elementary Education Act of 1870 were elected specifically to supply education where there were deficiencies. To their credit they acted quickly in St. David's. The need was great.

It was inevitable that the safe establishment of elementary schools would lead to the establishment of a post-primary system of education.

> An adequate supply of elementary schools increased the need for secondary schools and make the lack of them more obvious. The lack was great in England; it was greater in Wales, with its fewer endowments and lesser wealth. For the benefit of Wales therefore an Act was passed in 1889 making the counties the authority for intermediate education while empowering them to appropriate old benefactions and levy rates for the provision of it.

That quotation is taken from an article on the history of education in Pembrokeshire by David Salmon, Principal of Swansea Training College, in the booklet celebrating Education Week in Pembrokeshire, October 1925.

The Welsh Intermediate and Technical Education Act established a system of post primary education for Wales, and as one of its consequences a Joint Education Committee for Intermediate Education in Pembrokeshire met on 21 February 1891, in Haverfordwest, and decided that Fishguard and St. David's – the last two candidates – should have mixed secondary schools, the locality to provide suitable accommodation, including playground, for not less than 40 pupils, and for no less than five years – a probationary period – after approval of the scheme. There was to be a £5 capitation assessment, and this was to accumulate at compound interest until the expiry of the five years. On 5 June 1891, a public meeting was held at the Town Hall 'for the purpose of taking steps for securing an Intermediate School for St. David's'. In the absence of William Williams, Grove House, the chair was taken by William Davies, Rhosycribed. Very soon afterwards the Town Hall Committee gave its permission that the Town Hall be made available to accommodate the new school.

In September 1894 the County Governing Body for the proposed secondary schools of Pembrokeshire met at the Shire Hall in Haverfordwest. W. Watts Williams and H. W. Williams represented St. David's and Solva. At about the same time a Selection Committee met to discuss the appointment of a first headmaster. On it were Canon Lewis; H. P. Griffiths (Henry Phillips Griffiths) of Long House, Letterston; W. D. Williams, Gwalia; Richard Jenkins, Croftufty; and the Revd W. M. Lewis, Tyllwyd (grandfather of Lewis, John and Morris Mendus). And on 9 March 1895, the papers announced that an appointment had been made – of T. Lewis Williams, B.A., a Welsh-speaking Welshman, 26 years of age, educated at Lewis' Endowed School, Gelligaer, Llandovery College, and with a London Final degree, at the University College of Wales, Aberystwyth. Also on the short list was W. Butler Smith, B.A., of West Hampstead.

On 16 March 1895, the first advertisement of the St. David's District School appeared in the press:

> To be opened in the first week of March, 1895. Applications for admission to be sent to the Registrar on or before Monday, the 4th of March. Admission qualifications Standard V or examination equivalent thereto. The scholarships, eight in number, to be divided equally between boys and girls, will be awarded shortly after the Examination, for which due notice will be given. Subjects to be taught – English, Grammar and Literature, Latin, French, Mathematics, Book-keeping, Natural Science, and for girls Domestic Science and its branches.
>
> School fees – £4 per term.
> 2 of a family – £7
> 3 of a family – £10
>
> Pembrokeshire Intermediate Education.
> St. David's County School.
> Chairman Board of Governors – Ald. W. Watts Williams, J.P.
> Vice-Chairman – Rev. Canon Lewis, M.N.
> Headmaster – Mr. T. Lewis Williams, B.A. (London).
> Assistant Mistress – Miss W. L. James (Univ. Coll., Cardiff).
> Music Mistress – Miss Maud Thomas.
> Registrar – W. D. Williams, Gwalia.

It opened, as things turned out, on 29 April 1895, with a first day attendance of 25 pupils, as the first Register shows. There had been twenty applicants for the scholarships, which were awarded to Eleanor Ann Thomas of the Board School; Phoebe Davies of Carnhedryn; Minnie Thomas of the Board; and Martha Ann Williams of the Board; Henry John Thomas, Solva Board; E. B.

Jamieson, Llanrhian; Samuel Jones and Edwin D. J. Williams, both of the St. David's Board School.

Lewis Williams was the first headmaster of St. David's; Brown was first headmaster of Fishguard. Surprisingly, in under eighteen months both had resigned. In December of 1895 the County Governing Body appointed Owen Gledhill of Leeds as headmaster of Fishguard. In January 1897, Thomas Thomas, B.A., of Brynberian, was appointed headmaster of St. David's County School. There were nine applicants, and of the three shortlisted he was alone in being able to speak Welsh – some of the members of the appointing body had newly returned from a meeting in Shrewsbury, where a recommendation had been made that in appointments there should be preference for a Welshman if he were of sufficient merit. The salary of the St. David's post was £120 per annum, with the addition of £1 capitation for each pupil. These two newly appointed headmasters turned out to be men of great strength of character. In many ways they were ahead of their time in their outlook on school and education, and they established, each in his own way, a deep and characteristic imprint on their schools that long outlasted their thirty years of headmastership.

In May, 1899, the Pembrokeshire Governing Body informed the Charity Commissioners of its decision that the Charity Schools of Fishguard and St. David's were to be put on a permanent basis. In July of the same year it was announced that Benjamin Richard James, George Bentham Jamieson, and Thomas David Williams, three pupils of the school, had passed the London Matriculation.

In the same month a special meeting of the County School Governors met to discuss plans and specifications for a new school. In September of 1902 the new school was opened by Principal H. E. Griffiths of University College, Cardiff (of the family of James Griffiths and Howard Griffiths and Eiluned Lewis), seven years after the bare beginnings of secondary education in the Old Town Hall; and in the audience were three Fellows of the Royal Society, all connected with the parish. Much was said of the difficulties of the beginnings and of the old Hall, and its importance was given a further emphasis at the official opening of the Memorial Hall in 1922. J. Howard Griffiths of Priskilly revealed that when St. David's in 1895 had been offered a temporary school, to be made permanent after five years if results justified, there had been a great deal of opposition. He was doubtful whether a school would have been established had the Old Town Hall not been available as a temporary home.

At the official opening in 1902 it was revealed that the total cost of the new school had been £1,800, of which £450 had come from the

Governing Body and £500 from local contributions. The architect was D. E. Thomas of Haverfordwest; the contractors, T. Evans and Son, Solva; and the clerk of works, Archie Morgan of Cloisters Hall. Tribute was paid to the leaders of the movement: Dean Howell, who was chairman of the Committee; Captain Roach (Vice Chairman); J. Howard Griffiths, Priskilly (Treasurer); W. D. Williams, Gwalia (Secretary); and Captain Griffiths of Arfon Villa, Watts Williams of Menai, first chairman of the Governors, and Archdeacon Lewis. In those pioneering years they had had to work, to exert pressure, and as happened many times afterwards, to go out and talk to parents and enrol pupils from the farms and fields and, as in the parable, from the highways.

It is probably true to say that, over the centuries of its history, this parish has been too remote, too far removed from the main currents of thought, too scattered in population and too feeble in resources to have maintained schools of learning of a high standard. There was a Grammar School in Haverfordwest in the fifteenth century – an entry in the Episcopal Register of St. David's records that on 13 May 1488, the bishop had appointed 'our beloved in Christ, Richard Smyth, master in artes, chaplain in our church of the Blessed Mary', to be its master. After the Reformation the school was revived by the sponsorship and support of Thomas Lloyd of Cilciffaith, a member of a family that had contributed substantially to the history of this county. In St. David's was established one of the earliest foundations of Christianity, and in St. Mary's College a school which pre-dated Winchester (1387) and Eton (1441). St. Mary's College was closed down at the Reformation. The joint school of choristers and vicars choral that followed soon after was supported by a Church that was either too neglectful or too poor to maintain any excellence. Irrespective of other advantages or disadvantages, the secular foundation scored.

Since 1895 the Grammar School has seen many vicissitudes. Now as Ysgol Dewi Sant it is proving effectively what twenty years ago was held as heresy – that a small comprehensive school can be viable and educationally sound. Its strength in St. David's has always derived from two sources: from its teaching staff; and from roots deep in the compact and closely knit community of farm and city and parish. In an article in the *National Library of Wales Journal* (1976) Wynford Davies, former Director of Education of Pembrokeshire, points out that although the Aberdare Committee on Higher and Intermediate Education in 1881 recommended a few large schools for each county what actually happened was the establishment of many smaller schools, local, individual, strongly linked each with its own community. Their strength lay in their smallness and their community spirit. Thomas Thomas started with 22 pupils. In his last term as Headmaster, in 1929, he had 88, and three assistants and one part-time staff. He was then engaged in teaching for 32 out of 37 weekly teaching periods and was responsible for Latin, Mathematics and History to the stage of the First Examination. The argument, the whole point of the argument, is this: whatever the Aberdare Committee said, local loyalty had refused to contemplate any reduced curriculum, any reduction of subjects. The dedication of the teaching staff ensured that as many subjects as the locality demanded were taught, that broad historical and academic foundations were firmly laid.

Those two uplifts saved the school in more than one crisis in the past, usually a crisis of numbers emanating from a thinly populated community. The supporting strength came from the community of loyal supporters, both English and Welsh, and typically and very strongly from the farmers. The dangers? A widening and increasingly anglicised catchment area is one problem. Even more dangerous is a reduced farming community that is no longer fortified by the old strength that came from large and inter-related families.

CHAPTER NINE

Population – Past and Present

This combination of 'littlest city' and 'largest parish' has always been small in terms of population. Willis-Bund estimated that at the time of the *Black Book* St. David's had about a thousand inhabitants. Four hundred years later came what can be regarded as our first census. Edward Yardley's *Menevia Sacra* contains 'An account of ye number of houses and inhabitants in St. David's Parish as taken & communicated by ye late Revd Mr Henry Goffe, Sub-chanter of St. David's Cathedral.' Henry Goffe was appointed Master of the Cathedral Grammar School in July 1714 and Vicar Choral in July 1716, and his census made a total of 304 houses and a total population of 1316. In the four hundred years since the *Black Book* it had grown by three hundred.

Henry Goffe's census is important and useful as a statistical base. It also contains little insights into the history of place-names. It mentions Sheep Street, the present Goat Street – Sheep, not Ship – but makes no mention of the elusive Pit Street, which was mentioned in the bishop's Rent Book as far back as 1685. His Sceifog, phonetically true today, is, whatever it means, better than the mongrelised Skyfog. His Mechellich, which looks appropriate, is better than the O. S. Vachelich. He has Rossan, for Rhosson, using the old Gaelic word *rosan*, meaning a small wood. He has Tref-gweidd (the modern Tregydd), a form which suggests that here at one time may have been the home of a weaver, *gweydd* in Welsh. And he has Trefecca (Tref Becca?), a name that appears in the list of Griffith Jones's Circulating Schools, but could not be traced until Jenkin Davies found that there was a field of that name near Hendre Eynon.

Goffe's comments on *tref* are significant. 'Villages or inshipps', he said, 'were in some cases called trefs or towns, though consisting but of one house & most of them but two, but housing a very large number of people.' In the Laws of Hywel Dda the 'free tref' could be the isolated house in the country; the 'taeog dref' was the hamlet where the workers lived. Goffe tells us of these two types and of the patterned clusters of houses that will appear again in the Tithe Commutation Map and Schedule. There were 6 houses in Sceifog, 14 in Tretio, 11 in Gwrhyd Mawr, and 8 in both Hendre and Llandridian, and 15 in Treleddid Fawr, a settlement which a century after the Tithe Commutation investigation was strong enough to build and support two chapels of ease.

Browne Willis supplied some statistics for 1715. In the Town, he said, there were 78 small inhabited houses and about 292 inhabitants; in the Valley or Close 13 houses and 73 inhabitants; in 'Cylch-Fychan' 38 houses and 139 inhabitants; and in Cylch Mawr, or the Great Circle, 68 houses and 338 inhabitants. Cylch Mawr, the farming area, appropriately had fewer houses and a greater population than the town.

> In all 1203 Souls, and 261 houses, in the Parish of St. David's; and yet the Town and Country is so healthy, that from Easter-day, viz 17 April 1715 to 14 September 1715, there were but two buryed, and one of them was very old.

These were figures for the old days. Official census returns started in 1801. Here are the official census figures for parish and for county since the year 1801.

Year	*Parish*	*Close*	*County*
1801	1803 (+300)		56280
1811	1816 (+13)		60615
1821	2240 (+424)		73788
1841	2445 (+205)		88044
1851	2513 (+68)		94140
1861	2119 (−394)		96278
1871	2131 (+12)		91998
1891	1876 (−255		
1901	1739 (−137)	+29	87894
1911	1644	+23	89960
1921	1543	14	91978
1931	1580	25	87206
1951	1505	26	90906
1961	1690	30	94124
1971	1638	26	98968

The whole of the country in general, including Ireland and Wales, suffered a population rise and fall in the nineteenth century. What by mid-century, by 1851, one may ask, had brought so many people into a parish always lacking in work opportunities? What attracted them when housing and road conditions were primitive? And what drove them away again? The population of 1980, in spite of much building and in spite of a seemingly heavy but deceptive influx of newcomers, is less than it was at the beginning of the nineteenth century.

The Census return of 1841 gives separately the totals of males and females in each of the Cylchs, it specifies the number of occupied and unoccupied houses, and gives the numbers of servants in each Cylch, the male and female servants, and the agricultural labourers who presumably worked on the land but lived in their own cottages and small holdings as opposed to the servants, who lived in. In the total were 168 female servants, traditionally responsible for more hard work in the fields than was customary elsewhere. Twenty per cent of the total population came into this category of servants and agricultural labourers; and there were 250 more women than men, which must have created some unusual social and sexual problems. In a total of 476 houses there were just under five people in each. And on Ramsey were four occupiers, supported by ten male servants and one female.

Besides the workers on land were fishermen, seamen and mariners, the horse rider, thatcher, cordwinder, the washing women, the weaver, the cooper, and only a few shopkeepers. In the City were the miller, the baker, the hawker, the boot and shoe maker, the clog maker, lime burner, carpenter, slater, blacksmith, and nurse and schoolmistress. There were fifteen classical scholars in the Cathedral School, and canons and vicars choral in the Close, and very few professional people.

Each return sheet included one specific demand: the instruction to notify any temporary influx or temporary departure that had affected the returns in each and every area. Each sheet carried a blank or nil return. And yet, between 1712, Browne Willis's year, and 1801, the year of the first census in Britain, there had been an increase of nearly 600.

According to the 1851 census (the peak population year), a family of husband and wife and three daughters lived in Clegyr Farm. They were helped by one female servant and two farm labourers. Upper Clegyr had husband and wife, one son and three daughters, two farm labourers and one female servant. It was these extraordinary opening entries that led one to disregard the 'town' element in the census and concentrate entirely on the 'country', the farms, small holdings, and cottages.

According to the Royal Commission on Agriculture, Wales, which reported in 1881, four out of five of Pembrokeshire farms were under 50 acres, small holdings (in modern terms) farmed by husband and wife and children. In other words, they were family subsistence farms. Some were large, many were twenty to thirty acres, some as small as eight. They all had their quota of servants or labourers. In Penlan, husband and wife, two sisters and a nephew, farmed 260 acres with the help of four male and three female servants. Penarthur had husband and wife, two sons and two daughters, and five servants. Hendre had five servants. Husband and wife farmed Harglodd, 175 acres, with four sons and two daughters, and five servants, two of whom were farm labourers. In Lower Treginnis a widowed husband had six servants, two of whom were female house servants. Husband and wife in Pencarnan, with two children, had two servants and two 'visitors' to farm 57 acres. And Llaethty, with husband and wife and two sons and a daughter, had six servants to farm sixty acres. And Ty Gwyn, 14 acres, had husband and wife, three sons and a daughter, and one servant.

In Penpant lived a sailor's wife and three daughters; in Nine Wells, a labourer's wife, a wool spinner, who had one daughter; in Fachelich, one female pauper and three sons; in Nine Wells – a husband and wife, two sons, a male servant and three female servants, one acting as nurse: the husband superannuated from the Coastguard Service. Again in Nine Wells, husband and wife, a carpenter son, a schoolmistress daughter, one daughter doing domestic work, one son at school: the father a superannuated Inland Revenue Officer. Families of rich and poor, landed or otherwise, were large, and most had servants.

Professor David Williams in *The Rebecca Riots* gives no reason for this population explosion that had affected both England and Wales, except to say that it was a general and natural growth, naturally linked with the other social conditions of the time. More people were getting married, and more were getting married younger. Many, it has been said, were encouraged to do both and to have larger families because after 1800 the introduction of potatoes made it possible to feed larger families without any increase in cost. In the wisdom of hindsight, the *neithior* has been blamed, the growing custom of giving presents to young married couples encouraging a false sense of ownership and security. Even the Methodist Revival has been blamed. Fear of death and fear of hell have at other times in human history driven people to excesses, but the defenders of Welsh morality against the accusations of the *Blue Books* may well have been driven to anger at seeing that early marriage and too large families and promiscuity were being laid at the door of religious enthusiasm, and the extra opportunity for sexual fraternisation that followed the introduction of the evening service.

Other factors were involved in this growth, as the census returns for St. David's prove. Families became large in the 'Italian' sense – sons and daughters as part of the labour force; in-laws, grand-children, nephews and nieces, wife and children of a son, grand-parents, all swelled the composite hearth. Many older people obviously had come back to their native heath: superannuated coastguardsmen, a pensioner of the Royal Artillery, customs men, some undoubtedly coming home now that Waterloo had gone and the French wars had come to an end. There was also a frequent and cryptic mention of 'visitors' and 'lodgers', who may or may not have been genuine members of the family. Samuel Williams's report on education, looking back from 1871, hinted that there had been an influx of strangers to the parish and town 'during the last six years.'

The aftermath of war was not a time of agricultural prosperity. It is difficult to explain how now or at any other time there was justification for the presence of two labourers on small farms of fifty or twenty or fewer acres. It is clear also that these servants came from far afield – Middlesex, Carmarthen, Machynlleth, Meidrym, Scarborough, Letterston, as their census entries show. Labour, beyond doubt, was cheap and plentiful. And precarious. How many found themselves ultimately bound up in troubles of settlement and examinations for removal? Was St. David's again being turned into a sanctuary for the poor and for the deprived? There were folk in plenty, paupers and widows, not a few widows of seamen: the baptismal registers of 1814 showed that 14 out of 43 fathers of that year were seamen. Women worked hard on the land. The births registers of the early 1800s reveal a large number of what were (unintentionally) called labouring women, more than a few centred on Porth Glais. They tackled all the arduous work on the farm; and they were involved in a large number of irregular births.

The 1851 census showed no great change, and no reduction, in the range of occupations: mason, lathcutter, washerwoman, miller and miller's boy, blacksmith, thatcher, clogmaker, molecatcher, the spinner and the knitter, quilt maker, carrier, mariners and fishermen, and all the other basic craftsmen. Ebenezer Williams was druggist. Thomas Lewis was cloth-factor, and his wife, Mary Lewis, woollen spinner. There was a servant in husbandry, a nice convolution. William Morris, Mount Pleasant, was Methodist minister, Isaac Jenkins the Wesleyan. Martha Griffiths and Mary Appleby were school marms. There were many retired mariners. And in the Close, besides the clerics, there were groom and cook, agent, housemaids, shoemaker, doctor and tailor.

The immediate result of an expanded population was an overstrained economy. During the Napoleonic Wars agriculture was prosperous. Immediately after Waterloo came decline and depression, and the larger population, which the operation of the Poor Law helped. Lord Ernle's *English Farming Past and Present* instances the case of a woman in Swaffham, Norfolk – a long way from St.

David's, but we have seen how fast and far things travelled – who had five bastard children. As a consequence she received from the parish a weekly allowance of 18s, considerably more than the wages upon which a respectable married farm labourer was expected to keep his wife and family. Later, after the 1870s, the Green Revolution began, sales of land and farms increased in number, tenants bid for their holdings, and – after a succession of wet seasons and hard winters of which 'Black '79' was the worst – agriculture began to return to some prosperity but with a much reduced labour force. J. Howard Griffiths, county councillor and alderman of later years, sent his report on the agricultural labourer to the Lleufer Thomas Royal Commission on Labour, and gave the impression that the great post-1851 fall in population was partly due to the moving away of agricultural labourers, itself due to the agricultural depression. The number of married labourers living in their own cottages, he said, had greatly diminished; the younger population made for the industrial areas, tempted by higher wages. The 1861 census had declared that the decrease in population in Brawdy, Whitchurch, Mathry and the Cylch Mawr division had been mainly attributed to the removal of persons to the mining areas. A footnote in the 1871 Census Report said that 'The general decrease of population in the sub-district of St. David's is attributed to the introduction of machinery for agricultural purposes, which lessens the demand for manual labour.' And little items of news in the local papers prove the point. The *Haverfordwest and Milford Haven Times* in 1860 referred to the introduction of the reaping machine into the county. The *Western Telegraph* of August 1878 mentioned an interesting trial of one of Messrs. Hornby's reaping machines at Fenton. *The Dewisland and Kemes Guardian* of 14 June 1879, advertised a 'Mowing Machine for sale. Excellent condition, new last year. Apply Mrs Rees, City Hotel.' In September W. W. Beynon of Harglodd announced that he had a one horse power threshing machine for sale. And in June 1879 a *Dewisland and Kemes Guardian* advertisement announced that H. Phillips of Cwmwdig was prepared to cut hay with his machinery, at prices not exceeding 2/3d per acre.

Migration overseas had been in the news for some time. In 1729, in the earlier days of dissent when people emigrated to allow their conscience to breathe in freedom, a group of Pembrokeshire landowners organised a petition against what they called a very pernicious practice carried on by wicked and designing persons (this is almost verbatim from the petition, which is printed in full in Francis Jones's *Dissent and Dissatisfaction in Pembrokeshire*) to delude great numbers of ignorant inhabitants to migrate to 'Pensilvania'. The result was that the farmers of Pembrokeshire were hard pressed to find labour for harvesting time. Samuel Harries of Cruglas was one of the signatories. Economic difficulties, famine, depression and an insistence on human rights had driven Morgan John Rees to establish the Welsh colony in Philadelphia in 1798, and Samuel Roberts and his brother to try to establish the Tennessee settlement in 1856 and 1857, and Michael D. Jones and Lewis Jones to establish the Welsh colony in Patagonia in 1865.

No emigrant to Patagonia lived nearer to St. David's than Aberystwyth, and someone living in the quiet seclusion of Cylch Mawr might well never have heard of Patagonia or any other emigration target overseas. They might have heard that a daughter of Michael Raymond of Solva and Trecadwgan, shipowner and merchant, had married one of the Williamses of Llandigige, and that from that family came some of the migrants who made their way and their name in Jamaica and the United States, and linked themselves with the history of New York, Maryland, and Cornell University. They would hardly have missed the news that John Perkin (born in Llanfirn in 1812) emigrated on the *Wave* to Tasmania in 1838, and that another John Perkins, son of William Perkins, who was born in Hendrewen, near Fishguard, emigrated also to Tasmania in 1860. There is no doubt at all, if they were readers of the *Pembrokeshire Herald*, that they would have read the signs, and the advertisement in that paper on 26 December 1851:

> From St. David's to Quebec Direct
>
> To leave St. David's direct for Quebec, the first week in April, that fast sailing copper bottomed Brigantine *Talent*, Captain Prosser (provided a sufficient number of passengers can be obtained).
>
> for particulars Samuel Williams
Rock House, St. David's.

Rock House, incidentally, was the present-day Y Fagwr, built, according to Francis Green, by George Williams the merchant. And if those who were tempted to seek this far-flung freedom were not sufficiently assured that the *Talent* was a fast and copper-bottomed safe boat, there was the extra confidence that the man in command was Thomas Prosser of Nine Wells.

Two years earlier the prospective migrant would have seen an advertisement of passenger berths from Solva to New York: adult fare £3, under 14, 25/- and infants free. Obviously, some individuals and families migrated. The total we do not know. *The Pembrokeshire Herald* of January 1901 reported that migration from the county to Canada was heavier than 'in any previous year.' Chapel registers indicate migrations in small numbers between 1885 and 1910, but there is no evidence that any religious pressure compelled them to migrate. There is, however, proof that men of religion persuaded migration. The 1729 petition of the landowners against migratory movements to Pennsylvania had used the phrase 'pernicious practices'. Three years before the Captain Prosser advertisement a certain John Griffiths of Solva, afterwards of Llandovery, visited various neighbourhoods lecturing on the desirability of emigrating as a remedy for the growth in population and as an escape from the poverty of the small farm. It was a good text: the Welsh emigrated because they wanted a better life than was possible in an impoverished Wales, they disliked the Establishment, they yearned for freedom, they wanted a society of equals (*y gymdeithas gyfartal*); they were against king and church and tithes, they saw before them *Y Baradwys Bell*, the paradise on the far horizon, the land of promise. This was the urge that drove the Baptists to look towards America in the eighteenth century.

From 1850 on to the years of the First World War the population of the parish declined steadily, and most of the documentary evidence indicates that they moved, some overseas, but many more to industrial South Wales, and out of agriculture. The 1891 *Western Mail* reports on agriculture in Pembrokeshire suggested that farming now depended on old men and young boys. People recollected that during the Trevacoon sales farming actually meant a mere holding on. Yet from 1870 onwards St. David's, the City, was getting busier, rebuilding itself, and preparing for an obviously impending spate of tourism. The Directories prove the point.

The 1864 Rate Book tells us that every house in the parish, with the exception of four, had its garden, its little bit of land. There were eight shops only, occupied by Phillip Bowen, John Owens, Mrs A. Hicks, Thomas Davies, Thomas Hughes, William Jackson, Henry Rees and George Owen. But there were one hundred farms. Highest rated was the windmill at Twr y Felin; with its land it paid £14.10s. There were four stores, two occupied by William Williams of the Commercial, the others by William Davies, Rhosson, and William Jackson. Amongst them must have been two at least of the granary stores, still standing, of the golden age of the City.

From 1860 onwards was the time of building and rebuilding, chapels, schools, the Old Town Hall, churches. Almost all the dwelling houses of the City have been built or rebuilt since the middle of the last century. The 'Garth' of New Street is taken to belong to the seventeenth century, the solitary house of Speed's Map of the area, perhaps the 'long house' of the *Black Book*. The little cottage on the Square, now part of Cartref restaurant, has 1778 scratched on its pavement wall. 'Journey's End' in Nun Street, the home of the Moriartys, according to its date-stone was built by one of the Perkinses in 1788. The granary at the top of Deanery Hill carries the date 1758. And in the wall in the telephone kiosk inside the Old Cross Hotel, a wall that was once obviously an outside wall, is a date stone bearing the date 1766. Gwalia, on the Square, is now made up of three elements. The old building which is now the Boutique is part of the old thatched St. David's, one of the old buildings (visible in some photographs) that once lined the north side of the Pebbles. The shop area on the corner was built between Tithe Map year 1840 and 1857, when it was leased by George Jordan Harries of Priskilly to William Williams of the Grove and was in the occupation of William Williams and Henry Davies, master mariner. In 1876 it was leased from William Williams draper and general shopkeeper to William Davies Williams draper. What until recently was the dwelling house (now the right hand area of the shop) was older. The same sources of information that tell us of the three ages of this building also tell us that Glendower, with which Absalom the carpenter of Mount Gardens was involved, was built about 1877. Samuel Williams's letter books and papers indicate a considerable rebuilding in the 1870s, a filling in of gaps in the streets, the building of 'our Terrace', and of a house being pulled down in Nun Street and three houses built on the site by Captain John Davies. In his notes are also details for the erection of a stable, a straw-house and a cowhouse in Penlan, in 1863.

When Samuel Williams checked on the electoral roll about 1870 he made note of two builders of St. David's. One was John James of Pit Street. The other was James Stephens, who was born in 1828. His life coincided with the days when the old thatched cottages of St. David's were being replaced by the houses we know today. He built Goodwood, Emlych House, and Trevithan House in High Street, and rebuilt many of the farms. Between 1874 and 1877 he built Tabernacle Chapel. From 1846 onwards he rebuilt many of the bridges of the parish, although he was too late to carry out the orders of the Easter Quarter Sessions of 1834 – which ordered the rebuilding of the ancient bridge called 'Pont Kirwin Dowy' (the Merrivale Bridge) which had been 'almost entirely washed away about three months since by the floods.'

The other prominent builder of the time was Thomas Evans of Solva. As the local papers reported, he was the restorer of Seion Baptist Chapel in 1873, and built Capel y Cwm in Solva. In 1902 he built the original stone structure of the County School to which are attached the extensions of the last twenty five years.

There were others in the City who built houses or who ordered them to be built. They were the master mariners, the sea captains whose history has been so sadly neglected. They were men of character and distinction, and the houses they built have an equally distinctive personality – Lawn Villa in New Street, the Methodist Manse which was known as Arfon Villa in Peter's Lane, New Cross, across the road from 'The Beehive', the 'Stone House' of the novel, 'The Captain's Wife', and Glan-y-Môr, and Belmont on the Square.

Slater's Directory of 1880 is the best possible indicator of the growth of St. David's in these years. Trade was on the increase, houses and hotels were being built, the boats of Porth Glais were busy. And there was a very great increase in the numbers of its craftsmen. There were five blacksmiths in the City, three in Solva, one in each of Rhodiad, Waunbeddau and Fronwen; five carpenters, one in Skyfog and Penybont, and three in Rhodiad; four ironmongers; six stone masons, three wheelwrights, three painters and glaziers. Samuel Williams's account books show that slates and lime were being brought in through Porth Glais for this building work, and that some of the lime was used for whitewashing. Surprisingly, in 1876, thatch was being delivered for work on Park House in Solva, and wages paid to John Morgan the thatcher. There were two millers in St. David's, one in each of Middle Mill, Rhodiad, Dewston, Caerforiog and Caerbwdi; six boot and shoe makers; fifteen grocers and drapers and sellers of sundries; six milliners and tailors; and four butter merchants. William Williams was Postmaster, and deputy agent for Lloyds. James J. R. Nash was agent of the Bristol Traders, and George Owen Williams represented Manby's Apparatus for Wrecks. Albert David was the chemist, and Samuel Foley was the only doctor. Alliance, Provident Life, Provincial, Queen's, and Shipwrecked Fishermen and Mariners Benevolent were all represented by agents. There was one solicitor.

Traditionally and historically the blacksmith, maker of arms, was regarded as the most important of craftsmen, although according to the *Black Book* the best paid and senior craftsman of that time was Master John the carpenter. Francis Cornock (according to the 1870 Rate Book) had his forge on Cross Square, and his house and garden belonged to the Minor Canons. William Harries was in Waunbeddau; Henry Jenkins in Solva, and David Morris and Daniel Phillips; Ebenezer Rees was on Rhodiad Bridge; William Reed in Fronwen; and in addition there were David Johns and Henry Prees (Preece). In March 1889 John Roach of Priskilly Terrace advertised in the *Dewisland and Kemes Guardian* – To let, with immediate possession, a conveniently situated Smithy, established over sixty years, and formerly occupied by the late Mr William Roach. All the necessary tools, with 4 fixed anvils, are on the premises. Henry Roberts is mentioned in the 1906 *Directory*. He worked with Francis

Cornock on the Square. Was he, one wonders, related to another Roberts, a George Roberts whose name is in the Cathedral Burial Register for 1760? Alongside his name had been entered the phrase 'An ingenious blacksmith'.

These craftsmen – their number is sufficient proof of their importance in their time – deserve the few lines it takes to list and name them. They were the builders and rebuilders; and they belonged to families of craftsmen some of whom are still practising today. Here are the carpenters and joiners:

Thomas Evans, Solva; William Evans, Croesgoch; Thomas Hughes; William James, Skyfog; John Jenkins, Penybont; Francis John, Solva; James and Joseph Lloyd, Solva; William Lloyd, Upper Solva; Ebenezer Owen, Rhodiad; George Propert, with whom David Evans of Felin Wynt served his apprenticeship; James Raymond, Rhodiad; and James Rowlands and Benjamin Thomas.

Amongst the millers were David Evans, St. David's; Henry Griffiths, Middle Mill; John Harries, Rhodiad; Richard John, Caerforiog; John Owen, Dewston; Abram Rees, Caerbwdi; and John Williams of Solva.

The following were listed, curiously, as 'miscellaneous':

Assistant Overseer – William Perkins, Nun Street.
Bailiff of the Court Leet – John Phillips of Cross Square.
Deputy Steward of the Manor – John Harvey and Sons, Haverfordwest.
Medical Officer of Health and Public Vaccinator – Samuel Foley.
Registrar of Births and Deaths – John Phillips, Cross Square.
Town Crier – Lewis Lewis, Catherine Street.
Auctioneer – Wilkin Beynon.
Tidewaiter – Charles Brown.
Maltster – William Williams.
Lodgings – Ann Cornock.
Carding Mill – Benjamin Price.
Saddler – Isaac Evans, High Street.
Printer – Martha Williams, Solva.
Hotels – The City, The Grove, Prospect.

A combination of all these things – the variety and totals of craftsmen; the story of trade in Porth Glais; the numbers of captains and mariners; the building activities; the growth of tourism and the response in accommodation to meet it; William Williams's references to the gentry and the hunters after antiquity and the commercial gentlemen who stayed at Grove Hotel – in total they amount to trade and commerce and, of necessity, transfers of money. The first Bank had come to St. David's.

The original drovers' banks had been active in West Wales since the beginning of the nineteenth century. 'Bank y Llong' is said to have started in Aberystwyth about 1762. One of its partners, David Davies of Machynlleth, married Blanch Maria, daughter of one of the Rogers family of Carnachenwen, and retired to Carnachenwen to live. A Wilkin and a Beynon were married in Llanrhian Church in the mid-1700s, and that established the reputed link between the local family and that of the bank (Wilkins and Co.) that was established in Brecon in 1778. But the first bank to come to St. David's was the one most closely connected with the farming community. In 1891 Lloyds Bank opened, with Henry Owen as agent. He was followed as agent by John Morgan Williams, who lived in Spring Gardens, before Lloyds opened permanently in their present premises on the site of 'The Black Lion' on Cross Square. In 1890, before the official establishment in St. David's, Lloyds, which established a reputation for absorbing financial businesses in the nineteenth century (48 banks in 49 years), had also bought the Old Brecon Bank of the Wilkin family.

By 1906 the London and Provincial Bank Limited, manager A. J. Wright, had also opened on Cross Square. Barclays took it over in 1918, and opened on a daily basis on 1 December 1927. Midland was the third bank to come into the city. It started in its present day premises in July 1929, with a clerk in charge and a junior.

Commercial growth did not in any way affect the predominance of agriculture in the parish. Ninety-five men and women registered themselves as farmers in *Kelly's Directory* of 1906. What was surprising was the number of women, and of spinsters, who were registered as being in charge of farms. Some conceivably were widows, or the wives of men who were following the two-job tradition. Some years earlier the Solva 'local' had indicated that a large number of people were selling milk in St. David's. 'Judging from the number of people who now sell milk here,' it said, 'we think it must be a very profitable trade. We also think that it is time that the Inspector under the Food and Drugs Act should pay us an unexpected visit.' Dairy farming was economical from the labour point of view. Three persons designated themselves 'cowkeepers' in the 1906 Directory. Presumably they tended animals grazing the hedges and roadsides. Captain Davies of Nun Street took his herd out grazing on the Fishguard road, along the Glasfryn Lane, and on to fields on the Haverfordwest road. In one herd of fifty, it was not unusual to find the leaders – Willie Morris's herd from New Street, for instance – arriving home before the stragglers had left the field. It was a trafficless world, and the farmer's cowhouse was on the City street.

'Tidewaiter' was no less an unusual term than 'cowkeeper'. The tidewaiter of the Directory waited for and checked on ships coming into Porth Glais. He was Charles Brown, the excise officer from Solva.

On that note we conclude an imperfect and fragmentary description of what may be called the permanent and basic population of City and parish. But remote as the place is and quiet and peaceful as has been its later history, it has always been subject to intermittent invasion. The Irish have always come, tribe, raiding party, priest, from pre-Christian times and during the Age of the Saints; they came much later in fear-raising gangs when the Potato famine in Ireland was at its worst; they came in gangs to work on the reconstruction and restoration of the Cathedral; they still come. In these days the early potato industry demands seasonal and imported labour, and whole families make their annual trip across, and establish their little settlements of cars and vans and caravans on the potato farms.

From early Christian days the pilgrims came. The Reformation put an end to two of the greatest features of medieval Christianity, the worship of relics and the kindred cult of pilgrimage. The old Celtic Saints believed that it was good and godly to go on pilgrimage to holy places. The Normans made St. David's one of the great fanes of Christendom – and medieval belief made pilgrimage and the veneration of relics a protection against the terrors of hell and damnation, of physical and spiritual sickness. Pope Calixtus II bracketed St. David's with Rome and Jerusalem, and St. David's became famous when the Turks occupied Jerusalem and made it inaccessible. Hence the couplet:

> Dos i Rufain unwaith ac i Fynyw ddwywaith
> Ac un elw cryno a gei di yma ac yno.
> [Go to Rome once and to St. David's twice,
> And here and there you'll get the same reward.]

And so it carried on. It took the mock-heroic ribaldry of Iolo Morganwg to put it all in its post-Reformation perspective:

> Would haughty Popes your senses bubble,
> And once to Rome your steps entice,
> 'Tis quite as well, and saves some trouble,
> Go visit old St. Taffy twice.

They did. It was not an easy journey to St. David's, any more or less than it was by land and sea to other places. Bishop Adam Houghton in 1385 tried to protect his pilgrims by issuing a proclamation:

> I take all pilgrims into my special protection, and especially enjoin my officers not to permit them to suffer any molestation, damage or insult, and, if they should suffer any annoyance, satisfaction shall be made to them for it without delay.

They came, nevertheless, to see the shrine of St. David. Here also was, ironically, a chapel dedicated to St. Thomas a'Becket, the man who had given his life to defend the rights of the English Church and who had been responsible for the subjection of the Welsh Church to Canterbury. Whatever the irony, the presence of the Chapel of St. Thomas in our Cathedral must have been of great symbolic significance, and profitable. Tens of thousands flocked to Canterbury, amongst them Gerald the Welshman. How many came to St. David's, and how many passed through St. David's from Ireland on their way to the even more popular shrine of St. James of Compostella, we do not know. There was no Chaucer in St. David's. Even if there is neither detail nor description, we are told, and told again, of its medieval greatness as a place of pilgrimage. The hospitals on the way, and the Bishop's Palace itself, are our only proof of the mass invasions of the pilgrimages.

Medieval Kings and Queens made occasional visits. William the Conqueror in 1081, Henry II in 1171, Edward I and Queen Eleanor in 1282. Pilgrims and prelates naturally followed them. Archbishop Baldwin was the first primate of Canterbury to come. Bishop Vaughan, last of the builder bishops, could sit in his own Chapel and see and hear around him five masses being performed at five different altars. Then came the Reformation and the place stayed pilgrimless, beautiful and overgrown with weeds and ivy, till Connop Thirlwall and Gilbert Scott began the great restoration. That also began another and modern invasion – the age of the pilgrim-tourist had begun.

Before passing on to a description of this phase we must record that so great was the fame of St. David's and so deeply involved in the Christian tradition in these islands in the past that Royal personages and church dignitaries from home and overseas continued to be frequent visitors to the Cathedral. On 7 August 1955, Queen Elizabeth II and the Duke of Edinburgh attended morning service at the Cathedral, the first royal pilgrims since Henry II, and, said the programme, 'for the first time since the Stall was assigned to the reigning monarch it was occupied by its rightful owner'. This is the first prebendal stall in the Choir, which, uniquely to St. David's, belongs to the reigning monarch. Three explanations have been offered for the fact that it carries the Royal Arms: that Adam Houghton, made Lord Chancellor by Richard II, offered it to the king in gratitude; that the Master of St. Mary's College, whose stall it originally was, offered it to Henry VIII during the dissolution of the monasteries, thinking that it might help to keep the king's hands off the College; and, thirdly, that when Edward VI closed the College the prebend naturally went back to the Crown.

On 3 July 1969, a service of dedication in the Cathedral followed the Investiture of the Prince of Wales at Caernarfon Castle. The Prince himself attended. There is a legend that another Prince, the newly-crowned Edward VII, also visited the Cathedral, incognito, and sat on the royal stall, and then slipped away. That was in August 1902, when the royal yacht, on its way to the Isle of Man, anchored in Milford Haven.

On 14 July 1925, there was a massive pilgrimage when the Eastern Orthodox as well as the Western Church joined in. It was held to celebrate the sixteen hundredth anniversary of the Council of Nicaea and the acceptance by all Christians of the Nicene Creed. The patriarchs of Alexandria and Jerusalem were here together with the Archdeacon of Jordan and the Archbishop and Bishops of Wales. The Celtic Church in the sixth and seventh centuries, it was said in that service, was the daughter of the Church of Gaul, which itself derived its inspiration from Ephesus. Modern research has moved even further and can show that there was constant connection between Celtic Britain and the Eastern Mediterranean lands in the days of the Celtic Church – a contact most clearly shown in the way the Celtic Saints, including St. David, adopted the monastic traditions of the Early Fathers of the Egyptian Desert.

Before this section on pilgrimage is concluded, we must note that following the last stages of the restoration of the Cathedral there has been mass pilgrimage on very modern lines and with very modern transport. In July 1963, the ecclesiastical authorities made a unanimous decision to begin the restoration of the last remaining unroofed section of the Cathedral and its ancillaries: the restoration of the original Chapel of St. Mary's College. The restored Chapel, it was felt, would fill the need of a hall for parochial, Cathedral and diocesan purposes. What persuaded Dean and Chapter and the Society of Friends of the Cathedral to adopt this aim was made clear in the words used in their thirty-third Annual Report. St. David's Cathedral, said Dean Jenkins (it all happened in his time) is becoming once again, as it was in medieval times, a centre of pilgrimage. In June 1966 the new St. Mary's Hall was officially opened by Archbishop Morris as a most impressive meeting-place for pilgrims. In 1976 came 'Sunrise', a pilgrimage, and services in the Cathedral which included representatives and clergy of every parish in Wales, and the archbishop and the four bishops. Five hundred, on the eve of the Saturday, walked their way from Llanrhian along the old pilgrim road to the cathedral which John Speed had called 'a nursery to holy men.' In 1977 came 'Dayspring', when one and a quarter thousand turned up of all denominations from home and abroad, including eighty from Ireland to keep alive the old historic contact. They came because St. David's as a place of pilgrimage was established in the days of early Christianity.

The great tourist expansion of modern times is the last and most recent of invasions. As far back as 1871 the *Dewisland and Kemes Guardian* had been in the habit of printing lists of names of notables who had spent a summer holiday in St. David's. 'The ancient city has been well patronised . . . all seemed to be highly delighted. The Cathedral which is in course of restoration is the great attraction and in another 18 months or so, we shall expect to see this magnificent old building completely restored to its ancient and original grandeur.' And then, 'after having the long talked-of railway to the City, no doubt hundreds more will avail themselves . . .' There was severe criticism of lack of proper lodging houses, and worse criticism of the journey from Haverfordwest in 'that antiquated machine called a Bus', and very severe criticism of the treatment of horses. But it went on to announce that Mr James Davies of the Commercial had determined to speculate and open Brynygarn (the present Warpool Court) for visitors, and Captain John Rees's 'New and attractive Hotel, the City, will be open shortly.'

Travers J. Bryant's *Guide to St. David's Cathedral*, published in 1896, shows how people responded to the new possibilities. Miss Evans of The Windmill, Mrs Sime of Maldwyn House (now the Beehive), John Martin of The City, William Williams of the Grove, all advertised in the glossiest of terms. So did Mrs Cornock of Glasfryn. William Williams offered splendid autumn and winter shooting rights of over two thousand acres. When the Williamses were gone, Edward P. Mathias presided over the Grove. He baited his line with many hooks, as the G. W. R. Holiday Guide showed:

> The portals of the Grove, embowered in a clump of beech, sycamore, elms, ash and evergreen oaks . . . is well and favourably known to antiquaries and ecclesiologists, nor is it less favourably known by the ardent golfer or the enthusiastic sportsman in search of wild geese and ducks, woodcock, widgeon, snipe and golden plover. 'Mine host' is himself a dead shot, but he is also an astute collector of the curios which abound in the neighbourhood of the 'village city'.

The Cross House which is now Menai was a private hotel between 1887 and 1898, run by George Owen Williams and his wife and later by their daughter, Esther Sime. The hotel visitors' book for those years reveals the kind of people that holidayed in St. David's in those days: clerics and visitors from overseas (the Bishop of Pretoria was one); Royal Navy men, concerned with the Lifeboat; business people; the de Wintons and the Yorks of Langton, and the Wills family of Bristol; academics, men of the universities, Coolidge of Magdalen, Oxford, Parry of Aberystwyth, and O. M. Edwards of Lincoln College, Oxford, who delighted in the people, the place, and the flowers. The few lines he wrote delicately into the visitors' book ended with his greatest delight – he had seen, by the south wall of the Cathedral Yard, midway between Thirty Nine Steps and the Deanery, the grave of William Morris.

In 1896 Tŵr y Felin was still a windmill, one of three at one time in the parish. It is said that it was built in 1806 by the two Llewellyn brothers of Ty Gwyn, then passed into the hands of George Williams, and to 'Tommy' Williams, who built the dwelling house (Y Felin Wynt) nearby. In 1861 David Evans of Ty Gwyn bought it. A hundred and one years from its erection, after many mishaps, and after grinding corn till 1904, it was converted by Evan R. Evans into the landmark that it is today, the Tŵr y Felin Hotel. The hotels of St. David's (apart from those built in very recent years) were now established. They were not alone. The ordinary people also responded to the demands of this modern age; in the Directory of 1906 it was already evident that they were prepared to enter the trade. Then and henceforward there was to be a swelling list of 'Apartments to Let'.

'And so,' said Francis Kilvert, 'we come to the end of the world where the Patron Saint of Wales sleeps by the Western Sea'. To the enchanted land of the Mabinogion, to the 'gwlad hud a lledrith' of Pwyll Pendefig Dyfed. For one third of the year they come, these modern pilgrims, not in their hundreds as the *Guardian* of 1871 suggested, but in their tens of thousands. They present problems. One that faces many other parts of the country is that of preservation against thousands of tramping feet. There are physical problems of roads and parking places and accommodation, of roads in particular. The railway never came. Now it is the problem of car and caravan, the Cleddau Bridge, the Severn Bridge and the motorway. The greatest problem of all is not any more a problem of material things. Pilgrimage meant and means prosperity. The problem is now the preservation and conservation, in face of material prosperity, of the character of the place. This country, said *The Captain's Wife*, casts a spell on strangers. Hopefully some of that enchantment will remain. Two of its old elements we can neglect, or proceed to lose, to our cost. Walk the pathways of gorse and heather, look at rock and sea and island below Treginnis. Walk the old folkways around Treleddid or Tretio or Drws Gobaith. Walk into the Cathedral and altarwards into the finest perspective in all England and Wales, and around the ruins of the Palace or anywhere in the Close, and you will meet them. They will, if you let them, enfist and hold you. They are, in the first place, a sense of peace, clean-aired peace; and then, the redolence of age and sanctity. If the lovers of St. David's do anything that will let those go by, then all will be lost.

CHAPTER TEN

Chronicles and Chroniclers

One of George Ewart Evans's most delightful books on the rural life and customs of Suffolk is *Ask the Fellows Who Cut the Hay*. The title is a line from a verse translation by Ezra Pound, given in full in the book, together with a quotation from an eighteenth-century tract:

> We old men are old chronicles, and when our tongues go they are not clocks to tell only the time present, but large books unclasped; and our speeches, like leaves turned over and over, discover wonders that are long since past.

This is 'oral history', picked from the mouths of old characters, reminiscences and memories recorded, parchments of the spoken word, as valuable and authentic as any history found in document or book. Its basis, of course, is the art of asking questions, reminiscent of *Domesday* and the *Black Book*. Much can be lost through not asking questions (and not making records) as many in St. David's are prepared to confess, and the time for asking questions is always today. Tomorrow is too late. It is impossible to say what has been lost because those questions were not asked of Phillip Owen of Prospect House, who farmed Llanferran; or Sidney Mortimer, who knew the coast and all its tricks like the back of his hand, and whose family for two hundred years farmed Treginnis; or Ernest Martin of Trehenlliw or John Beynon of Penlan; or James Williams, carpenter humorist of 'The Beehive'; or Samuel Williams, whose son played the organ in Tabernacle; or Evan Evans, who drew the map, or Henry Evans, his brother, who compiled the *Twr y Felin Guide*; or W. D. Williams of Gwalia. Or, to go back still further, John Phillips, who with his grandfather totalled a century as Parish Clerks; or James Griffiths of Llanferran or Thomas Mortimer of Trewellwell, the farmer preachers; or the old deans of the Cathedral; or the strangely unrecorded sea captains and mariners, whose tales livened the shop in High Street of the other James Williams, the barber who sold boots.

Or the tough seventeenth century bachelor, Thomas Johnes, who gave two of his 'ambling mares' to Gilbert and Richard Johnes; and twenty lambs, in the custody of Hugh Harries, to another four of the Johnes; and three legacies which in effect were moneys owed to him; and ended up by giving all his household stuff and all 'that is lying in Llanungar haggards, and £10 in lieu of all the thirds of my land' to Mary Green, his 'bedfellow'. The wife could, 'according to the laudable habit of the country', claim one third of her husband's goods, and George Owen once deplored the fact that the custom was lapsing, but, confident of the capabilities of Welsh women, he suggested that they studied the law to defend their common cause, 'wherein I think that they were like to profit, for that there are of them many ripe wits, and all ready tongues.' Land was important, in St. David's of all places; and women were influential in the disposing of it.

The old Charles Dickens shops of St. David's – Gwalia in the days of the Davies Williams sisters; the ironmongery shop in Goat Street, with the Roberts brothers – are now changed out of all recognition. They belonged to a more leisurely age, gloriously confused in their wares, places where there was time for lovable idiosyncracy, and conversation and humour. In High Street was the barber's shop of James Williams, the old seaman. Here gathered the schoolmaster, Appleton; the sea captains, the two Roberts brothers of Epworth House, Captains Roach and Morse; sometimes Francis Green, solicitor antiquarian of Glanymor; J. J. Jenkins of the Board School, once of Carnhedryn; Captain Beer, father of Sidney Beer; Calder, coastguard and caretaker of the City Hall; and the minister, James Abel, gifted with the gentle art of provoking others to argument. And William Lewis of Goat Street, who once farmed Pencarnan, and who told wondrous tales of seals, and told them so often that he ended up by believing them. Into this gathering also came sometimes Walter Jones, the blacksmith of Nun Street, last 'elected mayor' of St. David's. And on the Square was James Rowlands, carpenter, teacher of navigation, a strong swimmer who hated boats. He collected the rates, and walked all the way to Haverfordwest to deliver them.

There were doctors, Williams, Lewis, Elliott. And chemists. Martin Hughes of Court House was the first; in the eighteen eighties he advertised sales of wines and spirits. Then came Albert David, small, dapper, a fine tennis player on the City's grass courts where the 'Hafan' is now and where Wimbledon stars played in the summer. After Albert David, for a brief spell, came Evans, whose widow became Post Mistress. And then the Menduses, John and Morris. Both were men of character and dignity, knowledgeable in local history, and Morris was a photographer whose work remains a standard documentary of Cathedral and parish.

There were other and stranger characters, the unsophisticated eccentrics of this tapestry. Lewis Williams, Lewsin Tinker of Town

Hall Lane (known also as Pwt's Lane or Tinker's Lane or Edmund Lane), was a professional rat catcher, who twice a year went to Ramsey to catch the rats that were major characters in Ivor Arnold's diary. Peggy Williams, Peggy Pwt, was the fortune teller who lived near Clegyrfwya Bridge. Those who have read *The Captain's Wife* will remember the death of Philip, the son of Lettice Peters. Among those who called at Lettice's back door to pay their respects was Peggy Pwt, in 'her jaunty clothes and soiled beauty'. William Miles, the illiterate ploughman, was a water diviner and expert on weather signs. The two sisters, Mally Dac and Mari Dac, herbalists, lived on Merrivale Hill; many of their customers were too poor to pay; some suffered ailments that were too private to divulge. Martha Fortune, a fiery Liberal in days when Liberalism was predominant in St. David's, was cleaner of the Board School. And Jane Elizabeth Stephens of Rhosson Terrace, acting solicitor for the illiterate poor, read their letters and answered them, 2d for those who could afford, nothing to the poor. Strangest of all was John Richards (John y Ffarm) who lived in one room at the back of premises where Isaac Evans had been saddler. A rough craggy bachelor, he spoke in the flaming tongue of Biblical prophets; and always carried a tall stick and wore a peaked sailor's cap. During service in Tabernacle the peaked cap perched on the tall stick in the corner of the pew.

Talfryn James, pupil of Thomas Thomas and Miss Green, graduate of Aberystwyth, spent most of his life in the United States, and his 'old chronicles' were letters from retirement in Florida. As in John Miles Thomas's *Looking Back*, printed posthumously in 1978, what was remembered was a boyhood in the very different St. David's of the turn of the century: the excitement when the lifeboat rocket was fired from a field 'back of High Street'; the arrival every Saturday morning of the lorry from Haverfordwest with supplies for the City's stores; the arrival of the mail coach; Spackman's butcher's shop in High Street and the slaughterhouse in Back Lane, and the smell of blood; farm hands on Saturday night (Jim Llewellyn shaved and cut hair till the early hours) having a little too much and being carted off in the wagonette to Solva jail; the old man with the long grey beard, of High Street, who could foretell deaths – farmers spread straw on the road to deaden the noise of horse and cart, for the benefit of the dying; and Willie Moss, the baker, who had a marvellous gramophone playing cylindrical records; and Miss Green playing hockey in a full length grey skirt; and Dr Williams's, the first car in St. David's, in 1903.

Before he left coastal waters and long before he became coxswain of the St. David's Lifeboat and 'mine host' of St. David's most famous mill, Dai Lewis spent two years on the 80 ton ketch *Portland*, whose master was Captain Bruford of Barnstaple, married to a Solva girl and living on the Square. From Pembroke Dock the *Portland* went to Hook for a cargo of culm for Solva; empty to Porth-gain to take on a load of crushed stone for Minehead; from Minehead to Swansea to load with house coal for the merchants of St. David's: that was the merry-go-round, the pattern, varied only by the odd load of culm for Ceibwr, or to Lydney for coal. The senior of St. David's captains, now retired but careful of his boat, is George Harries. He went to sea when fourteen and gained his certificate the hard way. For some time he served on a schooner owned by Hook Colliery, taking anthracite to France. His pay was 30/- a month, with food.

Willie Morris chronicled the story of coal and Porth Glais. In New Street, alongside his house, are the outbuildings where he and his father carried on, with another in Porth Glais alongside the Gasworks, where his uncle was manager. They unloaded the coal from boat to cart by basket and pulley, one basket one hundred-weight, seven baskets for a load. Dolly, Bess and Scot (always English names for horses, and commands always in English) did the rest, pulled the carts around town and country, a thousand tons a season (from March to November), weighed on the Hafod weigh-bridge by a wobbly old character called William Rowland. Willie Morris went down to Porth Glais as a lad, sometimes to help on the boats, sometimes to grow to manhood suddenly and eat his snack on board with the crew. He saw old women gathering lumps of strayed coal left on the going out of the tide, poverty gleaning the remnants. And he ran along the harbour wall before wind and waves got working on the cracks.

On her ninety-fifth birthday, alert and bright-eyed and full of humour, she talked of the days of her youth; completely forgetful of yesterday, she remembered the farm and seventy years back. May Evans was born on 29 August 1879, in Llandigige-fach, and her father was Henry Davies, conductor of a choir, precentor of Felinganol Baptist Chapel, true-life character in *The Captain's Wife*. Married, she lived in Penarthur. Her grandparents on her mother's side belonged to Kingherriot and Solva; her aunt lived and farmed in Hendre Eynon. She talked of her farming days in Penarthur: of the pride taken in good stock and good horses; of butter making – sixty pounds from one churning, patterned delicately with tools that are now lost and forgotten, sold by the pound or barrel, to Henry Richards, butter merchant, or taken to Haverfordwest. She remembered hard days when beggars were frequent in the country-side, trying to sell things and begging for food. There were nine children on her parents' hearth, and if there was lack of money there was no lack of food, nor any lack of identity with the community. She remembered the fairs on Cross Square, and competitions for eating hot pudding. She had tasted *bara tân matau*, bread baked on a peat fire. She remembered James John y Wern, with his four-wheeled covered wagon galloping to Haverfordwest. She remembered walking with her family to the Baptist chapel in Solva. And Mathry Fair, one of the great outings of the year. She remembered her father talking to the visiting tailor, and the visiting seamstress; and the pig slaughterer, and bacon hanging from the beams. The wool from their flock they sometimes took to the wool fair in Haverfordwest; oftener to the Felinganol Mill to be made into blankets. She remembered Morris, the clog-maker weaver in Upper Solva; and sports and pony races on Whitesands; and one disappointing eisteddfod in the Bishop's Palace.

Many of her reminiscences were a complement to those of *The Captain's Wife*, the novel based on memories of Eiluned Lewis's mother and grandmother: habits and customs, how people dressed, children's games; seasonal changes, the integrated whole of a farming life bound to the calendar of the months. The art of mixing culm with clay from the moors, trodden in by busy pairs of clogs, made into balls to seal the fire for the night, one glowing hole on top; the first steam engine tugging the first threshing machine through narrow lanes; the black pot on the kitchen fire, fed with gorse; oatmeal, *llaeth enwyn* (butter milk); how they ate sand eels and enjoyed first the game of catching them in the spring and under harvest moon. Plenty of vinegar, said Eliza in the novel, and then eat them with thin slices of brown bread and butter.

Children trundled iron hoops around the Square; adults made candles in the autumn, and samplers, some still to be seen in City homes. They baked bread in the open on Dowrog; in the farm baking belonged to Friday, and churning to Tuesday. In due course, wheat broke the grim monopoly of rye and barley, and white bread appeared on the farmer's table only on Sunday. That was how the ploughman, Shemi Trepuet, knew it. But one Sunday there was no white bread, and Shemi harnessed his horses and went to work in the fields. He was known as Shemi Bara Gwyn for the rest of his days.

People have written on these oddities of custom and character in St. David's, but very few have been Welsh or written in Welsh. Most have been anglicised lovers of the county or men interested in their family histories; or the English antiquarians, the travellers of the eighteenth and nineteenth centuries, and their material has dealt more with the cathedral than with the parish. So it is with the guide books, the best of which is still Henry Evans's *Twr y Felin Guide*. Some tourist books relished the primitive oddities, some were 'doing places' in the modern way. There is a skittish chapter in the *Cambrian Register* on the superficial tourists and on those who 'enthused with the spirit of embellishment'.

The oldest of writers was Rhygyfarch, who mentioned Hodnant, the Valley, and Porth-mawr, and Boia, and glorified the Saint.

The next was Gerald the Welshman, canon of St. David's, archdeacon of Brecon, prebend of Mathry, the keen-eyed journalist and analyst of Welsh character. He noted how the farmers loved their land and were watchful over boundaries, and eager to cross them when they belonged to someone else. They loved, he said, to extend their territory by every possible means. The Quarter Sessions Rolls of later centuries prove how right he was.

Four hundred years after Gerald lived George Owen of Henllys (1552–1613), direct descendant of Rhys ap Tewdwr, the Elizabethan squire who loved his county and the history of his family. His *Description of Pembrokeshire*, intricately and ornately written, and packed with detail, was the first historical geography of the county.

The first of the English antiquarians, and the first to write in detail on the Cathedral, was Browne Willis. Born in Blandford St. Mary's in 1682, and pupil of Westminster School, his great passion was antiquities, and he studied every cathedral in England and Wales with the exception of Carlisle. He admitted that the first forty pages of his *Survey of the Cathedral Church of St. David's and the Edifices belonging to it, as they stood in the year 1715* had been written with the help of a correspondent. The material supplied by this friend is now believed to have come from a history of St. David's written in Latin by Thomas Tomkin, Vicar Choral and Master of the Choristers.

Richard Fenton (1747–1821), gentleman historian and antiquary, was born in Rhosson (the names of his parents, Richard and Martha Fenton, are in the Cathedral Registers) and died in Glynymel, in Fishguard. His *Tour of Pembrokeshire* is graphic and somewhat discursive and not always accurate. Bishop Burgess, who disliked his episcopal accusations, called him 'our historical tourist'.

George W. Manby wrote an interesting *History and Antiquities of the Parish of St. David's*, published in 1801. The Manby family were Royal Navy people, and it was George Manby, born in Denver, near Newmarket, and settled afterwards in Clifton, Bristol, and in Carnwchwrn, who invented the Apparatus for Shipwrecks named after him.

By now the pioneer tourist writers, Defoe and Borrow and Pennant, had done their job. Wales had entered its romantic revival and the gentry's Welsh Tour became popular. The restoration of the

Cathedral drew many visitors who saw both cathedral and country. But this was the Nash restoration of the West Front. When Barber came to see it he found a deserted place of a village, a mouldering pile of a cathedral renewing its magnificence, and the episcopal palace a superb ruin. Four years later, in 1807, Malkin came and found the marks of desolation without pity.

The Fellow of University College and the Late Fellow of Trinity College, Oxford, came to St. David's with their reading parties, and saw the gap-toothed High Street, scarcely deserving the name of street, lined with the irregularities of courts and pigsties. That was how Basil Jones and E. A. Freeman, authors of *History and Antiquities of St. David's*, saw the place for the first time.

Walcott came in 1864, and saw a poor secluded village, severed from the busy world; but he was intrigued by two old houses in Nun Street, and by barrel vaulted wells.

The most interesting and observant and impressionable of all came with his father in October 1871. Francis Kilvert, the young English curate from Clyro in Radnorshire, started from Haverfordwest at 8 o'clock in the morning, to meet the people pouring into Haverfordwest Fair on foot and on horseback, and saw the four-horse bi-weekly omnibus from St. David's. 'Droves of black cattle and sheep were pouring along the muddy roads. Most of the men wore blue coats and the women long blue cloaks.' At last they rattled into the village city, were told by the driver that the inns were dirty and uncomfortable and were recommended to stay at a private house of 'one Mr Williams'. They saw the Cathedral Tower rising from its glen, and were dazzled by all the whitewash: 'kept on fancying that snow had fallen.' They went first to St. David's Head, directed and misdirected by natives who seemed to have hazy notions of its whereabouts. They came to it eventually, past the white-roofed farm house, where the old woman (with the 'usual flat black straw hat tied under her chin over a full white capborder') guided them; past rough swampy rushy pasture, and a row of 'three ruined cabins built of loose large rough stones without mortar (in the fold a huge evil pig, yellow and black, was meditating wickedness); past low stone walls, rough fields and open moorland, and ultimately to the cliffs where the sea roared and plunged booming among the cliff chasms. In the afternoon they came back and found themselves under the sea Cathedral, the moor Cathedral, the Cathedral by sea and moor, St. Mary's College, and the magnificent ruins of the superb Palace 'with a bush of red flowers by the wall'. After luncheon they approached the Cathedral, 'melancholy in its devastation made by time and neglect and execrable taste and Churchwarden's Gothic' (of Nash's restoration). It was when they entered that they became astonished by richness of arches, massive round pillars and splendour of piers, and the glory of the roof, and the solemn grandeur of the silent Choir. The old bowed Canon in his black fur cloak with his venerable white silver hair flowing from beneath his black skull cap took them round. They saw the shrine and the tombs, and his father 'mounted the pulpit in the window of the transept which was squalidly fitted up for the Welsh service and reeking with the stench of oil lamps'.

Next morning they were inspecting St. Thomas's Church in Haverfordwest, and watching 'the fishwives . . . moving about the streets crying their fish, dressed in their peculiar picturesque national costume, the tall conical hat and scarlet dress over a blue short petticoat, or a blue dress over a scarlet petticoat.' We could have done with more of Francis Kilvert.

Walford and Skrine came and went without saying anything out of the ordinary. Kilner (*The Story of Four Welsh Counties* 1891) was different. He was fascinated by the miserere seats. Their prominent features, he thought, were foliage, animals, men, boats. The priest was fox and the layman goose. Cowled bull and fox, a double faced head, monks drunk and gluttonous and seasick, coiled serpents; links with sea and boats, human frailties hidden under cowl and cassock and in the shape of animals and birds, irony, the wry comment of the medieval craftsmen, their humour, carved in wood.

Manby was disgusted with them: they were singular in device but contained representations utterly unsuited to a holy office. Baker (*A Dead City*) adored them – 'each little face, tiny as it is, full of varied impressions: anger, scorn, laughter, rage, imperiousness, disgust, apathy, imbecility, yokelism'. Some of these visitors saw the famous ears of the rabbits in the Lady Chapel, where three carved ears do the work of six. Many missed the painting behind Bishop Gower's rood screen, above the arch leading from choir to nave. Here is an owl, and on either side a magpie, from the Valley, doubtless, where there are plenty of them. The owl, presumably, stands for wisdom, the magpies for the chatterers and nuisances of this world. A thousand faces, animal and human, look down silently, often unseen, on the passer-by inside and outside the Cathedral. A pair of human faces, hardly one inch across, at the base of the scroll on each of the choir stalls; the swine set in the magnificent ceiling of the presbytery; the fox that looks down at the choir from the west. The camera reveals them, and the incipient richness of their colour.

The tourist writers occasionally painted a vivid little sketch of beauty or of oddness. Kilner found that the place had no gas and that the people went about with lanterns, for the queer oil lamps gave but little light. But 'the Service in Welsh in the Cathedral is unique and striking'. He saw prosperous looking homesteads by contrast, dotting the undulating and almost treeless country.

Fletcher Moss wrote ecstatically on the beauty of a cathedral whose floor was not level (there is a rise of 14 feet from the West Door to the Lady Chapel), whose arches did not correspond and whose pillars were not upright. He looked for peace in the Bishop's Palace, but got none. 'Every coign of vantage had its jackdaw.'

There were others who wrote. Fletcher Moss's *Pilgrimages to Old Homes* was his fourth. Warner twice walked through Wales. And A. G. Bradley one hundred and thirty years later wrote of the romance of Wales and Pembrokeshire. The guidebooks caught on and developed a profitable trade. *Cambrian, Murray's, Black's* were all in English, their target the tourists from England.

Francis Green, solicitor of Carmarthen and Glanymor, began to investigate and collect the history of the parish. Thirty fat volumes of deeds and wills, indentures, marriage settlements, family trees, and a growing number of volumes of newspaper cuttings in the Library in Haverfordwest are his contribution to the county's history, in addition to what he wrote for the series of *West Wales Historical Society Transactions* which he edited.

Like Fenton a gentleman scholar, Edward Laws published his *Little England beyond Wales* in 1888. His main interest lay in Pembroke and the south of the county, but he could not ignore the north-west and St. David's. Here in a footnote is an introduction to a royal romance not unconnected with St. David's, the story of Dorothy Bland, Dorothy Jordan the actress paramour of William Duke of Clarence who later became William IV. She came to Treleddin and the Duke came to visit her. In Treleddin she had a brother and sisters the records of whose burials in the Cathedral Yard can be found in the registers. Thomas Williams of Treleddin married Blanch Scudamor, and Blanch Scudamor was related to the mother of Dorothy Jordan. It is a wonderful story, despite the fact that Edward Laws was wrong in most of his facts.

Edward Yardley's *Menevia Sacra* is an immense storehouse of information on the history of the Cathedral. Its author (1698–1770) was born in London, and, after being given the sinecure rectory of St. Florence by St. John's College, Cambridge, became Archdeacon of Cardigan in 1739.

A. W. Wade-Evans, Fishguard born, Haverfordwest Grammar School and Oxford, spent the greater part of his clerical life in England. His books and articles (*Coll Prydain, Welsh Medieval Laws, Welsh Christian Origins*) were learned and controversial in their ideas. His edition of Rhygyfarch's *Life of St. David* is authoritative and indispensable, and many of his ideas are now fully acceptable.

John James Evans, ardent Welshman and headmaster of St. David's County School from 1936 to 1959, wrote books on Welsh history, language, and literature. His *Dewi Sant a'i Amserau* is an historical summary of the life of St. David and Rhygyfarch and the Age of the Saints.

Francis Jones, Herald Extraordinary of Wales, inveterate collector of family histories, searched in his native Llandeloy and spread outwards over the three counties that now form Dyfed. The results can be found in the publications of the Cymmrodorion Society, in the *Journal of the Historical Society of the Church in Wales*, in the *National Library of Wales Journal*, and in *The Pembrokeshire Historian*. No lover of St. David's can ignore his *The Holy Wells of Wales* (1954).

Among the books on Welsh folk lore and folk custom published in the 1930s was *Coelion Cymru* by Evan Isaac. He was a minister in St. David's for a time and collected details of local customs and elements of Welsh superstition, obviously in close collaboration with H. W. Evans of Solva, whose contributions were printed in the *Pembroke County Guardian* and in *Pembrokeshire Antiquities*. One strange story told of William Howells of Caerfarchell, a tailor who was commonly called Wiliet. He, to the consternation of the whole district, had forecast the sudden death of David Jones, minister with John Reynolds of Felinganol Baptist Chapel, and had added that at the funeral would be a man with a large loose white beard. In June 1849 William Jones died suddenly. Neither at the service in the house nor in the procession was there a man with a white beard. When the cortege reached Felinganol they found a man in the big pew who had come direct from Haverfordwest. He was David Davies of the Baptist College in Haverfordwest. He had a massive loose white beard.

Evan Isaac also had something to say about *y dyn hysbys*, the *consuriwr*, conjurer, wise-man of old, inheritor perhaps of old Druidic knowledge. On the slopes of Penbiri is a farm called Trehysbys. In Henry Goffe's census the house was called Oppidum Magi.

Baring Gould's novel, *In Dewisland*, is set in the two farms of Ty Gwyn and Rhosson, and Garn Llidi and Dowrog. Above all else it concerns itself with the farmer's inherited wealth, his land. The heather buds in August, it blooms in September, and withers in October. Fathers and mothers die and the children inherit the family land. Inheritance and parental influence and marriage are vitally important. There is violence outside the parish, the Rebecca Riots. The violence within is that of deep emotion, fierce love and hate, rivalry between brothers who, as in Gerald the Welshman's time, are contentious over land.

The Captain's Wife is deep set in the life of the farms, Llanfirn y Frân in particular, and in the life of men at sea. Here also is the Cathedral, and the Bishop's Palace: 'Compared with the Palace all other playgrounds were dull and commonplace; the vaults, the bats, an uneasy fear, the noise of endlessly cawing rooks, the loveliness of old grey stone and tender grass, the Wishing Well'. At the other end of the City was Back Lane, not forbidden country but the beginning of all adventure, where, uniquely, banks and hedges were so wide that there were pathways on top, where children played and looked down upon the world. In the country were the little Ebenezers, and cottages coloured in shades of apricot. And the farms, Llanfirn with its Flemish chimney, Llanmadoc (or was it Pwllcaerog?) with its vast fireplace and round black pot. Nantgwyn had a wide flagged passage, and 'Penisha', the parlour, and the great Flemish chimney as big as a room, from which you could look up at soot-lined walls and a patch of blue sky.

The country was stable, and peaceful. On the other side was the sea where the men of the farms risked their lives and lost them. In the third chapter of the book is the wreck of *The Mystic Tie* on the Bitches. *The Mystic Tie* went down on Ramsey in November 1877.

Neither artists nor poets have gone much out of their way to chronicle St. David's. The brothers Buck, Sam and Nat (1740), executed an engraving of the south-east of Cathedral and Palace and dedicated it to Bishop Nicholas Claggett. A copy is now in the Council Chamber. Also there are engraved views of the Cathedral by W. Byrne for Sir Richard Colt Hoare's edition of *Sylvester Giraldus Cambrensis* (1806). There are views of the Cathedral by Henry Gastineau and four engravings of Cathedral and Palace by G. W. Manby. Charles Norris (1779–1858) planned to compile a volume of the architectural antiquities of Wales, completed his engravings of St. David's, and gave up. Graham Sutherland spent a part of his apprentice years in Treleddid Fawr – his 'Porthclais' is now in the gallery dedicated to him at Picton Castle. It is only recently that artists in oils and water colours have begun to find beauty in cottages and old farmhouses, and in the moors and long low skylines of this place.

In Glasfryn, however, are landscapes and, more distinctively, a series of portraits in oils of characters of old St. David's, painted by Herbert Colbourne Oakley (no relation of the old St. David's family) who died in the mid-1940s. And in Tabernacle vestry are two striking oil paintings of William Morris and George Williams.

Michael Drayton is the only English poet to have sung of St. David's. From *Polyolbion* come the familiar lines:

> Here holy David's church, that far from all resort
> With contemplation seem'd most fitly to comport,
> That void of all delight, cold, barren, bleak, and dry,
> No pleasure might allure, nor steal the wander'ng eye.

What he did was to make rhyming couplets of Gerald the Welshman's prose description of the 'remote angle', 'rocky, barren and fruitless', which had been once the solitary habitation of religious men.

The Welsh Inspector of Schools, A. G. Prys-Jones, wrote gentle sentimental verses in praise of the islands, and of the old story of the pilgrim road to the west.

Waldo Williams was born on the slopes of the Preseli, and James Nicholas in St. David's. Theirs is authentic poetry in Welsh: it takes us back to the Age of St. David, to a seeming peace and dedicated contemplation. And in both there is the deep anxiety that arises from anglicisation, from an injurious materialism, from the twentieth century intrusion of militarism into a land where religion had been as native as the rocks.

Waldo climbed Carn Llidi –

> Ar gadernid Carn Llidi
> Ar hyd un hwyr oedwn i,
> Ac yn syn ar derfyn dydd
> Gwelwn o ben bwy gilydd
> Drwy eitha Dyfed y rhith dihafal,
> Ei thresi swnd yn eurwaith ar sindal
> Lle naid y lli anwadal yn sydyn
> I fwrw ei ewyn dros far a hual.
> Gwig, a siffrwd pêr paderau trwyddi –
> Rhyw si yn nrysi Rhosyn yr Oesau.

And James Nicholas –

> Lle mae'r brwyn islaw'r twyni – fe loriwyd
> Hen falurion meini;
> Tawel yw aelwyd Dewi
> A garw a llwyd ger y lli.
>
> Rhan o fur a'i hen fawredd – a welaf
> Yng nghiliau rhosdiredd;
> Yno erys cyfaredd
> Dyrys yr hwyr dros yr hedd.

Last of the chronicles, indispensable in spite of its missing files, is the local paper. John and Martha Williams began to issue the *Dewisland and Kemes Guardian* in 1860/61. There are two other and older county papers, the *Pembrokeshire Herald* (1844) and the *Haverfordwest and Milford Haven Telegraph* (1854). Two other and later papers belonged to Fishguard, but were begun by men who had been trained in Solva Printing House: Levi Evans began his apprenticeship with Henry Whiteside Williams on 21 July 1880, and completed it in November 1886 and started the *Fishguard Echo*; G. O. Davies was born in Clegyr, trained in Solva, and started the *Fishguard Times* which was later absorbed in the *Echo*.

Henry Whiteside Williams, proprietor of the *Pembroke County Guardian*, died in January 1907, forty-seven years after his father had established its predecessor, the Solva paper which eventually became the *Guardian*. It seems that the *Dewisland and Kemes Guardian* in its early days was printed in London, with blank pages for the local news to be printed in Solva. Its earlier editions were remarkably dry reading, in a style of language remarkably unsuitable for local reading. With the years more local news was included, correspondence columns grew, and chapel reports in Welsh, articles by Henry Evans and by J. Young Evans; and later still the influence of a newly appointed Welsh editor from North Pembrokeshire, Brynach, poet, preacher, teacher, made it into a genuinely bilingual paper.

In time it developed another feature, and a continuing feature – its interest in archaeology, in local history, in research into times past. Henry W. Williams was himself a keen archaeologist. In the files in the Record Office, and in Francis Green's newspaper cuttings files in the Library, can be found a series called *Yn Amsang Ein Tadau* (In the Footsteps of our Fathers): in it are reports on the excavations in Clegyrfwya (Clegyr Boia); R. M. Dawson's investigations into the meanings of place and field names; Ferrar Fenton on the life and work of his father; a series on the Saints and great men of the parish; Henry W. Evans's articles on the customs and superstitions of the Welsh, the will o' the wisp, Christmas and New Year customs, Y Mari Lwyd, the hunting of the wren; a very erudite series on the bishops of St. David's by J. Young Evans; articles by Francis Jones on well-known Pembrokeshire families; and the 'Pembrokeshire Antiquary', articles on the history of hill and castle forts, the history of querns, and the history of some of the old manorial homes.

Occasionally there were amusing and skittish articles on contemporary problems. Taffy of Cwmtwlc (there is a Cwm Twlc above Whitesands Bay) wrote on the controversial Tithe problem. In 1886 the Solva paper reported on a meeting, planned for Cross Square, in the middle of the anti-tithe agitation. The Revd Dr Macneill was guest speaker, and he was accompanied by local nonconformist ministers. He spoke of the Cross of St. David's as an example of ancient Celtic art, an Iona Cross associated with the Gaelic missionaries who had brought Christianity into these parts. Then he turned a caustic humour on the tithe laws, criticising the parish priests who had sold their tongues, their pens, their consciences to landlord statesmen. The landlords in return for this subserviency had established them in their ill-gotten Church exactions; tithe laws had grown with the corruption and greed of the Church. It was on this that Taffy of Cwmtwlc spent his ironic drollery; religion was again mixed with politics, and with the language question.

There can be no better way, perhaps, of ending this chapter than to look again at our history. Macneill had manifested some of its contrasts. There are many of them, starting, as he did, with that of Celtic and Norman. This is a land that is hard and windswept, and yet it basks in the equanimity of a drift of a Gulf Stream climate that produces richness of barley and a profusion of wild flowers in their season. The stones of its cromlechs are grey and hard, and yet in Caerbwdi are the richnesses of stones in ecclesiastical purple and soft green. In the bowl of the Valley we have the immensity of a Norman Cathedral set in a Celtic land once full of little nonconformist Ebenezers. The exterior of the Cathedral is a matter of plain and forbidding buttresses, but inside is an unforgettable richness.

There are other contrasts deeply embedded in the chronicles of our Celtic past. In Rhygyfarch's *Life of St. David* we see austerity, ascetism, the hard code of conduct of the monks. Rhygyfarch wrote his *Life* about 1090. The *Mabinogion* also may well have been written in the eleventh century. Both belong to Dyfed. But we cannot reconcile the austerity of the Saints with the golden richness of the story of Culhwch and Olwen. King Arthur and his knights went hunting, Culhwch with them, for Twrch Trwyth, the prince turned into a wild boar for his misdeeds. They travelled through the Celtic countries and came to Porth Glais and to Mynyw. It is an impossible world, where the monks of David pulled the plough with their bodies and lived on herbs and water, and Culhwch rode a steed with light-grey head, shell-hoofed, and a gold tubular bridle-bit in its mouth; and his saddle was of precious gold and his whetted spears of silver, and his mantle was of purple and an apple of red gold in each of its corners!

There is a third contrast with the Age of Saints and the Age of the Arthurian Romances. The father of Gruffudd ap Cynan was Cynan, King of Gwynedd, and his mother was the daughter of a King of Dublin. Driven out of his kingdom by treachery and the arms of Norman invaders, Gruffudd went to Ireland for help, and came eventually to Porth Glais with a mixed army of Danes and Irishmen and Britons. In the sanctuary of St. David's he met Rhys ap Tewdwr, Lord of Deheubarth and of the house of Dinefwr, himself in exile. They joined forces, were blessed by Sulien the bishop in his church of David, and set forth to reclaim their kingdoms in the battle of Mynydd Carn. They won the day, and while they were winning the Normans were waiting in the wings who were the conquerors of England and blood brothers of the Danes who had destroyed St. David's. By 1115 Bernard the Norman was bishop.

It is a tangled history, of early wars and religion and romance. There was fighting in the days of the Welsh Princes. The Norman enemy brought peace. And out of all that has grown the City and the community that we know today. An old crossroads of trade and Christianity has become a crossroads of modern European tourism. It has known richness, and a desperate poverty. There was a time, said Sir Richard Colt Hoare, of abject shabbiness – 'such I fear will every traveller find in his approach to the wretched village, where misery and beggary stare him full in the face, and whence the deficiency of even tolerable accommodation has driven away many an inquisitive tourist and antiquarian.'

Today, aware or perhaps unaware of all this past, the antiquity of the place, its clashes of old culture, its vicissitudes of poverty and richness, they come in their thousands, to a little city with a large history.

Everyone, said Manby, should come once to St. David's, dead or alive.

APPENDIX I

Census of St. David's Parish, 1720 – Henry Goffe

An account of ye number of houses and inhabitants in St. David's Parish as taken & communicated by ye late Revd Mr Henry Goffe, Subchantor of St. David's Cathedral, A.D. 1720, according to its divisions into four parts called there Circles.

1. Cylch Mawr which has 59 houses and 259 inhabitants in these following divisions:

	Houses	Inhabitants
1. Sceivog	6 houses	31 inhabitants
2. Caernedren Ycha or ye upper	3	17
3. Llandrigige Vach or ye lesser	3	19
4. Dreftio	14	58
5. Pwll Caerog	6	30
6. Dref Munny	5	30
7. Dref Fleidir or Furis Oppidum	5	24
8. Dref Hispiss, sive Magi Oppidum	6	15
9. Gwrid Mawr	11	35

2. Cylch Fychan, which has 52 houses and 227 inhabitants

	Houses	Inhabitants
1. Caerfarchell which denominate a Prebend	10	46
2. Hendref ie Oppidum Antiquam	8	43
3. Harglauddycha	6	29
4. Mechellich, in this is only in St. David's Parish	4	13
5. Clegir	5	26
6. Llandridian, of which ye Chantor of St. David's is Lord	8	32
7. Tillerrer	6	25
8. Penypant	5	13

3. Cylch y Dref which has 115 houses (all of them but about 4 in St. David's Town) and 457 inhabitants

	Houses	Inhabitants
1. Caerfai, which gives title to a Prebend: here are 3 houses and 7 inhabitants. About a half mile from hence is St. Non's Chapel, which has of late a little house built by it. Here is a celebrated spring arched over, which ye Chantor of St. David's has of late improved	3	7
2. Cylch y Dref without St. David's Town or City	20	92
3. There are within ye Town or City of St. David's in ye several streets these following		
In High Street	32	126
In Sheep Street	15	47
In Nun Street	20	77
In New Street	5	26
In ye Close or Valley	12	57

4. Cylch Gwaelod which has 49 houses and 205 inhabitants

1. Trefgynis Ucha	4	22
2. Treffaiddan	4	10
3. Rossan	5	23
4. Pencarvan	3	23
5. Consodigg	3	15
6. Llaethty	5	22
7. Lleithir	5	12
8. Trefleddid Vawr	15	54
9. Treffleddin	5	25

Besides ye villages or inshipps in ye several Cylchs of St. David's Parish, there are a great many houses to make up ye gross sum and some of these called Trefs or Towns, though consisting but one house & most of them but two, viz.

In Cylch Mawr	Trefgweidd	1	2
	Hendref Eynon	1	8
	Trefecca	1	7
	Trefjago	1	9
	Treferfin (only 1 inhabited)	2	3
In Cylch Fychan	Trefeithel	2	3
	Trefwellwell	1	11
	Trefadog	1	8
	Trefboeth	1	4
In Cylch y Dref	Trefarchan	2	10
	Trefenllue	2	11
	Trefpuet	1	3
	Trefcedny	1	7
	Trefinnert	2	12
In Cylch Gwaelod y Wlad	Trefgynnis Ycha	2	19
	Trefach	1	5
	Trefnergy	2	7
	Trefceny	2	9
	Trefgwillim	1	6
	Trefely	1	12
	Trefluyd	1	12

(Henry Goffe's census is taken from *Menevia Sacra*, by Edward Yardley, Archdeacon of Cardigan)

APPENDIX II

Highway Rate Book (Parish Chest) Data for 1870

Phillip Bowen had a shop and house in Nun Street.

Francis Cornock's forge was on Cross Square. His house and garden adjoining belonged to the Minor Canons.

Windmill land was owned and occupied by David Evans.

Mrs E. Griffiths owned and occupied a workshop in New Street.

Thomas Griffiths lived in a house owned by John Harding Harries.

Mrs E. Griffiths occupied a house and garden called Old Blue Bell.

Thomas Hughes had a house, shop and garden called the Carpenter's Arms.

A stable in High Street owned by Thomas Hughes was occupied by William Williams.

William Jackson occupied stores in Pit Street.

Danyrhiw, owned by the Dean, was occupied by David Morris.

A barn in High Street, occupied by Morris Stephen, was owned by the Bishop.

John Owen owned and occupied a house, shop and land on Cross Square.

Mill House and lane (Dewston), owned by the Bishop, was occupied by William Owen.

Caerbwdi Mill, owned by the Bishop, was occupied by Abraham Rees.

The mill house and land at Rhodiad, occupied by Ebenezer Richard, was owned by William Perkins.

Stables in the Valley were owned by Sir George Williams.

A house and haggard in High Street were owned and occupied by Samuel Williams of Menai.

Stores at Pantycyrill were owned and occupied by William Williams.

He had an outhouse and land in Backlane.

And a house, garden and shop – the Post Office.

And a house which he had recently bought and converted into an hotel – Grove House.

One set of lime kilns were owned by Charles Allen and in the occupation of Thomas Davies.

Lime kilns at Porthclais were owned by Charles Allen and in the occupation of William Williams.

Elizabeth Williams had a workshop in Pit Street Lane.

George Williams owned and occupied an outhouse in Catherine Street (one of the granaries).

John Foulkes (minister of Ebenezer) lived in a house in Ebenezer Square owned by Henry Griffiths.

Sarah Lewhellyn lived in a house in Pit Street owned by the Trustees of Tabernacle.

David Morris occupied a house and garden in Pig's Foot Lane owned by John Harding Harries. After his name and in brackets was inserted the word 'Miners', which seems to confirm that the Miner's Arms was situated in Pig's Foot Lane.

George Owen Williams lived in and owned a house and garden in High Street.

William Miles owned and lived in the 'Commercial'.

Henry Hicks lived in the Old Wind Mill.

Dr Thomas Jones had a house and garden in Whitewell Road.

Revd A. Green, one of the minor canons, lived in Penygarn (Warpool Court).
Ebenezer Thomas occupied a house in New Street owned by the Trustees of the Baptist Chapel.
James Thomas lived in a house in Cockwell (Quickwell) owned by the Trustees of Ebenezer Chapel.
Ebenezer Price had a house and forge in Gwrid.
William Reed had a house and forge in Fronwen.

At about the same time, Samuel Williams was checking the electoral list and adding some names and matters of interest:

Baker – William Miles of High Street.
Builders – James Stephens of Nun Street,
John James of Pit Street.
Carpenters – David Absalom, Mount Gardens,
Abel James, New Street.
Drapers and Grocers – William Miles, High Street,
Sarah Richards, Priskilly Terrace.
Masons and Stonecutters – William Rees, Edmund's Lane,
Thomas Bowen, Pit Street,
Thomas Harry, Cross Philip,
Henry John, Cuckwell,
David Roberts, High Street,
Jno Henry Morgan, Nun Street,
John Rodney, New Street,
William Rodney, Nun Street.
Private Lodging Houses – William Miles, High Street,
Caroline Appleby, Nun Street.
Shoemakers – William Perkins, Nun Street,
William Thomas, Back Lane,
William Morris, High Street,
John Williams, Pit Street,
David Morris, Pig's Foot Lane,
David Lewis, Clegyr Bridge.
Straw and Bonnet Maker – Elizabeth Davies, Nun Street.
Private School – Emily Jane Appleby, Nun Street.
Dressmakers – Mary Lee, Pit Street,
Margaret Perkins, Nun Street.
Butchers – Josiah Absalom, Nun Street,
James Charles, Fagwreilw,
Thomas John, Rhoscribed,
George Owen, High Street.
Public House – John Thomas, Boncath Cross.
Tailor – John Lewis, New Street,
Thomas Griffiths, Nun Street,
William Lewis, Cross Square,
Abraham Jones, Pit Street,
Eben Davies, Porthskilly Terrace (?).
Watchmaker – James Morse, Pit Street.
Weavers – John Lewis, Nun Street,
David Morris, Tanyrhiw (Samuel Williams's addition – 'and carding')
James George, Pit Street,
John George, Nine Wells.

APPENDIX III

St. David's Residents in 1906 – Kelly's Directory

Private Residences
Bateman Mrs W.P. Goat Street
Davies Jas. Cathedral vils. Nun st
Davies Mrs 2 Grove villas High st
Evans Revd Hugh B.A. (curate) Boncath Fach
Evans Revd Arthur Biggerston L.D. (vicar choral & Bishops vicar & Curate) 2 Cathedral villas
Gabriel Revd Gwillym Philip M.A. (minor canon, sub-chanter & curate) Brynmor house
Griffiths John Dodd, 6 Nun street
Griffiths Mrs New Cross
Howell Mrs Cross square
Jay Macdonald Henry, The Close
Jones Revd David James, B.A. (vicar of St. David's and vicar choral) The Vicarage
Lewis Revd Thomas (Congregational) Carnhedrynuchaf
Lewis Fredk., Honddu, Goat street
Lewis Henry William, Cross square
Lewis William Davies, Goat street
Lloyd Mrs Canonary
Martin Mrs Ivy House, Tower street
Mrs Martin Arvon villa
Morgan Miss, Brynteg, High street
Morris Herbert, F.R.C.O. (organist of cathedral), The Treasury
Morse Thomas, 8 New street
Perkins Mrs Oakley ho., Oakley street
Phillips Miss, 2 Bank house, Goat st
Propert William Peregrine, M.A., Ll.D., Mus. Bac., J.P., F.G.S., F.R.M.S., barrister-at-law, High st
Rees Revd David (Baptist), New st
Rees Mrs Ivy cottage, New st
Rees Miss, Myrtle cottage, Oakley street
Rees Thomas Blethyn, J.P., Tremynydd
Roach Samuel, Belmont house
Roberts Mrs Laurel cottage, Bryn road
Smith Very Revd James Allen, D.D. (dean & precentor), The Deanery
Thomas Revd John Edward (Wes), Honddu Villas, Goat street
Thomas Thomas B.A. (headmaster of county school), Brynmeirion
Tyson Thomas, Mona house, New st
Williams Revd Richard (Calvinistic Methodist), Cross Square
Williams David Propert, J.P. High st
Williams Inkerman, New Cross
Williams John Morgan, High street
Williams Mrs A. Lawn vil. New street
Williams Mrs Dewi court
Williams Samuel James Watts, Menai, Cross square

Williams Wm. Glendower ho. Nun st
Williams William Wilfred, Glendower house, Nun street
Wilson Miss, 3 Cathedral villas

Commercial

Appleton William P. apartments, Brynmor house, Goat street
Arnold M.C. City family and commercial hotel; splendid shooting over 1,000 acres; sea bathing within half a mile; buses leave this hotel twice weekly for Haverfordwest, returning same day, New st
Arnold Martha (Miss) frmr, Trevinert
Arnold William, farmer, Penarthur
Baines Miss Annie, frmr. Nine Wells
Bateman Jane (Mrs) Shopkpr, New st
Beynon Wm. Davies, farmer, Penlan
Bowen Thomas, farmer, Rhostwarch
Board of Trade Rocket Life Saving Apparatus (Thomas Tyser, officer in charge) Nun street
City Stores (John W. Evans, propr) draper, clothier, ladies & gents tailor & outfitter, dress maker, milliner, costumier & Welsh flannel & wool merchants, High street
Cornock Catherine (Miss) private lodging house, Glasfryn
Cornock Francis, blacksmith, High st
County School (Thomas Thomas B.A. headmaster; Miss Katherine M. Green, Ll.A. assistant mistress) Solva road
David Albert, chemist & druggist, Cross square
Davies Wm and Jn, frmrs, Rhos-y-cribed
Davies Elzbth (Mrs) farmer, Maendewi
Davies George, farmer, Tretio
Davies John, cowkeeper, Back Lane
Davies Lewis, farmer, Hendre Eynon
Davies Mary (Mrs) grcr, Boncath cross
Davies Thomas, farmer, Penberry
Davies Thos Jenkin, farmer, Treiago
Davies William, farmer, Clegyr-foia
Edwards David, farmer & mason, Caerfai
Edwards David, mason, Catherine st
Edwards Henry, farmer, Skyfog (Postal address, Solva S.O., Pembrokeshire)
England George Lim. dentists (attend alternate Thursdays from Tenby), Cross square
Evans David, grocer & baker, High st
Evans Henry, farmer, Carfarchell
Evans Isaac, saddler, Cross square
Evans John, farmer, Trelerwr
Evans John W. draper & clothier, ladies and gents tailor & outfitter, dressmaker, milliner, costumier & Welsh flannel merchant, City Stores, High street
Evans Richard, Morning Star P.H. Rhodiad
Evans Thomas, miller, Lower mill
Evans Thomas, farmer, Trelerwr
Evans Wm. Bennett, farmer, Clegyr
Eynon John, watchmaker & bootmaker, Nun street
Free Reading Room (Fredk. Lewis, hon. sec.) New st
George Thos. woollen weaver, Goat st
Griffiths James & Thomas, farmers, Treleddid Fawr
Griffiths Benjamin, woollen weaver, Nun street & Carding mills
Griffiths Emily Kate (Miss) sub-postmistress, Cross square

Griffiths James, butcher, Nun street
Griffiths John, cattle dlr. Catherine st
Griffiths John, farmer, Rhosson
Griffiths John, farmer, Y Waun-fawr
Griffiths Jn Howard, frmr, Lleyther
Griffiths Thomas, farmer, Carfarchell
Harries John, farmer, Trehyspye
Harries William, farmer, Trepuet
Heir Martbaan, baker, New street
Hicks Margaret (Miss), farmer, Lower Porthlysky
Hogan Margaret (Miss) Mary Ann, boot dealer, Goat street
Howells William, farmer, Cross Phillip
James Eleazor, boot maker & repairer, High street
James Eleazer, insurance agent, Priskilly terrace
James Elizh (Mrs) farmer, Llandridon
James Henry, farmer, Castle-rick
James Henry, farmer, Croeswdig
James Leonora (Mrs) cowkeeper, Mount Pleasant
James Louisa (Mrs) aparts, Goat st
James Peter, farmer, Rhosson
Jenkins Jn, woollen weaver, Cross sq
John James and Thomas, farmers, Skyfog (postal address, Solva R.S.O., Pembrokeshire)
John Henry, mason, Eyrallt
John Martha (Mrs) lodging house, 1 Goat street
John Richard, farmer, Porthmawr
John Sarah (Miss), dress maker, Nun street
John William, cowkeeper, Tudor terrace, Nun street
John William, mason, Eyrallt
Jones John, farmer, Llandridon
Jones Walter, blacksmith, Nun street
Jones W. Howard, auctioneer & valuer, Prospect hotel, Nun street
Lawrence Wm. carpenter, Cross sq
Lewis Elizh and Agnes Mary (Misses), farmers, Carnhedren
Lewis C. B. (Miss) farmer, Treithel
Lewis Ebenezer, farmer, Rhosson
Lewis Elizh (Mrs), farmer, Penypant
Lewis Frederick, board school master & Hon. sec. of reading room, Honddu villas, Goat street
Lewis Henry William, M.R.C.S. Eng. L.R.C.P. Lond. physician & surgeon, High street
Lewis Thomas, farmer, Carnhedryn-uchaf
Lewis Thomas, Penpant
Lewis William, farmer, Treleidir
Lewis William, tailor, Cross square
Lewis William Henry, tailor, 1 Grove terrace, Goat street
Llewellyn Maria (Mrs) grocer, Catherine street
Llewellyn Saml. town crier, Nun st
Lloyds Bank Limited (John Morgan Williams, agent) High st, draw on Lloyds Bank Limited, London
London & Provincial Bank Limited (A. J. Wright, manager) open on Wed. Cross square; draw on head office & Glyn Mills, Currie & co
Martin Alfred, farmer, Trehenlliw
Martin Edgar, farmer, Trevelly

Martin Ernest, farmer, Trehenlliw
Martin Florence (Mrs) Carpenters Arms P.H. Goat street
Martin John, jobmaster
Mathias Anne (Mrs) grocer, Goat street
Mathias Edward P. Grove family and commercial hotel
Miles John, farmer, Porthmawr
Morgan Peter & Wm, farmers, Clegyrboia
Morgan Claudia (Mrs) Windmill farm & boarding house
Morgan Maria (Mrs), farmer, Caerhys
Morgan Frederick, mason, High street
Morgan Frederick (Mrs), apartments, Ystwyth cottage, High street
Morgan Henry, farmer, Tygwyn
Morgan John, farmer, Carnhedrenisaf
Morris David, shoe ma. Trehenlleu terr
Morris David, farmer, Tretio fach
Morris John, school attendance officer
Morris William, boot maker & coal dealer, New street
Mortimer William Maurice, coal merchant, Goat street
Moss Wm. baker & grocer, Nun street
Owen Mary J. and Ada C. (Misses) drapers & fancy repository, Cross square
Owen George, farmer, Llanvirran
Owen John, miller (water), Lower mill and Gwyedbach
Owen Milton, farmer, Harglodd
Owen Levi Rees, grocer, ironmonger & auctioneer, Nun street
Palmer Mary (Mrs) aparts, High st
Parry Mary (Mrs) apartments, Trevithan house
Perkins Geo. Gibby, shopkpr, Nun st
Perkins John, farmer, Llanvirin
Philip James, farmer, Maenygroes
Phillips George, carpenter & builder, New street
Phillips James, farmer, Lletyrderyn
Phillips Martha (Mrs) dress maker, Coedegan terrace, Goat street
Phillips Sarah (Mrs) apartments, 2 Grove terrace, Goat street
Phillips William, farmer, Cwmwdig
Preece David and William, carpenters, Goat street
Price John, farmer, Treleddidfawr
Rawlings Mary A. (Mrs) apartments
Reed William, blacksmith and post office, Berea
Rees Elizabeth and Ann (Misses) dairy, Emlych house, Nun street
Rees Martha & Sophia (Misses), farmers, Porthclais
Rees Andrew, mason, Caerbwdy
Rees Henry, farmer, Emlych
Rees Henry, farmer, Carnwchwr
Rees James, farmer, Llandridon
Rees Luther, farmer, Clegyr
Rees Luther Bowen, farmer, Pwllcawrog
Rees Thos. Bleddyn, farmer, Tremynydd
Rees Wm. miller (water) Carforiog ml
Rhys Mrs Annie, apartments, Minerva house, Nun street
Rhys Thomas B. schoolmaster
Richards Jas. Farmers' Arms, Goat st
Richards Thomas, farmer, Crugglas
Roach Hy Perkins, farmer, Llanviran
Roberts John and David, farmers, Pencarnan

Roberts William & Martell, farmers, Upper Treginnis
Roberts Henry, blacksmith, Waun-y-Beddau
Roberts Henry, farmer, Trelethin
Rowlands James, carpenter, Cross sq
Rowlands Sarah Ann (Miss), dressmaker, Cross square
Rowlands Wm., bootmaker, Goat st
Sime Esther O. (Mrs) private hotel, Cross square
Sime Frederick J. relieving officer & registrar of births & deaths for the St. David's sub-district, Haverfordwest Union, Maldwyn house
Smith Arthur, grocer & baker, Goat st
Spackman George & Chas. T., butchers, High street
Stephens Captain James (coxswain of lifeboat) Mount gardens
Stephens Jn. cowkeeper, Mount gardens
Stephens Elizabeth Jane (Mrs) shop-keeper, Goat street
Stephens John, farmer, Vachelich
Thomas Edwin, cathedral carpenter, Brynhyfryn
Thomas Elizh (Mrs), baker, New st
Thomas Elizabeth (Mrs), grocer, Rhodiad
Thomas Henry, farmer, Tretio
Thomas John, blacksmith, Priskilly terrace
Thomas John, farmer, Lleity
Thomas Sarah (Mrs), farmer, Trelethydfawr
Thomas Thomas, insurance agent & draper, Cross square
Thomas William, farmer, Rhosson
Thomas William, frmr., Treleddid Fawr
Tossell James, grocer and confectioner, New street
Town Hall (Samuel J. W. Williams, manager), New street
Tudor Martha A. (Mrs), apartments, Goodwood House, Nun street
Waters David, farmer, Llandigigefawr
Waters
Walters Henry, farmer, Trevithan
Walters James, farmer, Hargloddisaf
Watkins Thos., farmer, Hendre Manor
Watts Mary Jane (Mrs) Laundress, Coedegan terrace, Goat street
Williams William Davies & Co. grocers, drapers, hatters, stationers & ironmongers, Cross square
Williams Adrian Owen Watts, general merchant, Cross square
Williams Catherine (Mrs), glass and china dealer, New street
Williams Edith (Miss), farmer, Carfai & Ramsey Island
Williams Edith (Miss) farmer, Mynydd Du
Williams Ellen (Mrs), farmer, Trelerwr
Williams James, carpenter & builder, New street
Williams John Morgan, solicitor, perpetual commissioner for oaths, agent for Lloyds bank & insurance agent, High street
Williams Thos., farmer, Low. Treginnis
Williams Thos., farmer, Tretio
Williams William D. clerk to County School Management, Gwalia
Williams William Wilfred, L.R.C.P., M.R.C.S., physician & surgeon, admiralty surgeon, certifying factory surgeon, medical officer of health and medical officer & public vaccinator, St. David's district, Haverfordwest union, Glendower house, Nun street

Farmers	95	Insurance agent	1
Dairies	1	Solicitor	1
Cowkeepers	3	Doctor	1
Cattle Dealers	1	Dentist	1
Guest houses, apartments, hotels	18	Chemist	1
Laundress	1	Banks	2
Drapers	2	Schoolmasters	3
Bakers	4	School attendance officer	1
Shopkeepers (unspecified)	4	Clergy	5
Grocers	10	Cathedral organist	1
Butchers	2	Nonconformist ministers	4
Watchmaker	1	Barrister	1
Boot makers and dealers	5	Weavers	3
Dressmakers	3	Millers	3
Tailors	2	Masons	5
Saddler	1	Blacksmiths	5
Glass & china dealer	1	Carpenters	5
General merchant	1	Jobmaster	1
Coal merchants	2	Town Crier	1

APPENDIX IV

Farmers and their Farms from the Tithe Schedule 1838

Caerfarchell – Henry Bevan
Thomas Jenkins
Caerhys – Henry Perkin
Carnhedryn – Thomas John
Carnhedryn Issa – Thomas David
Clegyr – John Williams
Clegyrvoia – James Bowen
John Davies
Elizabeth James
George Roberts
Croeswdig – William Rees
Cwmwdig – David Howells
Emlych – Thomas Rees
Gwrhyd – Thomas Martin
James Rowland
Gwrhyd Bach – William Owen
Hendre – William Harries
Hendre Eynon – William Davies
Llaethty – James Lewis
Llandigige Fach – James Nicholas
Llandrudion – William Lewis
John Perkin
James Rees
Llanverran – Thomas Evans
Llanvirn – Henry Perkins
David Roch
Lleithir – Dorothy Roberts
Lower Harglodd – Mrs Beynon
Lower Treginnis – Henry Harries
Mynydd Du – William Roberts
Penarthur – George Williams
Penberry – William Davies
Pencarnan – Thomas Lewis
Porthclais – David Rees
Porthllysky – George Perkins
Porthmawr – Thomas Greenish
John Price
William Rees
Pwllcawrog – Thomas and David Perkin
Rhodiad – James Propert
Rhosson – John Rees
Rhosycribed – George Williams
Skyfog – Thomas David
William David
Henry John
Eben Morgan
Trefhyspus – John Rees
Tregydd – William Thomas
Trehenlliw – Thomas Martin
Treiago – William Bowen
Trekenny – Henry Stephens
Treleddid Fawr – Elizabeth Arnold
George Harries
John Mortimer
Thomas Rees
Trelerwr – Anne Hughes
Abel Lloyd
Trelewyd – Revd James Griffiths
Treleddin – Phoebe Bland
Henry Bowen
Treleidir – William John
William Lewis
Tremunny – Henry Owen
Tresais – Henry Jenkins
Tretio – Edward Bevan
John Bevan
William John
Trevadog – John Lewis
Trevarchan – George Martin
Thomas Martin
Trevelly – Thomas Martin
Trevinnart – Jane Rees
Revd A. Richardson
Trevithan – William Walters
Trewellwell – Revd Th. Mortimer
Treythell – Watkin Lewis
Ty Gwynne – John Evans
Upper Harglodd – Levi Owen
Upper Treginnis – John Mortimer
Vagwrgaiad – Mary Anne Owens

APPENDIX V

The Cathedral Deans (1840–) and Nonconformist Ministers

Caerfarchell

1873–1875	John Griffiths
1888–1902	H. Solva Thomas
1905–1909	E. J. Herbert
1915–1922	E. R. Davies
1922–1925	A. H. Rogers
1927–1935	R.T. Davies
1940–1942	William Thomas
1961–1965	D. Haydn Thomas
1966–1975	D. T. Davies

Ebenezer

1784–1795	James Richards
1795–1833	William Harries
1814–1854	James Griffiths
1847–1857	John Lloyd Evans
1863–1866	Jenkin Jones
1868–1881	John Foulkes
1883–1888	William Powell
1889–1904	L. T. Jones
1909–1928	James Abel
1931–1933	James John
1933–1945	B. P. Protheroe
1948–1968	Emrys Evans
1975–	Elvet Lewis

Tabernacle

1838–1861	William Morris
1861–1881	George Williams
1882–1904	William Jenkins
1905–1909	Richard Williams
1912–1919	Eurfyl Jones
1920–1932	Thomas Bowen
1940–1946	D. Idwal Jones
1947–1952	R. Hugh Evans
1953–1959	W. O. Barnett
1961–1965	D. Haydn Thomas
1966–1975	D. T. Davies

Tretio and Seion

John Richards
Shon Clun
David Jones
William Reynolds
John Evans

1864–1871	Daniel Davies
1876–1878	Joseph Davies
1871	Benjamin Evans
1880	Henry Harries
1890–1903	J. S. Jones
1905–1913	W. D. Rees
1913–1916	Waldo Roberts
1919–1943	J. Gruffydd Davies
1945–1951	E. Dulais Jones
1953–1959	Awstin Henry
1961–1962	John M. Lewis
1969–1972	J. Watts Williams

Deans of the Cathedral

Llewellyn Lewellin 1840–1878 (The Dictionary of National Biography gives 1843)
James Allen, canon 1847–1870;
chancellor 1870–1878;
dean 1878–1895.
Evan Owen Phillips 1895–1897.
David Howell (Llawdden) 1897–1903.
Allan Smith 1903–1919.
William Williams 1919–1930
Watcyn Morgan 1931–1940
A. W. Parry 1940–1949
Witton Davies 1949–1956
T. E. Jenkins 1957–1972
Lawrence Bowen 1972–

APPENDIX VI

Headmasters

Headmasters

County School- Ysgol Dewi Sant

1895–1897	Lewis Williams
1897–1929	Thomas Thomas
1929–1936	Edgar Thomas
1936–1959	John J. Evans
1959–1974	David W. James
1974–	J. Glyn Owen

The Church or National School

January	1874	William Appleby
May	1883	Benjamin Hopkins
July	1883	Thomas Charles Kingdon
October	1890	J. S. F. Davies
January	1892	William Appleton
July	1930	Herbert George Perkins
January	1945	Bryn Davies
October	1951	Odo R. Saunders
May	1962	George J. Bird

The Council or Board School

March	1872	Thomas J. Polkinghorne
October	1875	William Jones
January	1880	Benjamin Hopkins
April	1883	Frederick Lewis
September	1920	Harold Heath
January	1921	J. J. Jenkins
	1948	W. O. Hughes
September	1957	J. H. M. Bateman
September	1975	David Salmon

APPENDIX VII

The First Log Book of the St. David's Rate Aided School 1872–1900

25 March 1872. Master – Thomas J. Polkinghorne (Certificated Second Class). These rooms (the Vestry Rooms near the Commercial Hotel) are preliminary . . . the number of children admitted was 17. The only member of the School Board that put in an appearance was the Revd Thomas Jones, D.D., Vice Chairman. Mr Foulkes, the Treasurer of the Board, also attended and two or three gentlemen from the neighbourhood. No furniture (desks not put up). Books not arrived.

19 April 1872. Improved attendance. Average nearly 64. Popularity of spelling lessons and competitions. One boy (Hedley Pearce) was sent to Solva by his parents in the morning and ran a considerable part of the way that he might be present at the exam.

7 June 1872. St. David's Fair. No school.

5 July 1872. William Griffiths of Tretio broke his leg when returning from school on Thursday, 27 June. He was riding a donkey and the animal went to lie down and lay on his leg.

26 July 1872. Many pupils kept at home 'about the hay'.

27 September 1872. Poor attendance. Late harvest. So much to do with the farmers and there are so many sales about and changing of houses.

December 1872. St. David's December Fair.

28 March 1873. Potato setting interfered with attendance.

16 May 1873. School visited by Mr Williams, late of Penarthur, and Revd Griffiths of Cilgerran, Calvinistic Methodist minister.

27 June 1873. Miss Edmunds, who has for many years past carried on a school in connection with the Calvinistic Methodist chapel, has been engaged as Assistant Mistress.

4 July 1873. 40 children admitted, 39 of whom were Miss Edmund's scholars.

1 August 1873. Ebenezer Williams left the school today. He is going as Clerk in the Ystradgynlais Post Office.

8 August 1873. Thomas James called for his books. He is going to work in the coalpit, coalcutting. It is a pity that such a sharp fellow is compelled to earn his bread by manual labour.

19 September 1873. School recommences. Country children are all absent, except one. Harvest.

28 November 1873. Attendance on Wednesday interfered with. Services held at Caerfarchell – recognition of their new minister, Mr Griffiths.

19 December 1873. Attendance low. Baptist Chapel being reopened.

16 January 1874. Holiday. Old New Year's Day.

13 March 1874. Few in school. Snow. Boys asked for a holiday to go snowballing.

20 March 1874. Attendance low. Potato setting, and the gardens.

2 April 1874. Large vessel wrecked in the bay. The neighbourhood has been wrecking all the week.

24 April 1874. Average attendance 126. Llandeloy Fair. Country boys away.

29 May 1874. Attendance low. Quarterly Meeting at Independent Chapel.

14 September 1874. New Bishop to be enthroned tomorrow. (William Basil Jones).

13 November 1874. Whitchurch Parish Church reopened after restoration.

18 December 1874. Removal of several families during the year. After Christmas, the Act regulating the employment of children in agriculture will come into operation.

9 July 1875. Two children, Jane and Rowena Morse, readmitted. They left some time ago and went to the Church School. As I suppose they did not find that so agreeable as they had expected, they have returned.

9 July 1875. George Owen of Beehive buried. His parents wished the children to attend. The Board consented.

18 August 1875. Average attendance 154. There is to be a treat tomorrow. That accounts for the unusually high attendance.

1 October 1875. Godwin Roberts and Thomas Jenkins have been appointed choristers in the Cathedral, in consequence left us and gone to the Collegiate and Chapter School.

18 October 1875. I, William Jones, late of Pontgarreg British School, commenced duties on Monday morning.

20 April 1883. Frederick Lewis took charge.

17 October 1884. Holiday. Reopening of Wesleyan Chapel. Abram John missing lessons. I think it useless to talk any more.

13 July 1900. The last entry.
Master – Frederick Lewis
Rosina Davies Rees
Pupil Teachers – Blodwen Thomas, Mary Jones, Hubert G. Perkins
Sewing Mistress – Miss Phillips.

APPENDIX VIII

First Log Book of St. David's Church School (1874–1919)

5 July 1874. Mr Appleby took charge. Bad attendance, bad behaviour. Talking and idleness.

20 April 1874. Admitted the choristers. They behaved very badly, were disobedient, noisy, idle, talkative, and generally troublesome.

21 May 1883. School conducted by Benjamin Hopkins.

16 July 1883. Thomas Ch. Kingdon (Certificated 2nd Class) takes charge today as Master. First impressions shocking.

18 July 1883. Punished few boys this evening for persistent idleness and impertinence with a rod picked from a hedge, a cane being unobtainable. Minerva Mortimer caned for imprudent conduct to Miss John, the sewing mistress.

1 December 1885. General election for county member. Holiday the whole day to enable master to go to Solva to record his vote.

14 December 1885. Small attendance, children having gone to see the new Lifeboat.

9 December 1919. School reopened.
W. P. Appleton – Master.
E. Perkins,
M. J. Richards.

Almost the last entry of this first log book notes that Lena Sime and Bowen Rees had entered the Intermediate School.

APPENDIX IX

First Register of St. David's County School 1895

1895	April 29	Williams I. Penry
		Davies W. Jenkin (Penberry)
		Lewis John Stephen (Herbert Lewis's brother)
		Harries Stephen
		Williams W. D. James
		Williams Ivor H. (printer)
		Evans Ernest D.
		Williams Edwin D.
		Jamieson G. B.
		Thomas Henry John
	April 30	Evans Dewi
	April 29	Williams Winnie (printer)
		Thomas Eleanor Ann
		Davies Phoebe (Kingherriot)
		Jenkins Henry (Croftufty)
		Williams T. D.
		Whitaker Frances
		Owen Mary Jane (Abereithy)
		Williams Martha Ann
		Thomas Minnie Maud
		Tudor Elizabeth Ann
		Beynon Eleanor A.
		Jay Dorothy
		Mortimer Olga
		Jones Samuel
		Davies Thomas Henry (Porthlyski)
	May 3	Williams Harry (Sampson)
	May 6	Arnold Lillian
		Howells George (Caerwen)
	May 7	Thomas Ethel Ince (baker)
	May 8	Jones Mary Ann (Sam Jones)
	May 9	Jenkins Edith
	May 13	Williams Mima (Porthgain)
		Phillips I. T. (traction engine driver)

The next term registered the addition of

Daniel Gronow
Margaret Ann Gronow
William Francis (Porthgain)
Edith Perkins
William Stephens
George Meredith Harries
and A. S. Whitaker.

(In brackets are comments written in pencil on the register).

APPENDIX X

The Welsh Port Books: St. David's (1566–1603)

11 April 1566.
Le Marie de portu Milford
Master – Thomas Stephens
Bristol
Merchant – Alexander Watkyns of St. David's
1 butt seck, 2 hnd metheglyne, 2 brls dry wares, 1 piece raisins,
½ cwt hops, 1 last emptye cask.

17 June 1566.
Le Salamon de Abothing
Barnstaple to St. David's
2 hnd iron, 60 qrs salt, 1 butt seck, 20 pieces calico,
12 lbs pepper, 1 burden fish.

25 May 1577.
The Steven of St. David's
inwards to Carnarvon
Master – Thomas ap John Philipe
Merchant – Thomas Williams
7 bushels dregge malt, 20 bushels peas, 80 bushels barley malt,
80 bushels wheat.

5 May 1586.
Le Jesu de Sancte David
St. David's to Dovey and Bermo
60 qrs barley malt, 20 qrs barley, 18 pilkorne.

10 June 1586.
Le Saviour de St. David's
St. David's to Bristol
Master – Thomas John Phillipe
Captain – Thomas Williams of St. David's.
60 st wool.
(This same ship had sailed from Milford Haven to Minehead on 9 November of the previous year to deliver 350 stone of wool to a merchant in Dunster, Somerset)

28 April 1587.
Le Angell de Bermo
St. David's to Bermo
20 qrs wheat, 100 qrs barley, 50 qrs pilcorn, 20 qrs rye.

4 February 1601.
The Mary of Wexford
Wexford to St. David's
20 Irish boards, 1,000 laths.

26 June 1601.
The Saviour of St. David's
Sailing out of Milford to Wexford
7 qrs malt, 2 qrs wheat.

19 June 1603.
The George of St. David
Captain – Thomas John Phillipe
Merchant – William Lewis
St. David's to Bermo
100 bushels wheat, 80 bushels barley malt.

30 July 1603.
The John of Wexford
Captain – Patrick Sinnett
Merchant – James Raymond
8 doz small poles and ashen timber, 1 piece of draught timber,
1 car full of bark.

APPENDIX XI

Boats of Abercastell, Solva, and St. David's 1828–1836

1828 Royal George (square) 95 tons. Built Solva 1802.
T. Raymond, Solva (landowner),
T. Williams, Solva (mariner).

1828 Industrious (sloop) 26 tons. Built Milford 1828.
R. Williams, Solva (mariner),
W. Roberts, Milford (shipbuilder),
R. Gwyther, Broadhaven (farmer).

1829 Felicity 159 tons. Built Lawrenny 1816.
R. Beynon, Solva (mariner),
T. Canton, Lawrenny (shipbuilder),
D. Vaughan, Milford (mariner).

1829 Kitty (sloop) 25 tons. Built Lawrenny 1829.
G. Williams, St. David's (merchant),
G. Perkins, St. David's (farmer),
H. Grinnis, St. David's (mariner).

1829 Betsy (sloop) 15 tons. Built Milford 1818.
W. Thomas, Solva (mariner),
J. Thomas, Solva (mariner).

1829 Milford 113 tons. Built Lawrenny 1808.
J. Owens, St. David's (mariner),
William Harries, St. David's (gentleman),
T. Canton, Lawrenny (shipbuilder).

1830 Expedition (sloop) 59 tons. Built Chepstow 1819.
J. Williams, Solva (mariner),
H. Williams, Haverfordwest (mariner),
W. Roberts, Milford (shipbuilder).

1830 Milford Packet 59 tons. Built Milford 1830.
H. Richards, Trevine (master mariner),
T. Richards, Haverfordwest,
W. Roberts, Milford.

1831 Union Packet 43 tons. Built Tenby 1820.
W. Lewis, Solva (mariner),
W. Bowen, Pembroke (victualler),
B. Thomas, Pembroke (draper).

1831 Alexander 28 tons. Built Solva 1821.
T. Raymond, Solva (Esquire),
W. Hughes, St. David's (mariner).

1831 Eliza Ann 20 tons. Built Lawrenny 1831.
T. John, Solva (mariner),
W. Thomas, Solva (farmer),
W. Roberts, Milford (shipbuilder).

1832 Hope 27 tons. Built Solva 1832.
S. Lewis, Solva (master mariner),
W. Lawrence, Solva (shipwright),
J. Phillips, Trenewydd (farmer).

1832 Flying Fish 24 tons. Built Kinsale 1818.
W. Thomas, Solva (mariner).
1832 Olive 89 tons. Built Lawrenny 1804.
S. Loyn, Solva (spinster).
1833 Britannia 33 tons. Built Solva 1810.
T. Raymond, Solva (Esquire),
W. Griffiths, Solva (mariner).
1833 Jane 28 tons. Built Solva 1809.
R. James. Solva (merchant).
1834 Pilgrim (sloop) 26 tons. Built Haverfordwest 1808.
John Davies, St. David's (mariner),
John Williams, Solva (merchant).
1830 John and Mary (sloop) 52 tons. Built Lawrenny 1829.
D. T. and J. Evans, St. David's (mariners).
1830 William (sloop) 17 tons. Built Lawrenny 1830.
T. Hughes, St. David's (mariner).
1835 William (sloop) 35 tons. Built Haverfordwest 1803.
John Howell, Solva (merchant),
William Roach, St. David's (mariner).
1835 Orielton (schooner) 114 tons. Built Lawrenny 1835.
William Morgan, Abercastle (Esquire),
D. Williams, Newport.
1835 Valiant (sloop) 18 tons. Built Lawrenny 1835.
H. Grinnis, St. David's (mariner),
T. Grinnis, St. David's (farmer).
1835 Margaret (sloop) 21 tons. Built Lawrenny 1835.
J. Thomas, Abercastle (merchant).
1835 Cecilia (smack) 22 tons. Built Solva 1835.
T. Bevan (malster),
H. Lawrence, Solva (shipbuilder).
1836 John and Mary (smack) 40 tons. Built Lawrenny 1829.
John Evans, St. David's (mariner).
1836 Flying Fish (smack) 90 tons. Built Kinsale 1818.
William Thomas, Solva (mariner).
1836 Favourite Nancy 17 tons. Built Milford 1817.
George Perkins, St. David's (farmer),
J. Rees, St. David's (mariner).
1836 Kitty (sloop) 15 tons. Built Lawrenny 1829.
George Perkins, St. David's (farmer).
1836 Orielton 100 tons. Built Lawrenny.
W. Morgan, Abercastle, (Esquire),
D. Williams, Newport (master mariner).
1836 Hope (sloop) 18 tons. Built Solva.
S. Lewis, Solva (mariner),
W. Lawrence, Solva (shipwright),
J. Phillips, Solva (farmer).
1836 Cecilia 15 tons. Built Solva 1835.
T. Bevan, Solva (mariner),
W. Lawrence, Solva (shipbuilder).

(Extracts from the Customs Register at Milford Haven, made by W. R. G. Lewis of Waterloo Road, Hakin, kept in the Library in Haverfordwest)

(Kitty, twice registered in Milford, was a one-mast one-deck boat of 15 908/1350 tons. Favourite Nancy, built in Milford in 1817, was of 17 38/350 tons. Her total ownership was spread amongst George Perkins, John Rees, William Davies, and the two brothers, John and George Williams. The Milford, whose master was John Owens, was a one-deck, two-masted brig of 113 84/94 tons, predominantly in the ownership of John Owens and William Harries, both of Hendre. She was finally sold to new owners in Bridgewater, and, having traded first in the Mediterranean and later with Ireland, foundered in Morecambe Bay in January, 1865.)

APPENDIX XII

Imports and Exports Coastwise (1827–1850) based on Bristol Presentments

Entered out coastwise:

21 May 1827.	The Mary (G. James) to Solva and Milford.
23 March 1840.	The Otter (Harris) to Solva.
5 September 1850.	The Kitty (Richards) to Solva and St. David's.
21 October 1850.	The Brothers (Davis) to Solva and St. David's.

Imports coastwise:

9 February 1850.	Eliza (J. James) from Solva. 155 qrs barley. Order. 1208 brls barley W. & E. Vining. True Bess (D. Williams) from Solva. 125 qrs barley. Order. 1220 brls barley. W. & E. Vining. Alligator (J. Reynolds) from Solva. 82 qrs 5 bush wheat 95 qrs 2 bush oats Order 700 bush wheat. J. Williams 700 bush oats. J. Williams
28 February 1850	Rechabite (T. James) from Solva. 155 qrs barley. Order. 1240 bush barley. W. & E. Vining. Kitty (W. Richards) from Solva. 85 qrs wheat, 35 qrs oats. Order 670 bush wheat W. & E. Vining 280 bush potatoe oats. W & E. Vining Alligator (J. Reynolds) from Solva 47 qrs 4 bush barley 96 qrs 2 bush oats
10 June 1850	Brothers (T. Davis) from Solva 194 qrs barley
15 July 1850	Brothers (T. Davis) from Solva 175 qrs barley 6 qrs 2 bush oats
10 October 1850	Brothers (T. Davis) from Solva 685 bush oats J. Williams 200 bush barley J. Williams 200 casks butter J. Williams
19 October 1850	Kitty (W. Richards) from St. David's 63 Casks butter. J. Williams
26 December 1850	Rechabite (T. James) from Solva 1088 bush wheat J. Williams 59 cheese J. Williams 8 casks butter J. Williams

23 December 1850	Kitty (W. Griffiths) from Solva 936 bush oats J. Williams 21 casks butter J. Williams 30 qrs wheat J. Williams

APPENDIX XIII

Wrecks in the St. David's Area 1748–1961

1	Alaric. Green Scar, Solva. Pitch pine balks.	March	1874
2	Albeona. St. Anne's Head.	March	1873
3	Albion. Jack Sound		1873
4	Alice Williams. 2 masted wooden topsail schooner. Skokolm		1928
5	Alicia. St. Bride's Bay.	January	1841
6	Amazonia. Gesail Fawr.	April	1881
7	Amity. St. Justinan's.	January	1875
8	Anne Davies. Smack. Ramsey Sound.	November	1870
9	m.v. Athel Duchess of Liverpool. Smalls.	August	1943
10	Beatrice. North Bishop.		
11	California		
12	The Cardiff Brig. The Bishops.		1838
13	Caroline. Porthgain.	October	1859
14	Cashair. Barque. Solva.	February	1900
15	Catherine. Porth Melgan. (a load of sugar)		
16	Chester. Ramsey Sound.	November	1870
17	Clara Felicia. The Bishops.	September	1899
18	Cymbric Prince		
19	Dan Beard. Strumble Head.	December	1944
20	Dorothy and Mary		
21	s.s Eagle. The Bishops.		
22	Edith Crossfield. North Bishop.	May	1904
23	Elizabeth of Newquay. Ramsey Island.	November	1882
24	Ellen. Grassholm.	December	1813
25	s.s. Ellerbeck. Hats and Barrels.	August	1914
26	Emmanuel. Ramsey Sound.	January	1925
27	Exeter. Ramsey Sound.	October	1879
28	Flora. Timber Spruce.	November	1852
29	Formosa. 3 masted barque. St. David's Head.	November	1915
30	Fortitude. The Smalls.		1812
31	Frederick. St. David's Head. General cargo.	February	1833
32	Friends. Y Gesail.		1819
33	Graffoe. South of Ramsey.	January	1903
34	Guiding Star. Whitesands.		1878
35	Gwen of Beaumaris. The Horse.	April	1882
36	Hope of Liverpool. North Bishop. 1000 tons guano	December	1847
37	Langton Grange (Houlder Line) Bell Rock.	August	1909
38	Le Courier. Porthclais.	October	1879
39	Lesmahagon. Llanunwas. Timber.	November	1861
40	Lewis of Beaumaris. Schooner. Crow Rock. (slates)	March	1894
41	Linen Hall. Druidston.		1810
42	Loch Shiel. Thorn Island.	January	1894

43	Louis Peros. South Bishop.		
44	Lyly Dale. Off Ramsey.	March	1895
45	Maggie Woodburn. The Smalls.	November	1872
46	Mar del Plata. Hats and Barrels.	February	1923
47	Margaret of Barrow. Crab Bay.	April	1878
48	Margaret of Swansea. Skokolm.	August	1893
49	Martha. St. David's.	October	1859
50	Mayflower. Porthclais.		1879
51	Morna. Crimea transport. North Bishop.	February	1855
52	Mersey of Liverpool. South Bishop Rock.	June	1871
53	Messenger of Exeter. Ramsey.	October	1879
54	s.s. Moleseley.	November	1929
55	Mladen. Whitesands.	November	1850
56	Molly. Sloop. Cardigan to Bideford. Ramsey.	September	1841
57	Mystic Tie. Cantor, Ramsey.	November	1877
58	Naples. Carreg y Wylan. Boston – wheat.		1849
59	Nimrod. St. Elvis. General cargo.	February	1860
60	Notre Dame de Fatima. Trawler. Skokolm.	November	1956
61	Oak of Belfast. St. Elvis.	October	1862
62	Ogmore of Dundee. Horse Rock. (potatoes)	April	1894
63	Orion. St. David's.	October	1859
64	Paulina. Iron. Porth Melgan.	March	1833
65	Perseverance of Yarmouth. St. Bride's Bay.	December	1841
66	Portland. Ramsey Sound.		
67	Prima. Smack. Ramsey Sound.	November	1870
68	Queen. Skokolm.	September	1843
69	Redcliff. Hats and Barrels.	January	1887
70	Resolution. Newgale.		1690
71	Rose of Liverpool. Y Dduallt.	January	1748
72	Rosina.	February	1873
73	St. Catherine. Whitesands Bay.		
74	St. Iztvan. Ramsey.		1907
75	Sarah Macdonald. The Smalls.	October	1913
76	Storjohann. Barque. Ramsey.	December	1882
77	Stumberlie. Hats and Barrels.	May	1891
78	Susannah Boulet. Ramsey.		1877
79	Suzanne Adriane. The Smalls.	December	1958
80	Tank Landing Craft (2). St. Anne's Head.	April	1943
81	Telegraph.	May	1876
82	s.s. Thomas Vaughan. Skomer.	January	1872
83	Thorold of Montreal. Smalls Lighthouse.	August	1940
84	Transit. Smack. Ramsey Sound.	October	1870
85	s.s. Trojan. Skomer.	October	1944
86	Turtle Dove. The Bitches.	May	1875
87	Two Brothers. Ramsey.	July	1872
88	Tynedale. Ramsey.	March	1877
89	Victoria of Waterford. Solva.		1848
90	Weima. m.v. The Smalls.	December	1961
91	Whitehaven. The Horse	May	1879
92	World Concord. South Bishops Lighthouse.	November	1954
93	Pearl. Schooner. Smalls Lighthouse	August	1913

(Confirmations from the Lifeboat Records, from local newspaper, from the Francis Green 'cuttings' files in the Regional Library in Haverfordwest, and from Mr D. A. Nash.)

Addenda

Commerce (26 ton sloop)	Ramsey Sound	1844
Myra (31 ton smack)	Jack Sound	1868
Atlantic (67 ton sloop)	Ramsey	1847
Wasp (29 ton sloop)	St. Bride's Bay	1870
Priscilla Eliza (74 ton schooner)	Porthgain	1869
Ellen Owen (131 ton schooner)	Smalls	1876

(The above from Ceredigion, Journal of the Ceredigion Antiquarian Society. Vol. 7. 1974–1975)

APPENDIX XIV

'Vessels wrecked or disabled since 1825'

(From Samuel Williams's Letter Books in the National Library)

1 Weasel of London. Cargo – slates. Abereiddy.
2 Jane of Bangor. Iron ore. Abereiddy.
3 *** of Dumfries. Tallow. Aberpwll.
4 John Ginzes of Newport. Ballast. Llechau.
5 Hannah of Aberystwyth. General. Llechau.
6 Star of Montrose. Copper ore. Porth***.
7 Naples. Indian Corn. Porth***.
8 Lady Mansfield of London. Hides. Y Dduallt.
9 *** of Aberaeron. Ballast. Y Gesail Fawr.
10 Morning Star. *** *** Y Gesail Fawr.
11 Brothers of Milford. Lime. Y Gesail Fawr.
12 Three Sisters of Aberaeron. Culm. Porthllong.
13 Nimrod of Cork. General. Porthllong.
14 Annie of Aberystwyth. Ballast. Porthllong.
15 Frederick of Liverpool. General. St. David's Head.
16 Catherine of Belfast. Sugar. Porthmelgan.
17 Atlantic of Newquay. Iron rails. Porthmelgan.
18 Flora of Waterford. Pit wood. Porthmelgan.
19 Acronian of Aberaeron. Iron ore (?). Porthmelgan.
20 Anne (?) of Barnstaple. Malt. Whitesands.
21 Bolina of Bideford. Pig ore. Whitesands.
22 Providence of Penzance. *** Whitesands.
23 M*** *** Wheat. Whitesands.
24 *** *** Lead ore. Whitesands.
25 Wasp of Newquay. Iron ore. Whitesands.
26 *** *** Pit wood. Pencarnan.
27 Xenia of Barmouth. China stone. Porth y Brag.
28 *** *** Caernarvon slate. Porth y Brag.
29 Sisters of Milford. Ballast. Cestyll.
30 Commerce of New Quay. Empties. Cestyll.
31 Jenny Jones of Cardigan. Limestone. Cestyll.
32 New Milford of Newport. Ballast. ***
33 John and Mary of Fishguard. Ballast. ***
34 Kitty of Kinsale. Potatoes. Carnarwig.
35 Anne of Cardigan. Ballast. The Bitches.
36 Hannah of Cardigan. Slate slabs. Y Watrin.
37 Daphne of New Quay. Iron ore (?). Gwaun-garreg.
38 Henry of Pwllheli. Slates. Gwaun-garreg.
39 Farmers Delight of Salcombe. Nuts. Abermawr.
40 William Irving of Cardiff. Ballast. North Bishop.
41 Aurora of Dinas. Iron ore (?). North Bishop.
42 Norma of Belfast. General. North Bishop.
43 *** *** Grain. Dau Fraich.
44 John and Henry. Iron ore. Dau Fraich.

45 Beatrice of Aberdovey. Iron rails. South Bishop.
46 Petite Louise of Dunkirk. Onions. South Bishop.
47 Gomez of Aberporth. Limestone. Ramsey Sound.
48 Rechabite of Fishguard. Culm. Ramsey Sound.
49 Flower of the South of Castletown. Potatoes. Ramsey Sound.
50 Victoria of New Quay. Coals. Y Bedol.
51 Gate of Cardigan. Limestone. Y Foel (Fawr of Ramsey).
52 Susannah of Bangor. General. Carreg y Fran.
53 Henry of Beaumaris. Oats. Carreg y Fran.
54 Belsey of St. David's. Ballast. Porthclais.
55 Eliza of St. David's. Limestone. ***
56 Alligator of Solva. Culm. Penpleidiau.
57 St. David of St. David's. General. Caerbwdi.
58 L*** *** Timber. Llanunwas.
59 Amelia of Cardigan. ?
60 *** *** Slates. Y Garreg Ddu.
61 *** *** Ballast. Traethgwyn.
62 Hannah of Milford. Ballast. Porthlagnewydd.
63 Providence of Shoreham. *** Pointz Castle.
64 Annie of Yarmouth. Ballast. Newgale.
65 Water Lily of Fowey. Ballast. St. Bride's Bay.
66 Mary of St. David's. Culm. St. Bride's Bay.
67 Veronica of Llanelly. Iron ore. St. Bride's Bay.
68 Defence of Porthmadoc. Slates. St. Bride's Bay.
69 Pilgrim of Solva. Limestone. St. Bride's Bay.

APPENDIX XV

St. David's Master Mariners and Captains

Thomas Jenkins and William Jenkins and John Evans of Caerfarchell.
The James family, father and sons, of Porth Glais, William, Thomas, Ebenezer, and John, who worked for the Hudson Bay Company.
John Rees and his son, John Rees, of Rhosson.
James Hughes, John Evans, Thomas Williams, Daniel Williams, David Williams, Henry Richards and John Davies, of St. David's.
John James of Trelerwr.
John Murrow, Henry Grinnis and Thomas Harry of St. David's.
John Hughes of Pentre Cyrill.
William Richard of Hafhesp and Ebenezer Harry of Gwrhyd Mawr.
Thomas Davies of Dyfrog Bridge, James Bowen of Clegyr, Thomas Hicks, James Brown, Thomas Harries, of St. David's.
Henry Rees. Thomas Davies of Trefaeddan House and Thomas Lewis of Grove Villa. George Beer of Maenor House.
Davies of Goodwood, John Tudor, William Oakley, Price of Berea, Henry Lewis, John Williams, George Lile.
John Mathias of Epworth who lost his life at sea in 1875.
Thomas Howell of Tir George Arnold.
James Davies of Nun Street, John Williams of Pantycyrill, James John of Pit Street, John Beynon of New Street, John Prosser of Naw Ffynon, James Webb of Porth Lisgi, Thomas Roach and Henry Beynon of Waunbeddau. George Lewis (Trinity House).
Thomas Griffiths.
John Roberts of Epworth.
David Williams, of s.s. Pembrokeshire, buried in Tretio.
John Stephens, coxswain of the Lifeboat from 1904 to 1910.
Tom Mortimer.
Peter Perkins, Samuel Roach, the Inkerman Williamses, Thomas Williams of Gwrhyd Bach, John Emlyn Davies, Leslie Owen.
George Harries, Jim Arnold, Dannie Evans, Bleddyn James.

(This list has been compiled primarily from the registers of chapels and churches, Rate Books, and newpapers)

APPENDIX XVI

The Police Force 1857–1968

From 1554, to 9 June 1857, the Parish Constable controlled the City of St. David's, under the supervision of the High Constable, later the Superintending Constable of the Hundred of Dewisland.

11 October 1840	– Thomas Davies appointed High Constable.
5 February 1842	– William Evans of Pencnwc (of Castle Morris).
4 April 1843	– William Thomas and Thomas Davies of Llanddwfi.
9 April 1844	– William Thomas and Thomas Davies.

From 31 December 1844 to 9 June 1857, George Jones was Superintending Constable.

The Pembrokeshire Police was formed on 9 June 1857, when George Jones became Superintendent in Charge of the Fishguard Division.

9.6.1857 – 29.6.63	John Davies PC15
17.12.1879 – 16.10.1883	William Smith PC37
16.10.1883 – 8.1.1886	David Pearce PC38
4.11.1887 – 17.8.1889	John James PC35 (father of C. B. James, later Chief Constable of the County)
30.9.1889 – 1.2.1891	Joseph Tudor PC46
4.2.1901 – 25.3.1901	William Morris PC8
12.11.1904 – 29.9.1910	Daniel Jenkins PC48
29.9.1910 – 30.9.1923	David Henry Lewis PC14
1.10.1923 – 27.10.1933	William Llewellyn PC43 (father of W. Llewellyn, High Street, present Honorary Secretary of the St. David's Lifeboat)

On 6 November 1933, St. David's was formed into a Sergeant's Section.

6.11.33 – 1.6.35	PS1 William George Wood
1.6.35 – 14.8.36	PS10 William George Victor Jones
14.8.36 – 18.1.39	PS11 Frederick James
18.1.39 – 11.3.40	PS Lemuel Trevor Rees
11.3.40 – 8.5.46	PS9 William Idwal Evans
8.5.46 – 3.1.50	PS Ernest Eynon Richards
30.1.50 – 8.8.51	PS Norman Wilnow
8.8.51 – 7.4.52	PS17 Percy Phillips
7.4.52 – 18.5.56	PS8 Robert Winston Jones
18.5.56 – 6.12.61	PS8 Elwyn Edwards
6.12.61 – 31.7.67	PS9 Daniel Ungoed
2.8.67 – 29.1.68	PS9 Walford Davies

On 1 April 1968, the Pembrokeshire Police amalgamated with the Dyfed Powys Police. At the west end of the nave of the Cathedral, on the south side of the West Door, is the plaque that commemorates the special service held in the Cathedral.

St. David's Cathedral (so runs the sub-title of the service leaflet) Pembrokeshire Police 1857–1968. A Service of Commemoration on Sunday, 17 March 1968, in the presence of Her Majesty's Lieutenant of the County of Pembroke (Col. the Honourable Hanning Philipps, M.B.E).

In 1976 St. David's ceased to be a Sergeant's Section.

(From Pembrokeshire Police Records – ex Inspector Winston Jones)

Bibliography

Abbreviations

CAA	Cambrian Archaeological Association
DKG	*Dewisland and Kemes Guardian*
HSPCW	Historical Society of the Presbyterian Church in Wales
JHSCW	*Journal of the Historical Society of the Church in Wales*
NLWJ	*National Library of Wales Journal*
THSC	*Transactions of the Honourable Society of Cymmrodorion*
WHR	*Welsh History Review*
WWHST	*West Wales Historical Society Transactions*

Archaeologia Cambrensis.

Baker, James. *Picturesque Guide through Wales and the Marches* (Winchester, 1795).

Barber, J. T. *Tour through South Wales* (London, 1803).

Baring-Gould, S. *In Dewisland* (London, 1904).

Bevan, W. L. *St. David's* (Diocesan Histories) (London, 1888).

Black's *Picturesque Guide through Wales* (London, 1865).

Bowen, E. G. *Wales: A Study in Geography and History* (Cardiff, 1941).

—— *The Settlements of the Celtic Saints in Wales* (Cardiff, 1954).

—— *Saints, Seaways and Settlements in the Celtic Lands* (Cardiff, 1969).

—— *Britain and the Western Seaways* (London, 1972).

Briant, Travers, J. *Guide to St. David's Cathedral* (London, 1896).

Broster, D. K. *Ships in the Bay* (London, 1931).

Browne-Willis. *Survey of the Cathedral Church of St. David's* (London, 1717).

Cambrian Register (London, 1799).

Chadwick, Nora. *The Age of the Saints in the Early Celtic Church* (Oxford, 1961).

Charles, B. G. *George Owen of Henllys* (National Library of Wales, 1974).

Davies, Walter (Gwallter Mechain). *General View of the Agriculture and Domestic Economy of South Wales* (1814).

Defoe, Daniel. *A Tour through England and Wales 1724–26* (Everyman).

Evans, Henry. *Twr-y-Felin History and Guide to St. David's* (1923).

Evans and John. *The Pembrokeshire Landscape* (Tenby, 1973).

Evans, J. J. *Cymry Enwog y Ddeunawfed Ganrif* (Aberystwyth, 1937).

—— *Dewi Sant a'i Amserau* (Llandysul, 1963).

Evans, Thomas. *Walks through Wales* (London, 1819).

Fenton, Richard. *A Tour through Pembrokeshire* (Brecknock, 1811).

Foord, Edward. *St. David's, Llandaff and Brecon* (London, 1925).

Foster and Daniel. *Prehistoric and Early Wales* (London, 1965).

Fox, Sir Cyril. *The Personality of Britain* (Cardiff, 1943).

—— 'The Round-chimneyed Farmhouses of Northern Pembrokeshire; *Aspects of Archaeology in Britain and Beyond* (1951).

Freeman, Eric. *Once in David's Royal City* (Llanblethian, 1959).
Friends of the Cathedral Reports.
Gastineau, Henry. *South Wales Illustrated* (London, 1830).
George, B. *Pembrokeshire Sea-Trading before 1900* (Dale Field Studies, 1964).
Giraldus Cambrensis. *The Itinerary through Wales* and *Description of Wales* (Everyman).
Hassall, Charles. *General View of the Agriculture of the County of Pembroke* (London, 1794).
Howells, Roscoe. *The Sounds Between* (Llandysul, 1968).
Hunt, J. Eric. *St. David's Cathedral* (SPCK, 1961).
Historical Society of West Wales Transactions.
Isaac, Evan. *Coelion Cymru* (Aberystwyth, 1938).
Jenkins, R. T. *Hanes Cymru yn y Ddeunawfed Ganrif* (Caerdydd, 1931).
Jones, Francis. 'Some Farmers of Bygone Pembrokeshire', THSC (1931).
—— 'Dissatisfaction and Dissent in Pembrokeshire', THSC (1967).
—— 'The Lordships and Manors of Dewsland', JHSCW (1966–9).
—— 'Rent Roll of the Temporalities of the See of St. David's', JHSCW (1976).
—— *The Holy Wells of Wales* (Cardiff, 1954).
Jones and Freeman, *History and Antiquities of St. David's* (London, 1856).
Jones, J. R. G. 'The Tribal System in Wales: A Re-Assessment in the Light of Settlement Studies', *WHR* Vol. 1 (1961).
Jones and Walker. *Links with the Past: Swansea and Brecon Historical Studies* (Llandybie, 1974).
Journal of the National Library of Wales.
Kelly's Directories.
Kilner, E. A. *The Story of Four Welsh Counties* (London, 1891).
Kilvert, Francis (Ed. Plomer). *Diary* (London, 1938–40).
Laws, Edward. *History of Little England beyond Wales* (London, 1888).
Leland, John. *The Itinerary in Wales, 1536–39* (London, 1908).
Leigh's *Guide to Wales and Monmouthshire* (London, 1835).
Lewis, Eiluned. *The Captain's Wife* (Batsford, 1943).
Lewis, Samuel. *Topographical Dictionary of Wales* (London, 1833).
Lloyd, Sir J. E. *A History of Wales* (London, 1939).
Mabinogion, The.
Mackinder, Sir E. J. *Britain and the British Seas* (Oxford, 1935).
Malkin, B. H. *The Scenery, Antiquities and Biography of South Wales* (London, 1801).
Manby, G. W. *History and Antiquities of the Parish of St. David* (London, 1801).
Moore, Donald (ed.). *The Land of Dyfed in Early Times*, CAA (1964).
—— *The Irish Sea Province in Archaeology and History*, CAA (1970).
Morgan, K. O. *Wales in British Politics 1868–1922* (Cardiff, 1980).
Moss, Fletcher. *The Fourth Book of Pilgrimages to Old Homes* (Didsbury, 1908).
Murray's Handbook (1806).
Nicholson, E. *Cambrian Traveller's Guide* (London, 1840).
Owen, E. E. *The Early Life of Bishop Owen* (Llandysul, 1958).
—— *The Later Life of Bishop Owen* (Llandysul, 1961).
Owen, George. *The Description of Pembrokeshire* (London, *THSC* 1892, 1936).
Payne, Archdeacon. *Collectanea Menevensia* (Bound ms. in the Cathedral Library).
Phillips, James. *History of Pembrokeshire* (London, 1909).
Pigot and Son's *Commercial Directory* (London, 1830).
Pembrokeshire Coast National Park Guide (HMSO, 1973).
Pembrokeshire Historian, The.
Rees, Thomas. *The Beauties of England and Wales* (London, 1815).
Rees, Thomas. *Byr Hanes Dechreuad a Pharhâd Pregethu gan y Trefnyddion Calfinaidd yn Nhy Ddewi* (Castellnewydd Emlyn, 1839).
Rees, William. *An Historical Atlas of Wales* (Cardiff, 1951).
Richard, Henry. *Letters and Essays on Wales* (London, 1884).

Richards, Melville. *Welsh Administrative and Territorial Units* (Cardiff, 1969).
—— 'The Irish Settlements in South West Wales', *Journal of Royal Society Antiquities, Ireland* (1960).
—— 'Places and Names in the Early Welsh Church', *WHR* (1971).
St. David's Parish Magazine (Bound volumes 1877–78–79 in Cathedral Library).
Saunders, Erasmus. *A View of the State of Religion in the Diocese of St. David's about the beginning of the eighteenth century* (Cardiff, 1949).
Sikes, W. *Rambles and Studies in Old South Wales* (London, 1881).
Skrine, H. *Two Successive Tours throughout the Whole of Wales* (London, 1798).
Slater's Directories.
Smith, Peter. *Houses of the Welsh Countryside* (London, 1975).
Timmins, E. Th. *Nooks and Corners of Pembrokeshire* (London, 1895).
Thomas, J. Miles. *Looking Back, A Childhood in St. David's* (Carmarthen, 1977).
Thomas, P. E. F. *'Purely Local'* (Cardiff, 1935).
Victory, Sian. *The Celtic Church in Wales* (SPCK, 1977).
Wade-Evans, A. W. *Life of St. David* (London, 1923).
—— *Welsh Christian Origins* (Oxford, 1934).
Walcott, Mackenzie. *St. David's and the Cathedral* (Tenby, 1864).
Warburton, F. W. *History of Solva* (London, 1944).
Williams, David. *The Rebecca Riots* (Cardiff, 1955).
Williams, Glanmor. *The Welsh Church from Conquest to Reformation* (Cardiff, 1976).
Williams, H. W. *Pembrokeshire Antiquities* (Solva, 1897).
Willis-Bund (ed.). *The Black Book of St. David's* (London, 1902).
Yardley, Edward (Ed. Francis Green). *Menevia Sacra*, CAA (1927).

Report on the Poor Law Commission, 1834, 1836–46.
Reports of the Commissioners on Municipal Corporations in England and Wales, 1835.
Report of the Commission on the state of the Roads, 1840.
Reports of the Commissioners of Inquiry for South Wales, 1843–44. (The Turnpike Trusts and the Rebecca Riots.)
Reports of the Commissioners of Inquiry into the State of Education in Wales, 1846–47. (The Blue Books.)
The Taunton Report on Endowed Schools, 1868.
Report of the Committee on Intermediate and Higher Education in Wales, 1881.
Royal Commission on Labour: The Agricultural Labourer, Volume 2. Wales. 1893.
Royal Commission on Land in Wales, 1896.
Report of the Royal Commission on the Church of England and Other Religious Bodies in Wales and Monmouthshire, 1910.
Royal Commission on Ancient and Historic Monuments in Wales and Monmouthshire. Pembroke, 1925.

Subscriptions

Financial contributions from the following sponsors towards the production costs of this book are gratefully acknowledged.

Dyfed County Council (Welsh Church Fund)
The Catherine and Lady Grace James Foundation (Pantyfedwen)
West Wales Guardian
William C. W. James, New York
St. David's Community Council
St. David's Assemblies
St. David's Art Group
St. David's Cathedral Library
St. David's Civic Society
Gwalia (C. B. S. and E. D. Davies)
Yr Oriel Fach (Christopher Taylor)
Lloyds Bank (R. O. J. Edwards)
Midland Bank (W. John Owen)